Considering Prose

Andrew Mayne and John Shuttleworth

HODDER AND STOUGHTON
LONDON SYDNEY AUCKLAND TORONTO

British Library Cataloguing in Publication Data

Mayne, Andrew
  Considering prose.
  1. Criticism
  I. Title   II. Shuttleworth, John
  801′.95   PN83

ISBN 0 340 32575 5

First published 1984
Second impression 1985

Copyright © 1984

Photo Typeset by Macmillan India Ltd, Bangalore

Printed in Great Britain for
Hodder and Stoughton Educational,
a division of Hodder and Stoughton Ltd,
Mill Road, Dunton Green, Sevenoaks, Kent
by Clark Constable
Edinburgh and London

Contents

Preface

This book on the criticism of prose is designed to meet the needs of both the student (and teacher) in the classroom and the individual reader who is working through the material on his or her own. In the first situation, teachers may wish the members of the class to read through and prepare particular sections of the book before they designate exercises to be covered in class. As far as possible we have tried to devise questions that can form the basis for either written work or oral discussion.

A. A. M.

J. A. S.

Introduction

READING PROSE

Reading prose; considering prose; looking closely and critically at prose: this is what we hope you will be doing as you read and work through this book. But we have made a large assumption already – that we know what 'prose' is! If you are unsure, then you are in good company, for Monsieur Jourdain, the hero of one of Molière's plays, had this same problem, and was surprised to find that he had been speaking prose all his life without ever having been conscious of the fact! Perhaps at this early stage, the Oxford Dictionary can help:

> *Prose*: the ordinary form of written or spoken language; the opposite to poetry.

This is a useful working definition, which we expect you will be able to sharpen and expand by the end of this book.

We all use prose in our daily lives, both in conversation and in reading and writing, whether it be the words we glance at on the back of our breakfast cornflakes packet, the report we peruse in our newspaper, the novel (or book of prose criticism!) we are currently reading or the essay we write for 'A' level English. We could not lead our normal, everyday lives without prose, and in an increasingly complex society, we encounter an immense variety. To be able to recognize the different types and different aims prose writers have is an essential first step to becoming critical and discriminating readers.

To help you take this first step, we have chosen a number of extracts from different types of prose. We suggest that you work in pairs or groups to discuss these, and try first to recognize what *kind* of written work they were taken from. You might find it useful to consider the following questions when discussing the passages:

1. Are there any words or groups of words that distinctively identify the type of writing?
2. How carefully do you think the writer has chosen the words he uses? Does it seem to you, for example, that the words used are part of common, everyday usage, or do they immediately suggest some specialized area of activity? Does the language draw attention to itself because of its 'new-minted' quality, or is the choice of word entirely predictable?

1

3. Does the structure of the sentences, or their rhythm, help in any way to indicate the kind of writing they are taken from?
4. Does the writer's attitude to the reader give any identifying clue?
5. Are there any special features of the writing – for example, use of description, inclusion of conversation – that provide any indication of origin?
6. Is it possible to identify the *purpose* the writer has in mind, or the effect he or she wishes to produce in the reader?

Prose extracts

A. Stretching from the Atlantic to the Pacific like a vast, multi-coloured canvas, America is a delight to behold and a joy to experience. It caters for every fancy of the imagination, and offers awesome natural beauty. Thundering Niagara Falls, the majestic Grand Canyon and the fiery Painted Desert of Arizona are just some of the wondrous sights that   5 could leave you breathless.

B. Socialization is a continuing process; it does not stop at a certain age, and on the whole, social psychologists seem to think of it as 'an interactional process whereby a person's behaviour is modified to conform with expectations held by members of the groups to which he   10 belongs.'

C. During the whole of a dull, dark and soundless day in the autumn of the year, when the clouds hung oppressively low in the heavens, I had been passing alone, on horseback, through a singularly dreary tract of country; and at length found myself, as the shades of the evening drew   15 on, within view of the melancholy House of Usher.

D. Now know ye that this document witnesseth that Insurance in accordance with the Terms, Exception and Conditions herein contained has been effected with certain Underwriters at Lloyd's, whose names and proportions underwritten by them appear on a written Form of   20 Authority . . .

E. Find a chopping board and a kitchen knife, a small basin, a lemon squeezer, a teaspoon, kitchen scissors and a measuring jug in which to make up the jelly. You will also need a dish in which to balance the orange halves while they set.   25

F. O Lord thou hast searched me and known me. Thou knowest my downsitting and mine uprising, thou understandest my thought afar off. Thou compassest my path and my lying down and art acquainted with all my ways. For there is not a work in my tongue, but lo, O Lord, thou knowest it altogether.   30

G. Hello! How are you? I am fine, trying to watch 'The Professionals' and dry my washing and listen to Lucy drying her hair. I try to pack a lot into my days off! Today my dad came to London and we managed to go for chocolate gâteau, an exhibition and a concert between 1 o'clock and 5.

H. 'Nuits St Georges,' I read from the label. 'How exciting that sounds! 35 Does it mean the Nights of St George? It conjures up the most wonderful pictures, armour and white horses and dragons, flames too, perhaps a great procession by torchlight.' He looked at me doubtfully for a moment and then, seeing that I had not yet tasted my wine, began to explain that Nuits St Georges was a place where there were vineyards. 40

Clearly these eight extracts are only a small sample of the many types of writing that are to be found in prose – no doubt you could think of many more yourself – but what we would like to draw your attention to is the broad distinction between the way prose is used in extracts A, C, F and H and the way it is used in the other passages. The distinction is between what we shall, for the moment, call 'imaginative' and 'non-imaginative' prose; between prose that communicates on the factual level only and that which communicates also to our feelings and emotions. For some people, a recipe or an insurance policy may be a matter of deep feeling, but for most of us this is not so and consequently the writers of recipes or insurance policies use 'neutral' words that are not expected to arouse an emotional response in their readers. The words chosen are intended solely to denote something, a 'chopping-board' or 'basin', for example, and we sometimes call this use of words 'denotative'. Such prose is used, for instance, when we wish to communicate information or ideas, or when we wish to give information about events.

When the conveying of information is paramount, we may feel that the prose should be a fairly transparent medium and that it would be undesirable for the reader to become too preoccupied *with the way in which* the information is conveyed.

In 'imaginative' prose, however, the texture of the language, the colouring of the vocabulary and the shape of the sentences are matters which, though integral to what is being said, are worth consideration in their own right. In this kind of writing we do not simply want to 'look through' the clear surface of the prose to find given information as easily and quickly as possible, as we do with 'non-imaginative' or 'denotative' prose.

The words in passages A, C, F and H are not used denotatively, because the intentions of the writers are to express emotions, feelings and attitudes as well as to transmit facts, ideas or information. We call such imaginative use of language 'connotative', because the words chosen are not neutral ones but are chosen for the *overtones* that they have. These words include something in their meaning beyond what they denote, for they imply an attitude or a feeling. The writer of the first passage, for instance, has chosen words like 'awesome' and 'majestic' because he or she wishes to create in the reader a desire to see the country which has sights of such grandeur. Similarly, the novelists of passages C and H aim, through their use of imaginative or connotative language, to appeal to the reader's feelings. By the use of words like 'dull', 'dark', 'soundless', 'oppressively', 'alone', 'dreary' and 'melancholy', writer C creates a suitable mood for a horror story.

Notice that we have referred above to the *use* of language in an imaginative or connotative way. We would not wish to leave you with the impression that all words by necessity fall into the two neat categories of denotative or connotative. Clearly there are many words which, according to the context, could fit into either category. The word 'rose', for instance, might be used in a purely denotative manner in a manual for gardeners; on the other hand, in imaginative writing, an author may wish to draw upon the many associations the word possesses – associations of religious martyrdom or romantic love or aesthetic appeal, and so on.

Now you may be interested to discover how close you were to identifying the original sources of our extracts. Here they are:

A. a travel brochure published by Trans World Airlines (TWA)
B. a report on the effects of television on people's attitudes, published by the Leicester University Centre for Mass Communication Research
C. the opening of Edgar Allen Poe's story, 'The Fall of the House of Usher'
D. an AA insurance policy
E. part of a recipe from *The Winnie-the-Pooh Cookbook*
F. the first three verses of Psalm 139, in the Authorized Version of the Bible of 1611
G. a letter from a university student to a friend
H. an extract from a novel, *Excellent Women* (1952) by Barbara Pym.

While we are not suggesting that there is always a clear or absolute dividing line between imaginative and non-imaginative prose, the distinction is, at this stage, a convenient and useful one, and in the following sections of this chapter, we are going to ask you to read some passages of imaginative prose and to analyse and criticize them. It is important that you become used to reading prose carefully, thinking about it and discussing it, for only in this way can you hope to become an informed and critically discriminating reader. We also suggest some different methods of working with prose and organizing your responses to what you have read, whether you are working on your own or in groups.

These methods of approach can be summarized as follows:

1. reading a passage and then making notes on your response
2. adopting three guideline questions to ask in connection with a passage
3. working in pairs
4. preparing a passage for reading aloud

5. preparing a passage for dramatic presentation
6. writing in imitation of a passage
7. preparing questions on a passage for a group to discuss
8. compiling an anthology of favourite passages.

We shall now look in more detail at these methods.

1. This is a method that can be used whether you are working on your own or in a group. We suggest you practise this approach on the passage from Thackeray's *Vanity Fair*, which follows shortly.

Read the passage selected for analysis at least twice, and then write down in note form your response to what you have read. You should not worry at this stage about producing highly polished writing – the notes are initially for your benefit alone. Concentrate more on getting your reactions clear in your own mind.

If you are working in a group, then use what you have written as a basis for discussion with other members of the group. This should help to sharpen your response and perhaps clarify any difficulties you might have had. It is important in working with literature to share your ideas with other people, and at the same time to listen to what they have to say.

Now you could write a more considered response to the passage, having more care for the ordering and organizing of your ideas. This would form your 'criticism' of the passage. We will give you a practical demonstration of how this may be done later (see pages 97–98).

This 'note-making' method is one which we will adopt frequently in the book, and sometimes before giving our own response, we will ask you to jot down your impressions. While we cannot, of course, stop you 'cheating', we do assure you that you will gain much greater benefits if you try the exercise yourself *before* turning to our suggestions.

Here Thackeray is describing the battle of Waterloo as the wives of the soldiers await news from the front line.

Towards evening, the attack of the French, repeated and resisted so bravely, slackened in its fury. They had other foes besides the British to engage, or were preparing for a final onset. It came at last: the columns of the Imperial Guard marched up the hill of Saint Jean, at length and at once to sweep the English from the height which they had maintained all day, and spite of all: 5
unscared by the thunder of the artillery, which hurled death from the English line – the dark rolling column pressed on and up the hill. It seemed almost to crest the eminence, when it began to wave and falter. Then it stopped, still facing the shot. Then at last the English troops rushed from the post from which no enemy had been able to dislodge them, and the Guard   10
turned and fled.

No more firing was heard at Brussels – the pursuit rolled miles away. Darkness came down on the field and city; and Amelia was praying for George, who was lying on his face, dead, with a bullet through his heart.

W. M. Thackeray: *Vanity Fair* (1847)

2. A second method uses three broad questions to be asked and answered about any passage of prose. They should help to guide your responses to what you read.

   (i) What is the passage saying? What effect is it designed to have on us? (Here it may be useful to start off by asking what kind of prose you are dealing with – descriptive, narrative, polemical etc.)

  (ii) How does the passage convey its subject matter? By what means is its effect achieved? (Think about the standpoint from which the passage is written; the types of words and imagery[1] used; the movement or rhythm of the writing; and the tone the writer chooses. Not all of these, of course, will be equally important in connection with any one particular passage.)

(iii) Do you find the passage successful? The basis on which your final judgement rests should be no vague, unsubstantiated value-judgement. The judgement should rest on your consideration of the first two questions: that is, one measure of success may be your assessment of the extent to which you think the writer has achieved what you take his or her purpose to be (question (i)); and another measure may be your judgement on the appropriateness and utilization of the methods adopted (question (ii)).

Now apply this approach to the following passage:

In this passage, Swift's narrator suggests a solution to the problem of hunger in Ireland, which Swift considers to have been caused by the effects on his country's economy of its exploitation by rich (English) landlords.

The number of souls in this Kingdom being usually reckoned one million and a half, of these I calculate there may be about two hundred thousand couple whose wives are breeders; from which number I substract thirty thousand couples, who are able to maintain their own children, although I apprehend there cannot be so many, under the present distresses of the   5 Kingdom; but this being granted, there will remain an hundred and seventy thousand breeders. I again substract fifty thousand, for those women who miscarry, or whose children die by accident, or disease within the year. There only remain an hundred and twenty thousand children of poor parents annually born. The question therefore is, how this number shall be   10 reared, and provided for, which, as I have already said, under the present situation of affairs, is utterly impossible by all the methods hitherto proposed; for we can neither employ them in handicraft or agriculture; we neither build houses (I mean in the country) nor cultivate land. They can very seldom pick up a livelihood by stealing till they arrive at six years old,   15 except where they are of towardly parts, although, I confess, they learn the

---

[1] Technical terminology is explained as it is introduced later: for *imagery*, see page 56. However, you may find it useful occasionally to refer to a work such as M. H. Abrams: *A Glossary of Literary Terms*. A good dictionary is certainly indispensable to a student of prose. Are you clear, for instance, what the word 'polemical' means? If not, you should have looked it up!

rudiments much earlier; during which time they can however be properly looked upon only as probationers, as I have been informed by a principal gentleman in the County of Cavan, who protested to me, that he never knew above one or two instances under the age of six, even in a part of the 20 Kingdom so renowned for the quickest proficiency in that art.

I am assured by our merchants, that a boy or a girl before twelve years old, is no saleable commodity, and even when they come to this age, they will not yield above three pounds, or three pounds and half a crown at most, on the Exchange; which cannot turn to account either to the parents or Kingdom, 25 the charge of nutriment and rags having been at least four times that value.

I shall now therefore humbly propose my own thoughts which I hope will not be liable to the least objection.

I have been assured by a very knowing American of my acquaintance in London, that a young healthy child well nursed is at a year old a most 30 delicious nourishing and wholesome food, whether stewed, roasted, baked, or boiled; and I make no doubt that it will equally serve in a fracasie, or a ragout.

I do therefore humbly offer it to public consideration, that of the hundred and twenty thousand children, already computed, twenty thousand may be 35 reserved for breed, whereof only one fourth part to be males, which is more than we allow to sheep, black-cattle, or swine, and my reason is that these children are seldom the fruits of marriage, a circumstance not much regarded by our savages, therefore, one male will be sufficient to serve four females. That the remaining hundred thousand may at a year old be offered 40 in sale to the persons of quality, and fortune, through the kingdom, always advising the mother to let them suck plentifully in the last month, so as to render them plump, and fat for a good table. A child will make two dishes at an entertainment for friends, and when the family dines alone, the fore or hind quarter will make a reasonable dish, and seasoned with a little pepper 45 or salt will be very good boiled on the fourth day, especially in winter.

Jonathan Swift: 'A Modest Proposal' (1729)

3. If you are working through this book as a member of a class, a method of approach that is suitable when you have two passages to consider is to split into pairs. Each partner reads both passages set for analysis, and then writes a reaction paper on *one* of the passages. The pair working together should then compare their findings. You could, if you wished, then arrive at an agreed view of the two passages and present this considered opinion to the larger group for discussion.

In the last section of this book you will find references to pairings of passages which present interesting stylistic contrasts.

Now try the approach on the following two extracts.

When in the Course of human events, it becomes necessary for one people to dissolve the political bands which have connected them with another, and to assume among the Powers of the earth, the separate and equal station to which the Laws of Nature and of Nature's God entitle them, a decent respect to the opinions of mankind requires that they should declare the causes 5 which impel them to the separation.

We hold these truths to be self-evident, that all men are created equal, that they are endowed by their Creator with certain unalienable Rights, that among these are Life, Liberty and the pursuit of Happiness. That to secure these rights, Governments are instituted among Men, deriving their just   10 powers from the consent of the governed. That whenever any Form of Government becomes destructive of these ends, it is the Right of the People to alter or to abolish it, and to institute new Government, laying its foundation on such principles and organizing its powers in such a form, as to them shall seem most likely to effect their Safety and Happiness.   15

The Unanimous Declaration of the Thirteen United States of America,
4 July, 1776

When things get so balled up that the people of a country got to cut loose from some other country, and go it on their own hook, without asking no permission from nobody, excepting maybe God Almighty, then they ought to let everybody know why they done it, so that everybody can see they are not trying to put nothing over on nobody.   5
All we got to say on this proposition is this: first, me and you is as good as anybody else, and maybe a damn sight better; second, nobody ain't got no right to take away none of our rights; third, every man has got a right to live, to come and go as he pleases, and to have a good time whichever way he likes, so long as he don't interfere with nobody else. That any government   10 that don't give a man them rights ain't worth a damn; also, people ought to choose the kind of government they want themselves, and nobody else ought to have no say in the matter. That whenever any government don't do this, then the people have got a right to give it the bum's rush and put in one that will take care of their interests.   15

H. L. Mencken: 'The Declaration of Independence in American', 1921
(from *The Mencken Chrestomathy*, 1949)

Another pairing of passages we recommend you to study at this stage, using the same approach, is to be found in a comparison of the opening paragraphs of Dickens's *David Copperfield* (1849) and J. D. Salinger's *Catcher in the Rye* (1951). Look them up for yourself.

4. To read a passage aloud is, of course, to suggest a kind of interpretation. You should approach the preparation rather like an actor deciding on the most effective way of performing a speech – though concentrate on the voice alone, unless you feel that gestures and movements about the room are absolutely essential! What tone of voice will you adopt? Will this vary? What about the pace of the reading? Are there any sections to which you wish to give a special emphasis? Any key words phrases you think it necessary to 'lean on'?
It is often interesting to ask two or three people to prepare a reading of the same passage. Listen to their different interpretations and then comment in a constructive way on the strengths and weaknesses of the various readings.

Here are two passages which you could prepare in this way. The first is from Dickens's *A Christmas Carol* (1843). As you probably know, Dickens was an author who clearly knew how effective a public reading could be, for he gave many such performances during his life. They were hugely popular with his audiences, both here and in America.

Master Peter, and the two ubiquitous young Cratchits went to fetch the goose, with which they soon returned in high procession.

Such a bustle ensued that you might have thought a goose the rarest of all birds; a feathered phenomenon, to which a black swan was a matter of course – and in truth it was something very like it in that house.   5
Mrs Cratchit made the gravy (ready beforehand in a little saucepan) hissing hot; Master Peter mashed the potatoes with incredible vigour; Miss Belinda sweetened up the apple-sauce; Martha dusted the hot plates; Bob took Tiny Tim beside him in a tiny corner at the table; the two young Cratchits set chairs for everybody, not forgetting themselves, and mounting guard upon   10
their posts, crammed spoons into their mouths, lest they should shriek for goose before their turn came to be helped. At last the dishes were set on, and grace was said. It was succeeded by a breathless pause, as Mrs Cratchit, looking slowly all along the carving-knife, prepared to plunge it in the breast; but when she did, and when the long expected gush of stuffing issued   15
forth, one murmur of delight arose all round the board, and even Tiny Tim, excited by the two young Cratchits, beat on the table with the handle of his knife, and feebly cried Hurrah!

There never was such a goose. Bob said he didn't believe there ever was such a goose cooked. Its tenderness and flavour, size and cheapness, were   20
the themes of universal admiration. Eked out by apple-sauce and mashed potatoes, it was a sufficient dinner for the whole family; indeed, as Mrs Cratchit said with great delight (surveying one small atom of a bone upon the dish), they hadn't ate it all at last! Yet every one had had enough, and the youngest Cratchits in particular, were steeped in sage and onion to   25
the eyebrows! But now, the plates being changed by Miss Belinda, Mrs Cratchit left the room alone – too nervous to bear witnesses – to take the pudding up and bring it in.

Suppose it should not be done enough! Suppose it should break in turning out! Suppose somebody should have got over the wall of the back-yard, and   30
stolen it, while they were merry with the goose – a supposition at which the two young Cratchits became livid! All sorts of horrors were supposed.

Hallo! A great deal of steam! The pudding was out of the copper. A smell like a washing-day! That was the cloth. A smell like an eating-house and a pastrycook's next door to each other, with a laundress's next door to that!   35
That was the pudding! In half a minute Mrs Cratchit entered – flushed, but smiling proudly – with the pudding, like a speckled cannon-ball, so hard and firm, blazing in half of half-a-quartern of ignited brandy, and bedight with Christmas holly stuck into the top.

Oh, a wonderful pudding! Bob Cratchit said, and calmly too, that he   40
regarded it as the greatest success achieved by Mrs Cratchit since their marriage. Mrs Cratchit said that now the weight was off her mind, she would confess she had had her doubts about the quantity of flour. Everybody had something to say about it, but nobody said or thought it was at all a small

pudding for a large family. It would have been flat heresy to do so. Any   45
Cratchit would have blushed to hint at such a thing.

At last the dinner was all done, the cloth was cleared, the hearth swept,
and the fire made up. The compound in the jug being tasted, and considered
perfect, apples and oranges were put upon the table, and a shovel-full of
chestnuts on the fire. Then all the Cratchit family drew round the hearth, in   50
what Bob Cratchit called a circle, meaning half a one; and at Bob Cratchit's
elbow stood the family display of glass. Two tumblers, and a custard-cup
without a handle.

These held the hot stuff from the jug, however, as well as golden goblets
would have done; and Bob served it out with beaming looks, while the   55
chestnuts on the fire sputtered and cracked noisily. Then Bob proposed:

'A Merry Christmas to us all, my dears. God bless us!'

Which all the family re-echoed.

'God bless us every one!' said Tiny Tim, the last of all.

Secondly, a passage that we certainly find enjoyable (and, as teachers,
just a little disturbing!).

A new teacher faces his class for the first time.

Ten boys sat before him, their hands folded, their eyes bright with
expectation.

'Good morning, sir,' said the one nearest him.

'Good morning,' said Paul.

'Good morning, sir,' said the next.   5

'Good morning,' said Paul.

'Good morning, sir,' said the next.

'Oh, shut up,' said Paul.

At this the boy took out a handkerchief and began to cry quietly.

'Oh, sir' came a chorus of reproach, 'you've hurt his feelings. He's very   10
sensitive; it's his Welsh blood, you know; it makes people very emotional.
Say "Good morning" to him, sir, or he won't be happy all day. After all, it is
a good morning, isn't it, sir?'

'Silence!' shouted Paul above the uproar, and for a few moments things
were quieter.   15

'Please, sir,' said a small voice – Paul turned and saw a grave-looking
youth holding up his hand – 'please, sir, perhaps he's been smoking cigars
and doesn't feel well.'

'Silence!' said Paul again.

The ten boys stopped talking and sat perfectly still staring at him. He felt   20
himself getting hot and red under their scrutiny.

'I suppose the first thing I ought to do is to get your names clear. What is
your name?' he asked, turning to the first boy.

'Tangent, sir.'

'And yours?'   25

'Tangent, sir,' said the next boy. Paul's heart sank.

'But you can't both be called Tangent.'

'No, sir, *I'm* Tangent. He's just trying to be funny.'

'I like that. *Me* trying to be funny! Please, sir, I'm Tangent, sir; really I
am.'   30

'If it comes to that,' said Clutterbuck from the back of the room, 'there is only one Tangent here, and that is me. Anyone else can jolly well go to blazes.'

Paul felt desperate.

'Well, is there anyone who isn't Tangent?' 35

Four or five voices instantly arose.

'I'm not, sir; I'm not Tangent. I wouldn't be called Tangent, not on the end of a barge pole.'

In a few seconds the room had become divided into two parties: those who were Tangent and those who were not. Blows were already being exchanged, 40 when the door opened and Grimes came in. There was a slight hush.

Evelyn Waugh: *Decline and Fall* (1928)

What elements in these passages lend themselves to public reading?

Of course, there are differing views about how to read prose. For instance, when one class was discussing this topic, an opinion was expressed to the effect that 'all good prose suggests the way it should be read aloud – like a musical score. All good readers should find themselves imagining an ideal reader uttering the words that pass silently through their mind'. On the other hand, it was also stated that 'only the barely literate link the printed word with the sounds of speech'. It would be valuable for you to examine your own experience of private reading in the light of these two comments, to see to what extent you find yourself imagining the tone and 'voicing' of prose. Perhaps your response will vary depending on what kind of prose you are reading.

5. If you wish to be more adventurous, you could take up our hints about acting given in the introduction to the previous method (4) and prepare a passage for dramatic presentation. Naturally, you would need to do this as a group and to concentrate not just on your voices alone, but on such matters as movement, gesture and positioning. We would advocate this approach, of course, for no more than a carefully selected part of the prose you will read in this book. However, you may come across some passages which suggest that they might make successful dramatic adaptations. The Royal Shakespeare Company has shown in its adaptation of a whole Dickens novel, *Nicholas Nickleby*, just how effective this method can be. Of course, we are not suggesting that you embark on a project of such scale yet! You would be wise to begin by selecting extracts from a novel which depend heavily on dialogue. The passages from both *A Christmas Carol* and *Decline and Fall* should give you ample scope – and you may feel like becoming even more enterprising later. This may sound an unusual approach to prose criticism, but in fact by considering in a most practical way how certain kinds of prose are to be presented in a dramatic format, you will quickly discover the relative strengths and weaknesses of the printed word.

6. It is certainly true that the best parodies, while often written in a spirit of fun, gentle mockery or satire, grow out of an intimate acquaintance with the original and usually, on some level, a responsive sympathy with the subject's distinctive stylistic qualities. After all, you can only copy effectively what you are very familiar with. To write a good parody, therefore, is not simply to adopt the same subject matter and general treatment as the original. You have to mimic and possibly exaggerate slightly – as in a caricature – the verbal gestures, the linguistic and stylistic idiosyncrasies of the writer you are parodying. Sometimes the cream of the jest may be to apply the characteristic method and style of an author to an incongruous subject.

Here for example, is a passage written with Dickens's description of the Cratchit ménage very much in mind.

Christmas afternoon

What an afternoon! Mr Gummidge said that, in his estimation, there never had *been* such an afternoon since the world began, a sentiment which was heartily endorsed by Mrs Gummidge and all the little Gummidges, not to mention the relatives who had come over from Jersey for the day.

In the first place, there was the *ennui*. And such *ennui* as it was! A heavy, 5
overpowering *ennui*, such as results from a participation in eight courses of steaming, gravied food, topping off with salted nuts which the little old spinster Gummidge from Oak Hill said she never knew when to stop eating – and true enough she didn't – a dragging, devitalizing *ennui*, which left its victims strewn about the living room in various attitudes of 10
prostration suggestive of those of the petrified occupants in a newly unearthed Pompeiian dwelling; an *ennui* which carried with it a retinue of yawns, snarls and thinly veiled insults, and which ended in ruptures in the clan spirit serious enough to last throughout the glad new year.

Then there were the toys! Three and a quarter dozen toys to be divided 15
among seven children. Surely enough, you or I might say, to satisfy the little tots. But that would be because we didn't know the tots. In came Baby Lester Gummidge, Lillian's boy, dragging an electric grain-elevator which happened to be the only toy in the entire collection that appealed to little Norman, five-year-old son of Luther, who lived in Rahway. In came curly- 20
headed Effie in frantic and throaty disputation with Arthur, Jr, over the possession of an articulated zebra. In came Everett, bearing a mechanical negro which would no longer dance, owing to a previous forcible feeding by the baby of a marshmallow into its only available aperture. In came Fonlansbee, teeth buried in the hand of little Ormond, who bore a popular 25
but battered remnant of what had once been the proud false bosom of a hussar's uniform. In they all came, one after another, some crying, some snapping, some pulling, some pushing – all appealing to their respective parents for aid in their intra–mural warfare.

Aunt Libbie, who lived with George, remarked from the dark corner of 30
the room that it seemed just like Sunday to her. An amendment was offered to this statement by the cousin, who was in the insurance business, stating that it was worse than Sunday. Murmurings indicative of as hearty

agreement with this sentiment as their lethargy would allow came from the other members of the family circle, causing Mr Gummidge to suggest a walk   35
in the air to settle their dinner.

And then arose such a chorus of protestations as has seldom been heard. It was too cloudy to walk. It was too raw. It looked like snow. It looked like rain. Luther Gummidge said that he must be starting along home soon, anyway, bringing forth the acid query from Mrs Gummidge as to whether or   40
not he was bored. Lillian said that she felt a cold coming on, and added that something they had had for dinner must have been under-cooked. And so it went, back and forth, forth and back, up and down, and in and out, until Mr Gummidge's suggestion of a walk in the air was reduced to tattered impossibility and the entire company glowed with ill-feeling.   45

Hallo! A great deal of commotion! That was Uncle George stumbling over the electric train which had early in the afternoon ceased to function and which had been left directly across the threshold. A great deal of crying! That was Arthur, Jr, bewailing the destruction of his already useless train, about which he had forgotten until the present moment. A great deal of   50
recrimination! That was Arthur, Sr, and George fixing it up. And finally a great crashing! That was Baby Lester pulling over the tree on top of himself necessitating the bringing to bear of all of Uncle Ray's knowledge of forestry to extricate him from the wreckage.

And finally Mrs Gummidge passed the Christmas candy around.   55
Mr Gummidge afterward admitted that this was a tactical error on the part of his spouse. I no more believe that Mrs Gummidge thought they wanted that Christmas candy than I believe that she thought they wanted the cold turkey which she later suggested. My opinion is that she wanted to drive them home. At any rate, that is what she succeeded in doing. Such cries as   60
there were of 'Ugh! Don't let me see another thing to eat!' and 'Take it away!' Then came hurried scramblings in the coat-closet for overshoes. There were the rasping sounds made by cross parents when putting wraps on children. There were insincere exhortations to 'come and see us soon' and to 'get together for lunch some time.' And, finally, there were slammings of   65
doors and the silence of utter exhaustion, while Mrs Gummidge went about picking up stray sheets of wrapping paper.

And, as Tiny Tim might say in speaking of Christmas afternoon as an institution, 'God help us, every one.'

Robert Benchley

(i) Locate and comment on particular features of Dickens's style which Benchley parodies. You should be able to find a number of fairly precise parallels and echoes.
(ii) What do you think Benchley is trying to say about the Dickensian version of Christmas in his parody?
(iii) How successful is the parody? And how amusing did you find it? What are the sources of the humour? Would Benchley's piece of writing lose all its humour and significance for a reader who was unfamiliar with *A Christmas Carol*?

If you are interested in reading more parodies you should consult Dwight Macdonald's *Parodies: An Anthology* (1960), from which the

Benchley passage is taken, and make a point of turning to the literary competitions which appear regularly in the *New Statesman*.

7. To find the important questions that need to be asked about a passage of prose is, rather like erecting signposts, a necessary recognition of the best direction or route to be taken. When you are formulating questions, you need to be aware that they fall into several categories. There is first the kind of straightforwardly factual question: What does this word or phrase mean? Answers in this area of basic comprehension – and it needs to be said that, unless we understand the original fully, all our attempts at more sophisticated criticism will fall flat – will be, within certain limits, either right or wrong. Then possibly more interesting questions can be put – of the kind which ask for some interpretative response or require consideration of some technical aspect of the language. (Remember our suggested 'three-question approach', page 6). In questions which aim to elicit an opinion or interpretation there will be, of course, a wider range of possible responses. However, beware of the naive, but rather fashionable fallacy that in this area 'anything goes' and 'your opinion is just as good as mine.' Clearly interpretation and opinion must always be supported by close reference to the text. While being flexible and open to the ideas of others, you should not be afraid to say, 'I think you are wrong', if somebody else's stated response goes beyond, or, in your opinion, cannot be justified by, the words on the page you are considering.

When you are formulating your questions for discussion by a group, do not feel that you necessarily need to have a comprehensive answer already worked out. We see no reason why you should not occasionally slip in a question in the spirit of 'I think this will lead discussion into an interesting and important area, though I'm not entirely sure of the final solution.' Even teachers of literature have been known to do this. The leader of a discussion does not need to know all: what *is* required is that sensible questions are asked and the discussion guided, without the leader's own viewpoint being imposed, in response to the emerging ideas and feelings of other members of the group.

8. As you read novels – some perhaps prescribed for an examination, some as a part of your wider reading – or literary criticism or your daily newspaper, it is likely that certain passages will strike you for one reason or another – possibly because they exemplify in your view good or bad features of prose style. We suggest that you make a note of such passages. Initially this may mean no more than jotting down a page reference. If you wish to be more diligent, you could keep in a notebook a record of your immediate impressions and the reasons why you singled out these chosen extracts. Or you could even assemble such material into a commonplace book.

If you are working in a group of students who are studying literature, it should be possible periodically to arrange a session during which, in turn, the students share their 'findings' with the other members: you may wish to limit each member to introducing, say, two passages of his or her own choice. Ideally, this material should be duplicated, so that everybody will have the opportunity of looking at it closely: to have passages under discussion actually in front of you for consultation is virtually a prerequisite. However, at least it will be possible for the chosen extracts to be read to the rest of the group, prior to a statement concerning why they have been selected and the wider discussion which should follow.

Students unused to the close discussion and analysis of prose – the activity you have been engaged on in this chapter and will continue to be throughout the book – are not slow to voice their uncertainties in the form of complaints; our own students are no exception. Consider the two following statements that they made. Do you agree with them? How would you answer their objections?

1. 'These writers did not intend us to take their prose to pieces in this way. When I read, I simply want to enjoy good writing. You can destroy good prose by dismantling it.'
2. 'It's all very well analysing a sentence of prose in great depth and discovering all kinds of technical devices and subtle effects. But that's not the way we read prose in practice. We don't stop all the time to scrutinize individual words and sentences. And if we did, we would never get beyond the first page of a book.'

Without unduly influencing your discussion of these points, we hope you consider the possibility that in good prose, as in all art, art is used to hide art, and that the techniques a prose writer uses – and which you can discover by careful analysis – are still powerfully operative (though usually unrecognized) when you are reading in a less critical manner.

2
Diction

We saw in the previous chapter that prose is used for a large number of different purposes as various as instructing would-be cooks and creating a character in a novel. Our intention in this and in the succeeding five chapters is to try to show you how prose writers achieve their aims, by examining what the tools of a writer's trade are and how they are used. In order to do this, we must look at the elements of prose individually. We are aware that this is an artificial device. For general purposes, most readers very rarely separate out these elements, responding rather to the effect of the prose as a whole. We would argue, however, that a reader's appreciation and enjoyment is increased by an understanding of how and why the writer has written in a particular way. Just as you can drive a car quite successfully without any knowledge of what a carburettor or a spark-plug is for, so you can read prose without knowing the part played by, for example, diction or rhythm in creating the effect of the passage upon you. However, an understanding of the way an internal combustion engine works can show you the difference between a poor car and a good one. Similarly, an understanding of the way prose works enables you to discriminate between good and bad writing. By working through these sections, you will, we hope, be helped to make distinctions of quality between different pieces of prose.

CHOICE OF WORDS

It seems to be stating the obvious when we say that a writer uses words; but it is in choosing which word to use and rejecting a great many alternatives that a writer can make us respond in a particular way. We can look at the sort of words chosen for a passage and learn from this something of the writer's intended effects upon the readers. It is this choice of words, and the implied rejection of the many possible alternatives, that we call 'diction'. Normally when we speak of diction, we are concerned with a writer's choice of nouns, verbs, adjectives and adverbs, rather than prepositions, conjunctions and pronouns, which, important as they are, do not usually give a passage its 'colour' or its own peculiar quality.

If we come across a word whose meaning is unfamiliar to us, we can look it up in a dictionary and some clarification is given. However, this is not always helpful to a writer who is searching for the exact word to convey his or her meaning. For example, most writers will know that a 'house' is a 'building for human habitation, especially a dwelling-place', but it may be that 'house' is not the word needed. Turning to a synonym-finder or a thesaurus and looking up 'house' the writer would find that there were a large number of synonyms to select from:

> house: home, residence, bungalow, villa, chalet, seat, place, mansion, hall, chateau, castle, manor, grange, palace, flat, flatlet, snuggery, box, cottage, cabin, hut, hovel, shed, shanty, shack, penthouse, apartment, suite, maisonette, mews . . .

One of these, it is to be hoped, would be the very word for the type of dwelling-place needed in the writing.

Which word do you think the writer would choose if the dwelling-place being written about were:

(i) where a noble English family had lived for hundreds of years without a break
(ii) where poor blacks lived in makeshift accommodation in South Africa
(iii) an ordinary suburban semi-detached house whose owners had pretensions to grandeur?

Clearly it would be incongruous to suggest that the noble family lived in a 'maisonette' or that the suburban house be called a 'cabin'.

You will presumably have remarked that it can be very difficult for a writer to convey the nuance required, for the range of words in English is great. While this is in fact one of the language's strengths, it means that a writer must constantly be on guard in selecting words. Look at this further example of the difficulties a writer faces. A seemingly simple action such as 'walking' can be described in any of these ways:

> step, tread, pace, stride, stride out, strut, stalk, prance, tiptoe, trip, tramp, goose-step, toddle, patter, stagger, lurch, limp, waddle, straddle, shuffle, dawdle, foot-it, stump, hike, plod, trudge, jog, ambulate, perambulate, take the air, take one's constitutional, march, ramble, stroll, saunter, rove . . . and so on.

Try writing your own sentences to illustrate clearly when to use some of these words in appropriate situations of 'moving from place to place'.

If you wish to take this kind of study further, you might like to look up some of the following words in a thesaurus and compose sentences that illustrate the subtle differences between the alternatives given: *speak*; *eat*; *writer*; *speedy*.

The examples we have so far given you have been fairly straightforward words, simple nouns, verbs or adjectives, but English is similarly rich in words describing abstract qualities. Take, for example, the word 'kindness'. Amongst the many synonyms for this we have:

> helpfulness, friendliness, harmlessness, benignity, heart-of-gold, kindliness, kindheartedness, charity, goodwill, consideration.

All are subtly distinct in the 'meaning they convey. 'Harmlessness' would seem to be the word to choose if a writer wanted to indicate the least degree of kindness, and 'heart-of-gold' the greatest. Try to place the others in ascending order of kindness, from the coldest to the warmest.

Doubtless in trying to do this, you will have had some difficulty and possibly some disagreement with other students, but this is to be expected when dealing with such fine distinctions in language. You will, however, have seen that in choosing one word or another, you have had to bear in mind subtle gradations of 'meaning' and to have been aware of the situation or context in which you would expect to use the word. Writers are for ever faced with this problem.

Perhaps you noticed that when we used the word 'meaning', we placed it, as here, within inverted commas. This, and the work you have done so far, probably alerted you to the fact that it is very difficult to pin down the 'meaning' of a particular word. A dictionary definition can be useful in establishing what we can call the *centre* of a word's meaning or reference, especially with fairly straightforward words such as 'photograph', 'potato' or 'proficient'; but such definitions can be useful only in a limited way, as many words have several meanings and the one intended depends very much on the context in which it is used. If you saw the word 'statement' on its own, you would have no idea whether it referred to the amount of money you had in a bank, the reply you gave to a policeman when charged with a driving offence or the pronouncement of the Prime Minister on the current economic situation. Words can only come alive when they are placed in relationship with other words.

A second difficulty in trying to establish a word's 'meaning' has already been mentioned in our opening chapter when we considered the difference between denotative (non-imaginative) and connotative (imaginative) prose. We saw that some words can be used not only neutrally (denotative prose) but also for their emotional colouring or associations (connotative prose). Indeed your work in the first part of this chapter will have shown you that words are chosen by imaginative writers very often for their emotional overtones, for much of the impact of a writer's work depends on the connotations of the words chosen. We have suggested that words come alive solely in context; not only do they have associations of their own, but also gain 'colour' from their relationship with the words around them. The following short examples should show you how the 'meaning' of one word – *old* – can vary with context. Read them and try to decide what these various 'meanings' are:

(a) It was a very special dinner, perfectly complemented by the old burgundy they drank.
(b) 'She's a very old friend; we have no secrets from each other.'
(c) I hadn't seen Brian for years and he now seemed an old man, though he couldn't have been more than fifty-five.
(d) I hadn't seen old Brian for years, not since 1955, in fact.

(e) He swore never to attend another school reunion, for all his fellow-guests were certainly old boys and behaved as such.

(f) The Headmistress introduced the speaker as a very distinguished old girl.

(g) She will insist on wearing old clothes, whatever the occasion.

(h) For one so young, he's very old in his ways.

(i) The old country still exerted an influence, though they had been gone some twenty years.

(j) 'I'm sorry to say that there's very little of the old London left now, though if we look hard enough I dare say we can still find something.'

LITERAL AND METAPHORICAL MEANING

We have already seen that when we use a word in its literal sense, we apply it in accordance with its standard usage to denote the generally accepted area of meaning that the word possesses, qualified by the context, of course. To find out what was meant, if you were unfamiliar with the word, you would generally simply have to consult a dictionary.

So, as an illustration of this, we can see that a literal usage of the word *blood* would be:

> He cut his finger and before long the handkerchief, with which he bound his hand, was covered with blood.

When, however, we extend the idea of blood to draw on the connotations that the word possesses, we are likely to be moving into the area of metaphorical meaning. Take, for example, the sentence: 'His blood is on your hands.' To be meant literally, this sentence would have to refer to some real blood which is actually on the hands of the person referred to. The words might be addressed to a surgeon after an operation: 'You still have some blood on your hands. Better wash it off.' But imagine that the words are addressed to the surgeon by an assistant who feels that, after a patient's death, the surgeon's faulty operating technique was definitely to blame. He is not using 'blood' in its *literal* sense: there is no blood, in fact, on the surgeon's hands. What is being said is something like: 'You are responsible; you carry the guilt'. This is a metaphorical usage of the word.

Read the following sentences, all of which contain the word 'blood'. After deciding what is meant, write down what seem to you to be the connotations of the word in each sentence. If you are working in a group, compare your findings. Do you think that the word is being used metaphorically in all the sentences?

(a) The blood of martyrs attests to the strength of their religious conviction.

(b) His blood became over-heated after imbibing too much wine.

(c) The manager decided it was time to blood the promising seventeen year old in the first team.

(d) The rose is blood-red.

(e) He was so anxious, he sweated blood.

(f) Blood is thicker than water.

(g) After his confinement, just to breathe fresh air again made the blood course through his veins.

(h) He prides himself too much on his blue blood.

(i) His father was a sailor, and you might say the sea was in his blood.

(j) Blood is notoriously difficult to wash out once it has stained clothing.

(k) The severe laws of Draco were written in blood.

It will probably have become clear that 'blood' is a word which possesses a wide range of connotation, embracing the ideas of physical vigour, sacrifice, family inheritance, and so on. Incidentally, notice how the word *literally* is often misused as a false intensifier in sentences such as: 'He was late for the train and literally flew down the high street'. (What does this mean?)

Now consider in closer detail, the metaphorical use of the word 'blood' in the following three short passages:

A. The dinner was very long, and the conversation was about the Aristocracy – and Blood. Mrs Waterbrook repeatedly told us, that if she had a weakness, it was Blood.

'I confess I am of Mrs Waterbrook's opinion,' said Mr Waterbrook, with his wine-glass at his eye. 'Other things are all very well in their way, but give me Blood!'

Charles Dickens: *David Copperfield* (1849–50)

B. When Pilate saw that he could prevail nothing, but that rather a tumult was made, he took water, and washed his hands before the multitude, saying, I am innocent of the blood of this just person: see ye to it. Then answered all the people, and said, His blood be on us and on our children.

St Matthew, 27, XXIV–XXV

C. And Mr Mick not only became a vegetarian, but at length declared vegetarianism doomed ('shedding', as he called it, 'the green blood of the silent animals') and predicted that men in a better age would live on nothing but salt.

G. K. Chesterton: *The Napoleon of Notting Hill* (1904)

A very large number of idioms and phrases in the language are generated by metaphorical meaning, though over a period of time it is often the case that this metaphorical origin is largely forgotten. Just how much we depend on metaphorical language is shown in light-hearted fashion by the American writer Louis Untermeyer, who traces a day in, the life of the ordinary man:

Having 'slept like a log,' he gets up in the morning 'fresh as a daisy' or 'fit as a fiddle'; he 'wolfs down' breakfast, 'hungry as a bear,' with his wife, who has 'a tongue like vinegar,' but 'a heart of gold.' He gets into his car, which 'eats up the miles,' 'steps on the gas,' and, as it 'purrs' along through the 'hum' of traffic, he reaches his office where he is 'as busy as a one-armed paper hanger 5 with the hives.' Life, for the average man, is not 'a bed of roses,' his competitor is 'sly as a fox' and his own clerks are 'slow as molasses in January.' But 'the day's grind' is finally done and, though it is 'raining cats and dogs,' he arrives home 'happy as a lark.'

Play in Poetry (1938)

Many of the examples are, of course, *clichés* – phrases which have been used so often that their original meaning has become dulled and hackneyed, though not all of these terms will strike an English reader as overfamiliar because Untermeyer is drawing on American English. In most kinds of prose we might therefore decide that this shop-soiled kind of metaphorical language is to be avoided, if we want our writing to possess freshness and vividness.

It should be clear to you by now that metaphorical language rests implicitly on a kind of comparison: our previous examples, using the word 'blood', have shown how a quality or connotation of the word is transferred and applied in a different context to another sort of action, quality or object, thereby generating a new meaning.

There are two terms connected with the use of comparative or figurative language that you need to be particularly aware of. These are *simile* and *metaphor*.

When we compare two distinctly different things and connect the comparison with the word 'like' or 'as', we call this a simile.

In the morning, the dust hung like fog, and the sun was as red as ripe new blood.

John Steinbeck: *The Grapes of Wrath* (1939)

If we make the comparison directly in the form of a statement which omits any connecting word such as 'like' or 'as', we call this a metaphor.

The King sits in Dunfermline town
Drinking the blood-red wine.

'Ballad of Sir Patrick Spens'

These two types of comparison are often referred to as *figures of speech*.
We will study the place of comparative language in prose more systematically in the following chapter; but at this stage, simply to make you more aware of some of the functions of simile and metaphor in prose,

we would like you to read and comment on the use of comparison in the following short extracts:

(a) It is often useful, particularly in the initial stages of analysis, to approach the diction of a passage of prose with a number of staple questions in mind which generally provide some helpful signposts.

Mayne and Shuttleworth: *Considering Prose* (1984)

(b) Mr Jones's pond was bubbling with life, and covered with great white lilies – they poured from their leaves like candle-fat, ran molten, then cooled on the water.

Laurie Lee: *Cider with Rosie* (1959)

(c) The Right Hon. was a tubby chap who looked as if he had been poured into his clothes and had forgotten to say 'When!'

P. G. Wodehouse 'Jeeves and his Impending Doom' (from *Very Good Jeeves*, 1930)

(d) At this crossroad in British Politics, the upward spiral of success of the Social Democratic Party looks destined to break the mould of the present party system, thus changing the face of politics and placing a time-bomb under the Labour and Conservative Parties.

(Newspaper article, 1981)

In this chapter so far, you have seen how the 'meaning' of words can alter with their context and give 'colour' to the passages in which they appear. You have also looked briefly at metaphorical language, which will be studied in depth later. However, before looking in detail at the questions we can ask about diction, we are going to take a more general view. Our first example is taken from Dickens's *Bleak House* (1852) and describes the Lincolnshire estate of Sir Leicester Dedlock during particularly bad weather. Read it through carefully, and then write notes on the diction, trying to show how Dickens's choice of particular words or groups of words helps to create the scene and the atmosphere of the estate.

The waters are out in Lincolnshire. An arch of the bridge in the park has been sapped and sopped away. The adjacent low-lying ground, for half a mile in breadth, is a stagnant river, with melancholy trees for islands in it, and a surface punctured all over, all day long, with falling rain. My Lady Dedlock's 'place' has been extremely dreary. The weather, for many a day   5
and night, has been so wet that the trees seem wet through, and the soft loppings and prunings of the woodman's axe can make no crash or crackle as they fall. The deer, looking soaked, leave quagmires where they pass. The shot of a rifle loses its sharpness in the moist air, and its smoke moves in a tardy little cloud towards the green rise, coppice-topped, that makes a   10
background for the falling rain. The view from my Lady Dedlock's own windows is alternately a lead-coloured view and a view in Indian ink. The vases on the stone terrace in the foreground catch the rain all day, and the

heavy drops fall, drip, drip, drip, upon the broad flagged pavement, called, from old time, the Ghost's Walk, all night. On Sundays, the little church in   15
the park is mouldy, the oaken pulpit breaks out into a cold sweat, and there is a general smell and taste as of the ancient Dedlocks in their graves.

Compare your notes on the diction with ours:

Words chosen to give cheerless, dismal tone: 'melancholy', 'stagnant', 'dreary', 'tardy', 'cold', 'lead-coloured', 'ancient', 'low-lying'; wetness of scene suggested by 'sopped', 'stagnant', 'wet', 'soaked', 'quagmires', 'moist', 'mouldy', 'drip', 'cold sweat'; Dickens appeals to our senses, especially that of sound, with 'no crash or crackle', 'drip, drip, drip', 'shot of a rifle' and senses of 'smell and taste'; an emphasis on endlessness: 'for many a day and night', 'all day . . . all night'; 'sapped and sopped' (note alliteration); 'punctured' suggests deliberate destructive activity of rain.

We have *underlined* certain words in the following passage. You will notice that they fall basically into two distinct groups: the first, words which describe the activity of the author's grandmother; and the second, words which name various parts of the house.

1. What contribution does each group make to the passage's effect (a) separately and (b) together?
2. Are there any other words in the passage which you would add to either of our groups?

My grandmother lived a very sedentary life, rarely moving outside an area of a few square yards during the whole course of the day. Yet she managed to be unceasingly active like a tense, irritable, continually fidgety, broody hen. All the morning she was on her knees, *scrubbing* the *oilcloth* or *polishing* the *furniture*; or *bending* down, *blacking* the *kitchen range*; or *sitting*   5
backwards, out of the *window-sill*, her lap wedged safe by the lower window frame, her arms *working* like a two-legged spider, *chamois-leathering* the outer *panes*. All afternoon, she was *baking* – sleeves rolled up, hands *dipping deep* into the *flour*, *kneading* and *scooping* and *trowelling* as if she were digging a hole big enough to plant an oak. All round her was an ironmonger's shop   10
of *tins* and floured *plates* and *basins* waiting ready for dough and pie-crust and plain cake-mix.

Norman Nicholson: Wednesday Early Closing (1975)

Finally, in this section on diction, we want *you* to decide what are the important questions to consider about the diction of the following two passages.

But the best time for the young children was when he made fuses. Morel fetched a sheaf of long sound wheat-straws from the attic. These he cleaned with his hand, till each one gleamed like a stalk of gold, after which he cut the straws into lengths of about six inches, leaving, if he could, a notch at the bottom of each piece. He always had a beautifully sharp knife that could cut   5
a straw clean without hurting it. Then he set in the middle of the table a heap of gunpowder, a little pile of black grains upon the white-scrubbed board.

He made and trimmed the straws while Paul and Annie filled and plugged them. Paul loved to see the black grains trickle down a crack in his palm into the mouth of the straw, peppering jollily downwards till the straw was full. 10
Then he bunged up the mouth with a bit of soap – which he got in his thumb-nail from a pat in a saucer – and the straw was finished.

D. H. Lawrence: Sons and Lovers (1913)

Enderby first thought of his mother, dead at his birth, of whom there had seemed to be no record. He liked to imagine a young woman of gentle blondeness, sweetly refined and slenderly pliant. He liked to think of her swathed in gold, in a beeswax-breathing drawing-room, singing 'Passing By' to her own accompaniment. The dying heat of a July day sang in sadness 5
through the wide-open french windows from a garden that flowed with Crimson Glory, Mme L. Dieudonne, Ena Harkness and Golden Spectre. He saw his father, become bookish, wearing bookman's slippers, O-ing out smoke from an oval-bored Passing Cloud, nodding his head in quiet pleasure as he listened. But his father had never been quite like that. A 10
wholesale tobacconist, ruling lines in the ledger with an ebony sceptre of a ledger-ruler, sitting in the office behind the shop in waistcoat and black bowler, always glad of opening-time. Why? To escape from that bitch of a second wife. Why had he married her? 'Money, son. Her first one left her a packet. Her stepson will, we hope, reap the benefit.' 15

Anthony Burgess: Inside Mr Enderby (1963)

QUESTIONS TO BE ASKED

When you were considering the diction of the two passages at the end of the previous section, you may have found that ideas came to you fairly easily. Indeed, it is perfectly reasonable to assert that the response of a sensitive reader to a passage of prose will, in itself, suggest the important questions to be considered. On the other hand, you may have taken up the hints we have already given you and approached the passages by asking, for example, 'In what way does the author's choice of word guide our response?' or 'What are the key words which seem to set the tone of the passage?'

It is often useful, particularly in the initial stages of analysis, to approach the diction of a passage of prose with a number of staple questions, which generally provide some helpful signposts, in mind. In this section, without being over-systematic or in any way suggesting that we are providing you with an 'all purpose diction analysis kit', we will suggest some of the questions which usually lead to productive answers. You may wish to regard these questions as suggested standard openings, as in a game of chess, though not all of them will always be relevant.

The questions we will consider are:

1. Does the diction produce any pervasive or predominant impression?

2. What are the key words? What are the words which are 'doing the work'?
3. Do the key words combine or interlock in any particular way – as regards, for example, their connotations?
4. Do the key words generally belong to the same part of speech?
5. Is there any sign that the key words belong predominantly to the Latin or Saxon sources of English?
6. Does the writer's choice of vocabulary make his or her own opinion or feelings very evident, or is the diction objective and neutral?
7. Does the diction appeal directly (a) to one or more of our senses, or (b) to our emotions or (c) is it indicative of abstract or generalized thought?
8. Does the diction belong to any specialized sphere of knowledge, or is it part of the common currency of language?

1. *Does the diction produce any pervasive or predominant impression?*

Read this passage by Gerald Durrell and jot down notes in answer to the question above.

Durrell is describing his first impression of Corfu, seen from a ship at sea. He has only recently left behind the leaden skies of an English seaside resort.

The sea lifted smooth blue muscles of wave as it stirred in the dawn-light, and the foam of our wake spread gently behind us like a white peacock's tail, glinting with bubbles. The sky was pale and stained with yellow on the eastern horizon. Ahead, lay a chocolate-brown smudge of land, huddled in mist, with a frill of foam at its base. This was Corfu, and we strained our eyes 5
to make out the exact shapes of the mountains, to discover valleys, peaks, ravines, and beaches, but it remained a silhouette. Then suddenly the sun shifted over the horizon, and the sky turned the smooth enamelled blue of a jay's eye. The endless, meticulous curves of the sea flamed for an instant and then changed to a deep royal purple flecked with green. The mist lifted in 10
quick, lithe ribbons, and before us lay the island, the mountains as though sleeping beneath a crumpled blanket of brown, the folds stained with the green of olive-groves. Along the shore curved beaches as white as tusks among tottering cities of brilliant gold, red, and white rocks. We rounded the northern cape, a smooth shoulder of rust-red cliff carved into a series of 15
giant caves. The dark waves lifted our wake and carried it gently towards them, and then, at their very mouths, it crumpled and hissed thirstily among the rocks. Rounding the cape, we left the mountains, and the island sloped gently down, blurred with the silver and green iridescence of olives, with here and there an admonishing finger of black cypress against the sky. The 20
shallow sea in the bays was butterfly blue, and even above the sound of the ship's engines we could hear, faintly ringing from the shore like a chorus of tiny voices, the shrill, triumphant cries of the cicadas.

My Family and Other Animals (1956)

We hope you found that the diction of this passage is principally directed to registering a sense of rich, dazzling colours and shapes under a glistening Mediterranean light. Your notes should record a large number of words which cluster around this central idea: the colours of 'smooth-enamelled blue' and 'the green of olive-groves'; the repeated use of words such as 'glinting', 'flamed' and 'flecked'. Contrast this with the diction we found in Dickens's description of the melancholy, sodden Lincolnshire landscape.

Though the main appeal of this passage is to our sense of sight, you should also have recorded some words which are directed to other senses. Where, for example, do we find diction connected with (a) sound, and (b) the texture that certain objects might be imagined to possess – their tactile quality? Did you also notice that two words are repeated three times? Why is this?

Your notes on the diction of this passage may contain a number of general descriptions ranging, perhaps, from 'colourfully exotic' and 'romantic' to 'overwritten' and 'self-indulgent'. This is fair enough: judgements will naturally vary. What we would like to stress at this point, however, is that any *general* comment you make on diction must be linked with close, concrete analysis. It is not enough to stick an all-purpose descriptive label on a piece of prose; you must first examine, word by word if necessary, the way in which the language is working.

To help you to be as *specific* as possible at this stage, we would like you to answer two final questions on the Durrell extract:

(i) Which words in the passage suggest (a) the sense of an exotic place, and (b) the idea that this scene is being observed for the first time by the author? Comment on the words you have chosen.

(ii) Select *five* words which you think clearly suggest Durrell's feelings about what he is describing. Comment briefly on the precise effect each word produces.

This next passage makes an interesting contrast with the description of sun-drenched Corfu. It is taken from a D. H. Lawrence short story.

Decide what you feel is the predominant impression of the diction, and then define in a short paragraph *how* this is achieved.

When I awoke I found the house darkened with deep, soft snow, which had blown against the large west windows, covering them with a screen. I went outside, and saw the valley all white and ghastly below me, the trees beneath black and thin looking like wire, the rock-faces dark between the glistening shroud, and the sky above sombre, heavy, yellowish-dark, much too heavy   5
for this world below of hollow bluey whiteness figured with black. I felt I was in a valley of the dead. And I sensed I was a prisoner, for the snow was everywhere deep, and drifted in places. So all the morning I remained indoors, looking up the drive at the shrubs so heavily plumed with snow, at the gateposts raised high with a foot or more of extra whiteness. Or I looked   10
down into the white-and-black valley that was utterly motionless and beyond life, a hollow sarcophagus.

Nothing stirred the whole day – no plume fell off the shrubs, the valley was as abstracted as a grove of death. I looked over at the tiny, half-buried

farms away on the bare uplands beyond the valley hollow. And the snow   15
seemed to lay me bare to influences I wanted to escape.

'Wintry Peacock' (from the collection *England, My England*, 1922)

2. *What are the key words? What are the words which are 'doing the work'?*

The importance of this kind of question may be judged by the fact that
virtually from the start of this chapter we have always, implicitly, been
asking it. When you considered the passage from Lawrence's story, you
probably found that you were constructing a word-list of key items – such
as 'darkened', 'white', 'thin looking like wire' and 'sombre' – as crucial
elements in the creating of this haunting wintry landscape of austere black
and white.

There is one further related question that you may have gone on to
consider in connection with the Lawrence passage:

3. *Do the key words combine or interlock in any particular way – as
regards, for example, their connotations?*

As we look more closely at the diction of some prose, we may discover an
underlying network of interconnections which draws on implicit parallels
or reinforces a related set of connotations. To make this clearer, consider
this sentence in the Lawrence passage in which, possibly, the narrator
strikes the key-note of his response: 'I felt I was in the valley of the dead'.

The same note is sounded again when he tells us that the valley 'was as
abstracted as a grove of *death*'; and the same idea is explicitly embodied in
such diction as 'shroud' and 'hollow sarcophagus'. Once we have
observed this, do we not quickly notice how a whole range of diction in
the passage *implicitly* revolves around the notions of death and burial?
Consider, for example, the connotations of the following: 'ghastly',
'sombre', 'utterly motionless', 'nothing stirred', 'half-buried' and the
suggestiveness of the colour black which recurs in the passage. You
should be able to locate other features in the passage which reinforce this
pervasive idea.

Now examine these two short passages and then note, in each case, the
ways in which the key words are arranged to create a unified impression.

*Both extracts are set in foreign parts. In the first, the scene is Mexico; in the
second, a couple in a car approach a city in the West Indies.*

Mr Tench went out to look for his ether cylinder, into the blazing Mexican
sun and the bleaching dust. A few vultures looked down from the roof with
shabby indifference: he wasn't carrion yet. A faint feeling of rebellion stirred
in Mr Tench's heart, and he wrenched up a piece of the road with splintering
finger-nails and tossed it feebly towards them. One rose and flapped across   5
the town: over the tiny plaza, over the bust of an ex-president, ex-general,
ex-human being, over the two stalls which sold mineral water, towards the

river and the sea. It wouldn't find anything there: the sharks looked after the carrion on that side. Mr Tench went across the plaza.

Graham Greene: *The Power and the Glory* (1940)

In a list of key words we might arrange some of the items in three separate categories.

(i) bleaching dust; shabby; splintering finger-nails
(ii) vultures; carrion (used twice); ex-president, ex-general, ex-human being; sharks
(iii) faint; feebly.

What is the common denominator of the items in each list? In what ways do these separate elements overlap to produce a dominant impression?

What does Greene suggest about Mr Tench's mood and feelings?

Now approach the following passage in a similar way by making a list of the key words and deciding in what ways they relate to reinforce a predominant impression.

Past the junked cars in the sunken fields, past the factories, past more country settlements, the suburbs, they approached the city, the rubbish dump smoking yellow-grey, the smoke uncoiling slowly in the still afternoon, rising high and spreading far, becoming mingled with the pink pall from the bauxite loading station, the whole shot through with the rays   5
of the declining sun. Sunlight gilded the stilted shacks that seemed to scaffold the red hillsides. The land began to feel choked. But the shanty-town redevelopments were subdued; those repetitive avenues of red earth showed little of their usual human overspill. There were few lorries amid the smoke and the miniature multi-coloured hills and valleys of the rubbish   10
dump, and not many scavengers. On each fence post a black carrion corbeau sat undisturbed; others on the ground hopped about awkwardly, two feet at a time.
    Jane rolled up her window, to keep out the oily smoke and the deep dead smell.   15
    Roche said, 'Picking the carcase clean. They'll pick the carcase clean.'

V. S. Naipaul: *Guerrillas* (1975)

Not all prose, of course, will reveal this kind of internal organisation. In what type of writing do you think we are most likely to come across it?

4. *Do the key words generally belong to the same part of speech*?

Sometimes it may be the case that the selection of words belonging to a particular part of speech stands out as a distinctive feature of a writer's style. This will generally involve an author's choice of nouns, verbs, adjectives and adverbs – though this is not to say that the more basic units of language, such as prepositions, conjunctions and pronouns, have no part to play in the creation of certain stylistic effects.

You might find it instructive to extract, in the form of a list, all the adjectives from the extract from D. H. Lawrence's 'Wintry Peacock', page 26. Do you find that, in this passage, adjectives produce the predominant – though that is not to say exclusive – effect? What important words are *not* included in your list? To what part(s) of speech do they belong? Is it true to say that in *all* descriptive writing adjectives will always be the crucial part of speech?

An author can sometimes produce the desired effect by deliberately limiting the use of a particular part of speech. For instance, Graham Greene, in his autobiography *A Sort of Life* (1971), writes of the difficulty he once experienced in creating drama and excitement in his writing; he found something of a solution to his problem in a wariness of using too many adjectives. His reason for this is that 'an adjective slows the pace or tranquillizes the nerve'. When he wants to create exciting action, he aims for plainness and simplicity: 'action can only be expressed by a subject, a verb and an object, perhaps a rhythm – little else'. Greene quotes with approval a couple of sentences from R. L. Stevenson. Do you agree with Greene's view that Stevenson's bare prose conveys the action effectively?

> It came all of a sudden when it did, with a rush of feet and a roar, and then a shout from Alan, and the sound of blows and someone crying as if hurt. I looked back over my shoulder and saw Mr Shuan in the doorway crossing blades with Alan.
>
> *Kidnapped* (1886)

Greene adds that a common fault among young writers of prose is to be led astray by a fatal love for words: 'Discrimination in one's words is certainly required, but not love of one's words – that is a form of self-love.' What do you think he means? Do you agree?

The American writer, Ernest Hemingway, frequently aimed at a style in which adjectives were used sparingly: the result often looks deceptively simple. Consider the following short passage.

> They came around a bend and a dog came out barking. Ahead were the lights of the shanties where the Indian bark-peelers lived. More dogs rushed out at them. The two Indians sent them back to the shanties. In the shanty nearest the road there was a light in the window. An old woman stood in the doorway holding a lamp.   5
>
> Inside on a wooden bunk lay a young Indian woman. She had been trying to have her baby for two days. All the old women in the camp had been helping her. The men had moved off up the road to sit in the dark and smoke out of range of the noise she made. She screamed just as Nick and the two Indians followed his father and Uncle George into the shanty.   10
>
> She lay in the lower bunk, very big under a quilt. Her head was turned to one side. In the upper bunk was her husband. He had cut his foot very badly with an axe three days before. He was smoking a pipe. The room smelled very bad.
>
> 'Indian Camp' (from *The First Forty-Nine Stories*, 1938)

Adjectives are not, of course, completely absent, but in general they are used in a denotative way: 'wooden', 'young' or 'lower'. Somebody commented that, because of his descriptive restraint, Hemingway's use of adjectives which we might normally regard as impoverished – 'big' or 'bad' – makes them 'possess a new, hard ring'. Do you agree?

What is the general emotional impact Hemingway is aiming for here?

The final extract in this section is taken from another story, 'Adolf', by D. H. Lawrence. To what part of speech do you think the key words belong? And how well-chosen are they?

> Suddenly the rabbit was alert. He hobbled a few tiny paces, and reared himself up inquisitively at the sugar basin. He fluttered his tiny fore-paws, and then reached and laid them on the edge of the basin, whilst he craned his thin neck and peeped in. He trembled his whiskers at the sugar, then did his best to lift down a lump.

5. Is there any sign that the key words belong predominantly to the Latin or Saxon sources of English?

This is a complex question and we can do no more than scratch at its surface. However, it is probably worth pointing out that in our reading of English prose, we may be made aware of a broad distinction between the words in English which have a Latinate origin and those which derive from the language's Anglo-Saxon roots. English is a uniquely rich, flexible and subtle language, and for this we have to thank its capacity to absorb words from other languages[1]. However, for general purposes of prose analysis, we may distinguish the two main tributaries which have flowed into our language as (i) Latinate or Romance, which covers words deriving from Greek, French and Italian as well as Latin, and (ii) Saxon or Teutonic, which refers to words having their origin in Old English or the related Scandinavian or Germanic languages.

Consider these pairings of words:

Latinate origin	*Saxon origin*
narration	tale
pediatrics	child-care
garrulous	talkative
termination	end
maternal	motherly
fatal	deadly
sovereign	king (queen)
exterminate	kill

---

[1] If you wish to study this topic, called *philology*, further, you should consult books such as Jespersen's *Growth and Structure of the English Language* or Anthony Burgess's *Language Made Plain*.

What different connotations do each of these synonyms have?

In *general*, we can say that words of Saxon origin tend to be shorter, less formal and possibly 'earthier' than those of Latinate derivation, though it would be easy to find many exceptions to this statement. Words of Latinate origin are liable to come into play, for example, when we are dealing with more general or abstract matters: they lend themselves to the language of formal inquiry and scientific writing – and, at one extreme, this kind of vocabulary can degenerate into vapid abstraction, jargon and euphemism (compare, for example, the difference between 'exterminate' and 'kill').

Consider, however, this passage from Dr Johnson's *Preface to Shakespeare*, written in 1765.

> Antiquity, like every other quality that attracts the notice of mankind, has undoubtedly votaries that reverence it, not from reason, but from prejudice. Some seem to admire indiscriminately whatever has been long preserved, without considering that time has sometimes co-operated with chance; all perhaps are more willing to honour past than present excellence; and the   5
> mind contemplates genius through the shades of age, as the eye surveys the sun through artificial opacity. The great contention of criticism is to find the faults of the moderns, and the beauties of the ancients. While an author is yet living we estimate his powers by his worst performance, and when he is dead we rate them by his best.   10

Are the roots of the diction predominantly Latinate or Saxon? Why has Dr Johnson chosen language of this particular type? Clearly you will have been struck both by the precision and by the majesty of his prose style, which in no small way derives from his choice of diction.

6. *Does the writer's choice of vocabulary make his or her own opinion or feelings very evident, or is the diction objective and neutral?*

With this question in mind, read the following passage. You may find it useful to ask yourself what kind of reader it is aimed at.

> It took hundreds of millions of years to produce the life that now inhabits the earth – aeons of time in which that developing and evolving and diversifying life reached a state of adjustment and balance with its surroundings. The environment, rigorously shaping and directing the life it supported, contained elements that were hostile as well as supporting.   5
> Certain rocks gave out dangerous radiation; even within the light of the sun, from which all life draws its energy, there were short-wave radiations with power to injure. Given time – time not in years but in millenia – life adjusts, and a balance has been reached. For time is the essential ingredient; but in the modern world there is no time.   10
> The rapidity of change and the speed with which new situations are created follow the impetuous and heedless pace of man rather than the deliberate pace of nature. Radiation is no longer merely the background radiation of rocks, the bombardment of cosmic rays, the ultra-violet of the

sun that have existed before there was any life on earth; radiation is now the   15
unnatural creation of man's tampering with the atom. The chemicals to
which life is asked to make its adjustments are no longer merely the calcium
and silica and copper and all the rest of the minerals washed out of the rocks
and carried in rivers to the sea; they are the synthetic creations of man's
inventive mind, brewed in his laboratories, and having no counterparts in   20
nature.

To adjust to these chemicals would require time on the scale that is
nature's; it would require not merely the years of a man's life but the life of
generations. And even this, were it by some miracle possible, would be futile,
for the new chemicals come from our laboratories in an endless stream;   25
almost five hundred annually find their way into actual use in the United
States alone. The figure is staggering and its implications are not easily
grasped – five hundred new chemicals to which the bodies of men and
animals are required somehow to adapt each year, chemicals totally outside
the limits of biological experience.   30

Among them are many that are used in man's war against nature. Since
the mid-1940s over two hundred basic chemicals have been created for use in
killing insects, weeds, rodents, and other organisms described in the modern
vernacular as 'pests'; and they are sold under several thousand different
brand names.   35

These sprays, dusts, and aerosols are now applied almost universally to
farms, gardens, forests, and homes – non-selective chemicals that have the
power to kill every insect, the 'good' and the 'bad', to still the song of birds
and the leaping of fish in the stream, to coat the leaves with a deadly film,
and to linger on in soil – all this though the intended target may be only a   40
few weeds or insects. Can anyone believe it is possible to lay down such a
barrage of poisons on the surface of the earth without making it unfit for all
life? They should not be called 'insecticides', but 'biocides'.

Rachel Carson: *Silent Spring* (1963)

While the opening sentences are straightforwardly factual and the
passage contains numerous words which have a strong scientific ring, you
should have been quickly aware that the diction of the passage reveals
that Rachel Carson is no dispassionate commentator. She has a case to
argue and this clearly colours her choice of words.

Consider carefully the way in which the key words in the following
three examples from the second paragraph reveal the writer's own feelings
and attitudes.

(a) The rapidity of change and the speed with which new situations are
created follow the impetuous and heedless pace of man rather than the
deliberate pace of nature. (lines 11–13)

(b) . . . radiation is now the unnatural creation of man's tampering with the
atom. (lines 15–16)   5

(c) they [chemicals] are the synthetic creations of man's inventive mind,
brewed in his laboratories, and having no counterpart in nature. (lines
19–21)

Rachel Carson is writing for the general, educated reader and her prose style is designed to alert the reader to changes in the natural environment which she considers dangerous and to persuade us that urgent action is necessary. She has strong feelings on the matter – that should be obvious from your analysis of the quotations above – and she wishes to enlist our feelings too.

Decide what effect you think Rachel Carson wishes to achieve in this extract from the last paragraph:

> . . . to still the song of birds and the leaping of fish in the stream, to coat the leaves with a deadly film, and to linger on in soil . . . (lines 38–40)

If Rachel Carson were writing for a scientific journal, how would this affect her choice of vocabulary?

It is vital to be aware of the shades of feeling or attitude that are communicated by a writer's choice of word. Sometimes this may be subtle or ambivalent, though in the extract quoted above you probably found that an obvious, though perhaps slightly contrived, charge of feeling ran through a phrase such as 'to still the songs of birds'. We often call this kind of diction 'emotive language': it is designed to trigger a strong emotional reaction in the reader – what we often term, colloquially, 'a gut reaction'.

In this next passage, taken this time from a novel, consider how Joseph Conrad employs emotive language to guide our response to the old terrorist, Karl Yundt.

On the other side of the fireplace, in the horse-hair armchair, Karl Yundt giggled grimly, with a faint black grimace of a toothless mouth. The terrorist, as he called himself, was old and bald, with a narrow, snow-white wisp of a goatee hanging limply from his chin. An extraordinary expression of underhand malevolence survived in his extinguished eyes. When he rose   5 painfully the thrusting forward of a skinny groping hand deformed by gouty swellings suggested the effort of a moribund murderer summoning all his remaining strength for a last stab. He leaned on a thick stick, which trembled under his other hand. 'I have always dreamed,' he mouthed, fiercely, 'of a band of men absolute in their resolve to discard all scruples in the choice of   10 means, strong enough to give themselves frankly the name of destroyers, and free from the taint of that resigned pessimism which rots the world. No pity for anything on earth, including themselves, and death enlisted for good and all in the service of humanity – that's what I would have liked to see.'

His little bald head quivered, imparting a comical vibration to the wisp of   15 white goatee. His enunciation would have been almost totally unintelligible to a stranger. His worn-out passion, resembling in its impotent fierceness the excitement of a senile sensualist, was badly served by a dried throat and toothless gums which seemed to catch the tip of his tongue.

Joseph Conrad: *The Secret Agent* (1907)

The following extract from one of Churchill's wartime speeches in 1940, after the formation of the Coalition Government, certainly falls into this category of prose designed to produce a gut reaction. Several words and phrases have been italicized for you to consider the kind of emotional response each is designed to produce. This will involve you in some discussion of the range of connotations of these key words.

Having received *His Majesty's commission,* I have formed an administration of men and women of *every party* and of almost every point of view. We have differed and quarrelled in the past, but now *one bond unites us all* – to wage war until *victory* is won, and never to *surrender* ourselves to *servitude and shame,* whatever the cost and the *agony* may be. This is one of the most *awe-* 5 *striking* periods in *the long history of France and Britain.* It is also beyond doubt *the most sublime. Side by side,* unaided except by their *kith and kin* in the great Dominions and by *the whole wide Empires* which *rest beneath their shield* – side by side, the British and the French peoples have advanced to rescue not only Europe but *mankind* from *the foulest and most soul-* 10 *destroying tyranny* which has ever *darkened and stained the pages of history.* Behind them – behind us – behind the armies and fleets of Britain and France – gather a group of *shattered States and bludgeoned races*: the Czechs, the Poles, the Norwegians, the Danes, the Dutch, the Belgians – upon all of whom *the long night of barbarism* will descend, unbroken even by 15 *a star of hope,* unless we *conquer,* as conquer we must; as conquer we shall.

As a general discussion topic, consider the view that, by the nature of language itself, it is impossible to be *completely* objective when we write. Take the following statement as a starting-point: 'It is simply a question of the *degree* to which the writer's feelings are apparent, running on a scale from Churchill's emotive diction to the instructions on how to roast a chicken which, though apparently emotionally neutral, will nevertheless convey some traces of feeling and attitude.'

Our next question grows naturally out of matters we have already been considering:

7. *Does the diction appeal directly (a) to one or more of our senses, or (b) to our emotions or (c) is it indicative of abstract or generalized thought?*

To try to help you make the distinctions which are taken for granted in this general question, read these statements about some of the passages you have already read in this chapter, and decide whether the statements are true or false. To assist you, we have done the first one for you.

(i) Dickens, page 22.
   Dickens pursues his argument about climatic changes to its logical conclusion.   True/False
   Clearly false. Dickens's aim is not to argue logically, but to evoke the damp, dank atmosphere at Chesney Wold. To this end, he uses words that appeal directly to our senses, especially of hearing and touch. Reread our notes on page 23 to see how he does this.
(ii) Anthony Burgess, page 24.

Burgess presents a purely cerebral view of his characters.

True/False

(iii) Graham Greene, page 27.
Greene's description is a sensuous evocation of a decaying Mexican town. True/False

(iv) Dr Johnson, page 31.
Johnson is arguing about the influence of the past on the present and his diction is therefore indicative of abstract and generalized thought. True/False

(v) Churchill, page 34.
Though clearly diction here is designed to appeal to our emotions, the author is not neglectful of language that appeals also to our senses. True/False

(vi) None of the passages we have reread in this section involves all three elements of diction singled out in question seven.

True/False

8. *Does the diction belong to any specialized sphere of knowledge (science, philosophy, politics, etc.) or is it part of the common currency of the language?*

When we were discussing Rachel Carson's diction (page 31), we noticed that, while she used a number of terms of scientific origin – words such as 'radiation', 'cosmic rays' and 'ultra-violet' – these were terms which were not going to mystify the general reader because of their general and widespread currency. Her diction is not in any way specialized, and the passage is concerned to find a level of discourse which is accessible to the ordinary person who knows little of natural science.

In modern times, particularly with the expansion of knowledge in areas such as sociology, psychology and the sciences, there has been a marked tendency for such disciplines to develop their own specialized language, or jargon. The study of literature has not been immune from the general trend, and in this book we make use of some elements of the vocabulary of literary criticism which we suggest can assist in pin-pointing important ideas succinctly – though it would clearly be undesirable to write at this level in a critical vocabulary which excluded the general reader from the debate. Obviously, jargon may be perfectly justified as a shorthand when one expert – for example, a doctor or a professional philosopher – communicates with a colleague: they share the same specialized language. Sometimes in the course of time, words from a relatively narrow discipline can become a part of the vocabulary of everyone, so that most people today would have some idea what was meant if you referred to, for example, 'class conflict', 'neurosis' or 'genetics'. The danger is, however, that jargon can sometimes be used in an attempt to mystify or browbeat the reader, or to add an entirely spurious authority to a piece of writing. This can even happen in conversation: is not a doctor, for example, parading his professional credentials a little obviously if, when talking to a patient's relative who clearly does not understand, he repeatedly refers to a case of 'cardiac arrest'? Do we really welcome throat specialists who portentously wish to dignify themselves with the title of 'laryngologist', or 'otorhinolaryngologist'?

The following piece from the opening of an article written as a parody of a certain kind of sociological jargon is, unhappily, representative of a kind of English which insidiously creeps into other kinds of writing:

> The purpose of this scheme is to present a taxonomic dichotomization which would allow for unilinear comparisons. In this fashion we could hope to distinguish the relevant variables which determine the functional speci-ficities of social movements. Any classificatory scheme is, essentially, an answer to some implicit other scheme. In this instance, it is an attempt to   5
> answer the various hylozoic theories which deny that social categories can be separable.
>
> > Daniel Bell: 'The Parameters of Social Movements: A Formal
> > Paradigm' taken from *Parodies: an Anthology from Chaucer to
> > Beerbohm – and After*, ed. Dwight Macdonald (1964)

  (i) Can you make *any* sense of this? Offer a brief, clear summary, if you can.
 (ii) What might be the motives of somebody who wrote seriously in this fashion?
(iii) Select three examples of jargon from the extract, and, after defining what each one means, consider whether they serve any useful purpose in writing of a more general kind.

You may be amused to learn that when Daniel Bell sent this parody to three of his fellow sociologists, two of them took it seriously!

It is true, of course, that a writer may wish to use the sectional vocabulary of a class, trade or profession to add authenticity to a work. So in a spy novel, such as John Le Carré's *Tinker, Tailor, Soldier, Spy* (1974) we find an abundance of words connected with the practice of espionage such as 'moles', 'housekeepers', 'lamplighters', 'tradecraft', and 'pavement artists', and the reader is given sufficient information to work out what they mean. It should also be noted that there is a level of diction appropriate to certain kinds of writing. An insurance or legal document (see the extract in our Introduction, page 2) or a formal business letter tend to generate their own conventional vocabulary. However, in general, one should beware of jargon: so often it is the cloak for confusion, exhibitionism or emptiness of real thought. The jargon-obsessed writer simply stitches together ready-made phrases to give an impression of importance to what is essentially trite, and as a result, any sense of language as an expressive and flexible medium is abandoned.

Every year the *Plain English Campaign* awards a prize to outstanding examples of official gobbledegook. We include here the first prize winner of the 1981 competition – which earned its writer two pounds of best Lancashire tripe. We want you:

(i) to summarize (use as few words as possible) in clear English what is really meant;
(ii) to comment on the most glaring examples of jargon and gobbledegook;
(iii) to look at the structure of the sentences. In what way(s) does this also hinder clear communication?

A reply to a disgruntled traveller on British Rail who had complained about the absence of a buffet service.

Whilst I can readily appreciate your frustration at the loss of breakfast, since in the circumstances you describe it is unfortunately true that in many cases where a catering vehicle becomes defective and both stores and equipment need to be transferred into a replacement car, this can only be done during the train's journey. We are very conscious of the need to reduce instances of 5 failure and provide the advertised service to a minimum, and each case is recorded and the reasons closely scrutinised in an effort to avoid a repetition.

You might like to collect the examples of jargon and gobbledegook you come across in your own reading, both as a source of amusement and as a warning to yourself of the type of writing to avoid!

Another exercise along similar lines. George Orwell takes a well-known verse from *Ecclesiastes* (a) and 'translates' it into (b).

(a) I returned and saw under the sun, that the race is not to the swift, nor the battle to the strong, neither yet bread to the wise, nor yet riches to men of understanding, nor yet favour to men of skill; but time and chance happeneth to them all.

(b) Objective consideration of contemporary phenomena compels the 5 conclusion that success or failure in competitive activities exhibits no tendency to be commensurate with innate capacity, but that a considerable element of the unpredictable must invariably be taken into account.

Orwell says of his translation: 'This is a parody, but not a very gross one'. What does he mean?

After wading through the seas of treacly prose in the previous exercises, some light relief may be in order, though you will quickly see how the following passage relates to some of the questions we have been discussing.

Read through this extract and then write your views on the points the author is making about a certain kind of journalistic style.

Goldwasser works on a research project dedicated to demonstrate that 'in theory a digital computer could be programmed to produce a perfectly satisfactory daily newspaper with all the variety and news sense of the old handmade article'. This involves feeding into a computer 'standard variables and invariables' of news stories.

Goldwasser sometimes took himself out of himself by pretending to be a computer, and going through one of the completed sets of cards observing the same logical rules and making the same random choices that a computer would to compose a story from them. The by-election set and the weather story set soon palled. So did "I Test New Car" and "Red Devils Fly in to   5
Trouble Spot". But the set for composing a loyal leader on a royal occasion seemed to Goldwasser to have something of that teasing perfection which draws one back again and again to certain pictures.

He opened the filing cabinet and picked out the first card in the set. *Traditionally*, it read. Now there was a random choice between cards   10
reading *coronations, engagements, funerals, weddings, coming of age, births, deaths*, or the *churching of women*. The day before he had picked *funerals*, and been directed on to a card reading with simple perfection *are occasions for mourning*. Today he closed his eyes, drew *weddings*, and was signposted on to *are occasions for rejoicing*.   15

The wedding of X and Y followed in logical sequence, and brought him a choice between *is no exception* and *is a case in point*. Either way there followed *indeed*. Indeed, whichever occasion one had started off with, whether coronations, deaths, or birth, Goldwasser saw with intense mathematical pleasure, one now reached this same elegant bottleneck. He   20
paused on *indeed*, then drew in quick succession *it is a particularly happy occasion, rarely*, and *can there have been a more popular young couple*.

From the next selection Goldwasser drew *X has won himself/herself a special place in the nation's affections*, which forced him to go on to *and the British people have clearly taken Y to their hearts already*.   25

Goldwasser was surprised, and a little disturbed, to realise that the word 'fitting' had still not come up. But he drew it with the next card – *it is especially fitting that*.

This gave him *the bride/bridegroom should be*, and an open choice between *of such a noble and illustrious line, a commoner in these democratic times, from*   30
a nation with which this country has long enjoyed a particularly close and cordial relationship, and *from a nation with which this country's relations have not in the past been always happy*.

Feeling that he had done particularly well with 'fitting' last time, Goldwasser now deliberately selected it again. *It is also fitting that*, read the   35
card, to be quickly followed by *we should remember*, and *X and Y are not merely symbols – they are a lively young man and a very lovely young woman*.

Goldwasser shut his eyes to draw the next card. It turned out to read *in these days when*. He pondered whether to select *it is fashionable to scoff at the traditional morality of marriage and family life* or *it is no longer fashionable to*   40
scoff at the traditional morality of marriage and family life. The latter had more of the form's authentic baroque splendour, he decided. He drew another *it is fitting that*, but thinking three times round was once too many for anything, even for a superb and beautiful word like 'fitting', he cheated and changed it for *it is meet that*, after which *we wish them well* followed as   45
the night the day, and the entertainment was over.

What a piece of work had the school of Goldwasser wrought here! What a toccata and fugue! How remote it was from the harsh cares of life!

Goldwasser started all over again with the churching of women. He had got as far as a choice between *it is good to see the old traditions being kept up* 50 and *it is good to see old usages brought more into line with our modern way of thinking*, when Nobbs came shambling out of his room, the word 'mate' written all over his face.

'Now look here, mate,' started Nobbs, 'this Paralysed Girl Determined to Dance Again . . . ' 55

But at this point, as it said on one of the cards in the 'They Are Calling It the Street of Shame' story cabinet, *our investigator made an excuse and left.*

Michael Frayn: *The Tin Men* (1965)

Now would be a good time to turn back to the list of questions we started off with (page 24) – before we add one or two more.

The next list of questions is couched in the form of a series of opposing qualities that prose may possess. They are offered, again, in the belief that when you are puzzled by a passage of prose and uncertain how to react, it is far better – certainly under the pressure of having to produce an examination answer – to begin a kind of 'interrogation' than to sit back passively in the hope that a response will begin to form.

(i) Is the diction: informal or formal?; literary, colloquial or even slangy?; elevated, everyday, or perhaps 'prosaic'?

(ii) Is the vocabulary drawn from current usage or is it consciously archaic? (It is vital to take into account the period at which the prose was written: diction which may seem archaic to us may have been common usage at the time of writing.)

(iii) Does the language draw attention to itself, perhaps as a result of its obscure diction, unusual syntax, metaphorical pyrotechnics or complex word-play, or is the prose style a straightforward, unobtrusive medium?

(iv) Is the diction in the same key throughout (e.g. elevated, grandilo-quent or mundane); or are there shifts in the kind of language at work, perhaps in response to a different purpose the writer has in mind; or a mixing of different registers to produce effects such as irony or bathos?

With all these questions to guide you, look at the following passages, which are grouped in pairs, and comment on their diction. You will hardly need the hint that, in the case of each pairing, you should be on the look-out for significant *contrasts* in the diction.

A. . . . It was the same in the next round; but the balance of power was thus restored – the fate of the battle was suspended. No one could tell how it would end. This was the only moment in which opinion was divided; for, in the next, the Gas-man aiming a mortal blow at his adversary's neck, with his right hand, and failing from the length he had to reach, the other 5 returned it with his left at full swing, planted a tremendous blow on his cheek-bone and eye-brow, and made a red ruin of that side of his face. The Gas-man went down, and there was another shout – a roar of triumph as the waves of fortune rolled tumultuously from side to side. This was a settler. Hickman got up, and 'grinned horrible a ghastly 10 smile', yet he was evidently dashed in his opinion of himself; it was the first time he had never been so punished; all one side of his face was perfect scarlet, and his right eye was closed in dingy blackness, as he advanced to the fight, less confident, but still determined. After one or two rounds, not receiving another such remembrancer, he rallied and 15 went at it with his former impetuosity. But in vain. His strength had been weakened, – his blows could not tell at such a distance, – he was obliged to fling himself at his adversary, and could not strike from his feet; and almost as regularly as he flew at him with his right hand, Neate warded the blow, or drew back out of its reach, and felled him with the return of 20 his left. There was little cautious sparring – no half-hits – no tapping and trifling, none of the *petit-maitreship* of the art – they were almost all knock-down blows: – the fight was a good stand-up fight.

B. It goes along like that for three rounds more. They don't talk any. They're working all the time. We worked over Jack plenty too, in between the rounds. He don't look good at all but he never does much work in the ring. He don't move around much and that left-hand is just automatic. It's just like it was connected with Walcott's face and Jack 5 just had to wish it in every time. Jack is always calm in close and he doesn't waste any juice. He knows everything about working in close too and he's getting away with a lot of stuff. While they were in our corner I watched him tie Walcott up, get his right hand loose, turn it and come up with an uppercut that got Walcott's nose with the heel of the glove. 10 Walcott was bleeding bad and leaned his nose on Jack's shoulder so as to give Jack some of it too, and Jack sort of lifted his shoulder sharp and caught him against the nose, and then brought down the right hand and did the same thing again.

Walcott was sore as hell. By the time they'd gone five rounds he hated 15 Jack's guts. Jack wasn't sore; that is, he wasn't any sorer than he always was. He certainly did used to make the fellows he fought hate boxing. That was why he hated Richie Lewis so. He never got Richie's goat. Richie Lewis always had about three new dirty things Jack couldn't do. Jack was as safe as a church all the time he was in there as long as he was 20 strong. He certainly was treating Walcott rough. The funny thing was it looked as though Jack was an open classic boxer. That was because he had all that stuff too.

A. William Hazlitt: 'The Fight' (1822)

B. Ernest Hemingway: 'Fifty Grand' (from *Men Without Women*, 1928)

C. A splendid Midsummer shone over England; skies so pure, suns so radiant as were then seen in long succession, seldom favour, even singly, our wave-girt land. It was as if a band of Italian days had come from the South, like a flock of glorious passenger birds, and lighted to rest them

on the cliffs of Albion. The hay was all got in; the fields round Thornfield   5
were green and shorn; the roads white and baked, the trees were in their
dark prime; hedge and wood, full-leaved and deeply tinted, contrasted
well with the sunny hue of the cleared meadows between.

On Midsummer-eve, Adele, weary with gathering wild strawberries in
Hay Lane half the day, had gone to bed with the sun. I watched her drop   10
asleep, and when I left her, I sought the garden.

It was now the sweetest hour of the twenty-four: "day its fervid fires
had wasted", and dew fell cool on panting plain and scorched summit.
Where the sun had gone down in simple state – pure of the pomp of
clouds – spread a solemn purple, burning with the light of red jewel and   15
furnace flame at one point, on one hill-peak, and extending high and
wide, soft and still softer, over half heaven. The east had its own charm
of fine deep blue, and its own modest gem, a rising and solitary star: soon
it would boast the moon; but she was yet beneath the horizon.

I walked a while on the pavement; but a subtle, well-known scent –   20
that of a cigar – stole from some window; I saw the library casement
open a hand-breadth; I knew I might be watched thence; so I went apart
into the orchard. No nook in the grounds more sheltered and more
Eden-like; a very high wall shut it out from the court on one side; on the
other a beech avenue screened it from the lawn. At the bottom was a   25
sunk fence, its sole separation from lonely fields; a winding walk,
bordered with laurels and terminating in a giant horse-chestnut, circled
at the base by a seat, led down to the fence. Here one could wander
unseen. While such honeydew fell, such silence reigned, such gloaming
gathered, I felt as if I could haunt such shade for ever.

D. Sometimes we'd have that whole river all to ourselves for the longest
time. Yonder was the banks and the islands, across the water; and maybe
a spark – which was a candle in a cabin window; and sometimes on the
water you could see a spark or two – on a raft or scow, you know; and
maybe you could hear a fiddle or a song coming over from one of them   5
crafts. It's lovely to live on a raft. We had the sky up there, all speckled
with stars, and we used to lay on our backs and look up at them, and
discuss about whether they was made or just happened. Jim he allowed
they was made, but I allowed they happened; I judged it would have took
too long to *make* so many. Jim said the moon could 'a' laid them: well,   10
that looked kind of reasonable, so I didn't say nothing against it, because
I've seen a frog lay most as many, so of course it could be done. We used
to watch the stars that fell, too, and see them streak down. Jim allowed
they'd got spoiled and was hove out of the nest.

Once or twice of a night we would see a steamboat slipping along in   15
the dark, and now and then she would belch a whole world of sparks up
out of her chimbleys, and they would rain down in the river and look
awful pretty; then she would turn a corner and her lights would wink out
and her powwow shut off and leave the river still again, and by and by
her waves would get to us, a long time after she was gone, and joggle the   20
raft a bit, and after that you wouldn't hear nothing for you couldn't tell
how long, except maybe frogs or something.

After midnight the people on shore went to bed, and then for two or three hours the shores was black – no more sparks in the cabin windows. These sparks was our clock – the first one that showed again meant   25 morning was coming, so we hunted a place to hide and tie up right away.

C. Charlotte Brontë: *Jane Eyre* (1847)

D. Mark Twain: *The Adventures of Huckleberry Finn* (1884)

E. The corn was orient and immortal wheat, which should never be reaped, nor was ever sown. I thought it had stood from everlasting to everlasting. The dust and stones of the street were as precious as gold: the gates were at first the end of the world. The green trees when I saw them first through one of the gates transported and ravished me, their sweetness   5 and unusual beauty made my heart to leap, and almost mad with ecstasy, they were such strange and wonderful things. The men! Oh what venerable and reverend creatures did the aged seem! Immortal cheru- bims! And young men glittering and sparkling angels, and maids strange seraphic pieces of life and beauty! Boys and girls tumbling in the street,   10 and playing, were moving jewels. I knew not that they were born or should die; but all things abided eternally as they were in their proper places. Eternity was manifest in the light of the day, and something infinite behind everything appeared, which talked with my expectation and moved my desire. The city seemed to stand in Eden, or to be built in   15 heaven. The streets were mine, the temple was mine, the people were mine, their clothes and gold and silver were mine, as much as their sparkling eyes, fair skins and ruddy faces. The skies were mine, and so were the sun and moon and stars, and all the world was mine; and I the only spectator and enjoyer of it. I knew no churlish proprieties, [private   20 possessions] nor bounds, nor divisions but all proprieties and divisions were mine: all treasures and the possessors of them. So that with much ado I was corrupted, and made to learn the dirty devices of this world. Which now I unlearn, and become, as it were, a little child again that I may enter into the Kingdom of God.

F. Often, at this stage he acquires an imaginary playmate with whom he plays for hours. He greets his 'friend' in the morning, and talks to 'him' about all manner of things. They get on splendidly together, though sometimes they will argue with one another. He will chat to his mother about his "friend" (to whom he refers by name) and the wise mother will   5 co-operate in the imaginary venture because the child is getting much joy from it. Furthermore, it probably serves a very useful function. Through it, the child experiments with the skills and techniques of social intercourse in a setting created by himself and which is, therefore, one that he can manipulate. As such, it is preparatory activity for the real   10 world of social give-and-take which he is now beginning to enter.

The child may tell tall stories; the lion he saw in the garden, the uncle from the other side of the world who spoke to him in the street, the tree which he lifted up by the roots. These stories are an offshoot of the child's growing capacity for imaginative thought, as are also the   15 creativity and originality that we see and hear in the games children play and the intriguing things they say. They are not lies in the adult sense of

the word but exaggerated fantasies, an expression of the dramatic, of the
extraordinary. An adult will often exaggerate in the same way (though
not perhaps to the same extent) about some extraordinary event he has   20
experienced or some deed he has executed. In the case of both, the child
and the adult, part of the motive is to gain attention and feel important.

E. Thomas Traherne (1637–1674): *Centuries of Meditation*

F. John Gabriel: *Children Growing Up* (1964)

In this final contrast, the two passages are taken from the same work

G. There were two white men in charge of the trading station, Kayerts, the
chief, was short and fat; Carlier, the assistant, was tall, with a large head
and a very broad trunk perched upon a long pair of thin legs. The third
man on the staff was a Sierra Leone nigger, who maintained that his
name was Henry Price. However, for some reason or other, the natives   5
down the river had given him the name of Makola, and it stuck to him
through all his wanderings about the country. He spoke English and
French with a warbling accent, wrote a beautiful hand, understood
bookkeeping, and cherished in his innermost heart the worship of evil
spirits. His wife was a negress from Loanda, very large and very noisy.   10
Three children rolled about in sunshine before the door of his low, shed-
like dwelling. Makola, taciturn and impenetrable, despised the two
white men. He had charge of a small clay storehouse with a dried-grass
roof, and pretended to keep a correct account of beads, cotton cloth, red
kerchiefs, brass wire, and other trade goods it contained. Besides the   15
storehouse and Makola's hut, there was only one large building in the
cleared ground of the station. It was built neatly of reeds, with a
verandah on all the four sides. There were three rooms in it. The one in
the middle was the living-room, and had two rough tables and a few
stools in it. The other two were the bedrooms for the white men. Each   20
had a bedstead and a mosquito net for all furniture. The plank floor was
littered with the belongings of the white men; open half-empty boxes,
town wearing apparel, old boots; all the things dirty, and all the things
broken, that accumulate mysteriously round untidy men. There was also
another dwelling-place some distance away from the buildings. In it,   25
under a tall cross much out of the perpendicular, slept the man who had
seen the beginning of all this; who had planned and had watched the
construction of this outpost of progress.

H. The two men watched the steamer round the bend, then, ascending arm
in arm the slope of the bank, returned to the station. They had been in
this vast and dark country only a very short time, and as yet always in the
midst of other white men, under the eye and guidance of their superiors.
And now, dull as they were to the subtle influences of surroundings, they   5
felt themselves very much alone, when suddenly left unassisted to face
the wilderness; a wilderness rendered more strange, more incomprehensible by the mysterious glimpses of the vigorous life it contained.
They were two perfectly insignificant and incapable individuals, whose
existence is only rendered possible through the high organization of   10
civilized crowds. Few men realize that their life, the very essence of their

character, their capabilities and their audacities, are only the expression
of their belief in the safety of their surroundings. The courage, the
composure, the confidence; the emotions and principles; every great and
every insignificant thought belongs not to the individual but to the   15
crowd; to the crowd that believes blindly in the irresistible force of its
institutions and of its morals, in the power of its police and of its opinion.
But the contact with pure unmitigated savagery, with primitive nature
and primitive man, brings sudden and profound trouble into the heart.
To the sentiment of being alone of one's kind, to the clear perception of 20
the loneliness of one's thoughts, of one's sensations – to the negation of
the habitual, which is safe, there is added the affirmation of the unusual,
which is dangerous; a suggestion of things vague, uncon'rollable, and
repulsive, whose discomposing intrusion excites the imagination and
tries the civilized nerves of the foolish and the wise alike.

Joseph Conrad: 'An Outpost of Progress' (from *Tales of Unrest*, 1898)

SHIFTS IN THE LEVEL OF DICTION

The passage you have just been considering were selected, in the main, to
show fairly clear-cut contrasts between different levels of diction.
Remember, it will often be the case that when you pose a question such as,
'Is the diction formal or informal?', the needle on the answering gauge
will register some point in between these two extremes. You need also to
be aware of the fact that the level of diction can vary considerably within
the same passage (see our Question (iv), page 39). For example, place side
by side two characteristic sentences from the last extract you studied –
from Conrad's story 'An Outpost of Progress':

   (a) He had charge of a small clay storehouse with a dried-grass roof, and
       pretended to keep a correct account of beads, cotton cloth, red
       kerchiefs, brass wire, and other trade goods it contained.
   (b) But the contact of pure unmitigated savagery, with primitive nature and
       primitive man, brings sudden and profound trouble into the heart.

The language of passage (a) is very concrete – it is grounded in the
close observation of people and things. In contrast with this opening
passage of the story, extract (b), which occurs just a couple of paragraphs
later, contains diction which shifts to a more abstract and discursive level.
Conrad here is introducing his own views in a magisterial way: some
might even claim he was moralizing rather too obviously. It is likely that,
while the diction of (a) presented few problems, you had to read
(b) through two or three times before you were entirely clear about what
was being said. Did you notice that the change in diction went hand in
hand with a move to a much more complex sentence structure?

Levels of diction can vary even more abruptly, within the space of the
same paragraph or sentence. Sometimes, this will be a 'bad thing' – if it
results from the writer's insensitivity to different registers of language (i.e.
differences of vocabulary, tone and syntax which reflect the various

situations and uses of language). Consider, for example, the following sentence from an 'A' level student's essay on *King Lear*:

> The unfolding action of the play which produces the physical reduction of the hero to the lowest bedrock of humanity is mirrored by a progressive pattern which occurs within Lear himself whereby his layers of pretension and his insulation from fellow-feeling are gradually stripped away, though by the time he perceives how irrationally he has acted, the old king is 5 virtually right off his rocker.

Until the last few words of the sentence, the writer is wearing the clothes he thinks appropriate to literary analysis – a dress suit of some stiffness. Then in those last words, with their sudden descent into hackneyed slang, the effect is rather like seeing him turn round to reveal a gaping hole in the seat of his trousers. The careful reader might have been prepared for this by a certain mixing of the metaphors in what has gone before; but the writer's cardinal sin is to shift registers of diction without considering the effect of unintentional bathos that this is bound to produce.

It cannot, however, be laid down as a rule: 'Do not change the gear of your diction'. In the field of the most elegant literary criticism, the calculated descent into the colloquial mode, the introduction of a down-to-earth phrase, can be tellingly effective. The main requirement is that the writer is able to judge the desired effect. In another sphere of writing, Raymond Chandler, one of the masters of the detective story genre, once wrote angrily to an editor who had allowed a proof-reader to 'improve' his prose:

> When I split an infinitive, God damn it, I split it so it will stay split, and when I interrupt the velvety smoothness of my more or less literate syntax with a few sudden words of bar-room vernacular, this is done with the eyes wide open.

The crucial emphasis is in the last eight words. Again, in a certain kind of humorous writing, the aim may consciously be to produce the effect of bathos: the humour is generated in the mock-heroic style, for example, precisely as a result of the incongruity between subject matter and style.

In certain kinds of prose, you must be alive to the effects produced by suddenly deploying a different kind of diction from what you are accustomed to or expecting. With this in mind, consider the following passage:

Ida Arnold and Mr Corkery have just arrived in the Pompadour Boudoir of a Brighton hotel

> While Mr Corkery was gone she made her preparations for carnival, the taste of the sweet cake between her teeth . . . She gazed round the big padded pleasure dome of a bedroom with blooshot and experienced eyes: the long mirror and the wardrobe and the enormous bed. She settled frankly down on it while the clerk waited. 'It springs,' she said, 'it springs,' and sat 5

there for quite a long while after he'd gone planning the evening's
campaign . . .
    Then she got up slowly and began to undress. She never believed in
wearing much: it wasn't any time at all before she was exposed in the long
mirror: a body firm and bulky: a proper handful. She stood on a deep soft   10
rug, surrounded by gilt frames and red velvet hangings, and a dozen
common and popular phrases bloomed in her mind – 'A Night of Love',
'You Only Live Once', and the rest. She bore the same relation to passion as
a peepshow. She sucked the chocolate between her teeth and smiled, her
plump toes working in the rug, waiting for Mr Corkery – just a great big   15
blossoming surprise.

Graham Greene: Brighton Rock (1938)

The reader who does not pause for a moment over phrases such as 'a
proper handful' or 'a great big blossoming surprise' is insensitive to the
effect Greene wishes to produce – the sense that the way in which Ida
Arnold thinks about her sexuality is cheap and common. We are surely
intended to wince slightly at the vulgarity and the 'cheapness' of the
language. The judgement on Ida suggested here is made explicit by
Greene when he states: 'She bore the same relation to passion as a
peepshow'.

Movements from one level of diction to another can be just as
significant in a more discursive kind of prose. Consider the following
extract:

Democracy has another merit. It allows criticism, and if there is not public
criticism there are bound to be hushed-up scandals. That is why I believe in
the Press, despite all its lies and vulgarity, and why I believe in Parliament.
Parliament is often sneered at because it is a Talking Shop. I believe in it
because it is a talking shop. I believe in the Private Member who makes   5
himself a nuisance. He gets snubbed and is told that he is cranky or ill-
informed, but he does expose abuses which would otherwise never have
been mentioned, and very often an abuse gets put right just by being
mentioned. Occasionally, too, a well-meaning public official starts losing his
head in the cause of efficiency, and thinks himself God Almighty. Such   10
officials are particularly frequent in the Home Office. Well, there will be
questions about them in Parliament sooner or later, and then they will have
to mind their steps. Whether Parliament is either a representative body or an
efficient one is questionable, but I value it because it criticizes and talks, and
because its chatter gets widely reported.   15
    So Two cheers for Democracy: one because it admits variety and two
because it permits criticism. Two cheers are quite enough: there is no
occasion to give three.

E. M. Forster: Two Cheers for Democracy (1939)

The language draws on political terminology – 'Parliament', 'public
criticism', 'the Private Member', 'the Home Office' etc. – and parts of this
extract read in a fairly formal way:

Whether Parliament is either a representative body or an efficient one is questionable . . .

But there is also another level of diction at work here: 'hushed-up', 'a talking shop', 'makes himself a nuisance', 'cranky', etc.

What kind of relationship is Forster trying to establish with his reader through the use of such diction? Is he successful in his aim?

GOOD DICTION: WHAT IS LEFT OUT?

We wish to remind you of something we said some time ago: looking at diction from the standpoint of our own writing, we should regard good diction as the choice of the words which come closest to expressing the feelings or thoughts we wish to embody in a piece of writing. To find the word which at least comes near to the inner ring of the bull's eye of what we wish to express will often involve the rejection of three or four words. To write clearly and expressively will often entail revision – the jettisoning of the unnecessary word which simply repeats what has already been said; the striking out of the cliché, the hackneyed metaphor or piece of jargon. In other words, what is omitted can be just as important as what is included.

As an illustration of this, examine the following passage, which reads like a 'bloated cliché', according to one critic. After the passage are the comments of the critic, followed by his own version. (We have italicized the words and phrases in the original on which he comments.)

As Andrew turned off the main road and *turned* into the *old* pathway, he fell into a *set* routine of behaviour, *a sequence* of actions he had repeated many times in the past. *Firstly*, he *glanced* down at the *rotating* front wheel of his bicycle, and listened carefully, *intently* to the spluttering, *crunching* sounds the tyre made as it *ran along* that *endlessly* unfolding *rough* surface of the   5
cinder *carpet. Like someone performing a task which required the most careful and precise concentration*, he bent low over the handlebars and looked with *a sort of* squint, *his eyes half-closed* but *full of rapt attention*, at the thin wheel and *its crunchy splutter. For some time* he *cranked* his head round, so that he was looking directly into *green*. Then *at that so concentrated moment in time*,   10
he *made a bet with himself* to close his eyes and count to ten before opening *his eyes* again. *His heart was in his mouth*, there was only red now against his closed eyelids and he seemed even *closer* to that *indescribable* crunching sound the *bicycle wheel made as it ran over the rough cinder surface*.
Four . . . five . . . six . . .

Elias Bell and Nathaniel J. Corrigan: *Have Bike, Will Ride* (1986)

The critic's comments:

turned: clumsy repetition.
old: ambiguous. Does the writer mean the *old* as distinct from some *new* pathway or (more probably) does he want to suggest the pathway was well-known to Andrew?

set and *a sequence...in the past*: simply duplicates the idea of *routine*.

Firstly: superfluous. Not only does no 'secondly' appear later, the description that follows is so clearly a sequence of actions that no signpost is necessary.

glanced: as Andrew is still looking fixedly at the wheel a sentence later, this is hardly an accurate word-choice.

rotating: unnecessary adjective. We know the bicycle is in motion.

intently: merely duplicates *carefully*.

crunching: another duplication, as the word follows *spluttering*.

ran along: colourless diction in a passage given to recording, or even exaggerating impressions of sound.

endlessly: the pathway may be long, but it must end somewhere! Moreover, is Andrew looking to where the pathway ends?

rough: superfluous adjective. A surface of cinder must be rough.

carpet: suggestions of smoothness and domesticity are possibly in conflict with the description of a cinder surface.

someone performing . . . precise concentration: rather vague simile. What kind of task?

a sort of: when is a squint not a squint?

his eyes half-closed: duplicates the idea of a squint.

full of rapt attention: surely already strongly suggested in the simile that opens the sentence.

its crunchy splutter: can you look at a sound? *Synaesthesia* – the description of one kind of sense impression in terms of another – is a legitimate device, but here probably only denotes the writer's confusion. Moreover, the writer has already told us what the sound is like, using virtually the same words.

For some time: unnecessarily vague.

cranked: odd, inexact word. Does the head make a full rotary movement? This could suggest an absurd picture!

green: probably too impressionistic. Do we not want to know what Andrew was actually looking at?

at that so . . . in time: "at that moment in time" is an ugly cliché which says no more than "then". We know it is a *concentrated* moment from what has gone before.

made a bet with himself: unidiomatic phrase and, with the slangy ring of *bet*, out of keeping with the general tone of the passage.

his eyes: why include this clumsy repetition when the use of the pronoun is so easy? Possibly the whole phrase *before opening his eyes again* is implicit in the first part of the sentence?

His heart was in his mouth: hackneyed expression. And does the emotion need spelling out? Why not simply let the situation suggest what the boy is all too obviously feeling?

closer: possibly the slightly ugly repetition of sound after *closed* could be eliminated? Is it really necessary to say his eyelids are *closed*?

indescribable: is it really so, particularly as the author has spent some time describing it?

the bicycle wheel . . . cinder surface: unnecessary repetition. We know all about the sound by now – and how it is produced. Why not keep the expression short and straightforward?

You may feel inclined to comment that our critic is being over-pedantic in some of his comments. Do you find yourself in agreement with *all* the criticisms he makes?

The following revised version is some sixty words shorter than the first. Is it better and more streamlined than the original? Or have some essential elements been lost? Are there any further changes you would like to make?

As Andrew turned off the main road into the familiar pathway, he fell into an old routine of behaviour. He fixed his eyes on the front wheel of his bicycle, and listened to the tyre's splutter as it bit into the unfolding strip of cinder. With the intentness of someone tuning a muscial instrument, he bent low over the handlebars and squinted at the thin wheel. For three or four   5 seconds, he cocked his head so that he was looking into the green blur of a hedge. Then he dared himself to close his eyes and count to ten. Now there was only red against his eyelids and he seemed even closer to the loud crunch of wheel on cinder.

Four . . . five . . . six . . .   10

The extent to which we can lay down definite rules about prose style is a contentious area. We enter it gingerly by finishing the chapter with an extract for discussion from George Orwell's essay 'Politics and the English Language' (1946). The passage is followed by some discussion topics which either relate to what Orwell has to say or to the wider range of questions covered in this chapter.

What is above all needed is to let the meaning choose the word, and not the other way about. In prose, the worst thing one can do with words is to surrender to them. When you think of a concrete object, you think wordlessly, and then, if you want to describe the thing you have been visualizing you probably hunt about till you find the exact words that seem   5 to fit it. When you think of something abstract you are more inclined to use words from the start, and unless you make a conscious effort to prevent it, the existing dialect will come rushing in and do the job for you, at the expense of blurring or even changing your meaning. Probably it is better to put off using words as long as possible and get one's meaning as clear as one   10 can through pictures or sensations. Afterwards one can choose – not simply *accept* – the phrases that will best cover the meaning, and then switch round and decide what impression one's words are likely to make on another person. This last effort of the mind cuts out all stale or mixed images, all prefabricated phrases, needless repetitions, and humbug and vagueness   15 generally. But one can often be in doubt about the effect of a word or a phrase, and one needs rules that one can rely on when instinct fails. I think the following rules will cover most cases:

   (i) Never use a metaphor, simile or other figure of speech which you are
        used to seeing in print.   20
  (ii) Never use a long word where a short one will do.
 (iii) If it is possible to cut out a word, always cut it out.
  (iv) Never use the passive where you can use the active.
   (v) Never use a foreign phrase, a scientific word or a jargon word if you
        can think of an everyday English equivalent.   25
  (iv) Break any of these rules sooner than say anything outright
        barbarous.

These rules sound elementary, and so they are, but they demand a deep change of attitude in anyone who has grown used to writing in the style now fashionable.   30

1. In your own words, describe the various stages Orwell charts in the process of writing. Do you think the approach he suggests here is a good one?

2. What are the principal qualities Orwell emphasizes as an essential part of good style? What elements of bad style does he take particular exception to?

3. What do you think Orwell has in mind when he refers to 'the style now fashionable'?

GENERAL DISCUSSION TOPICS

We end this chapter with a number of comments on diction that you might like to use as a basis for discussion. We feel that they raise a number of important issues that students often feel strongly about, but are fearful of expressing because they seem to go against official 'Eng. Lit.' policy. What do you think?

1. What Orwell does not seem to realize is that, for many writers, the whole point of putting pen to paper is to discover what they really think or feel. How can you always know this before you begin to write?

2. Orwell's prescriptions might lead to formally correct and controlled prose, but it would also be colourless and drab in most cases. He seems to want to take all the excitement and experimentation out of writing. He leaves no place for the writer who is wildly eccentric, the writer who wants to smear paint on canvas, to take risks in the desire to create a new style.

3. I find too much talk about prose style makes me very self-conscious about my own writing. I hardly dare to write a sentence now for fear of

committing some blunder. Must we always be judging what is 'good style'? I would much prefer just to let what I write flow naturally.

4. What really matters is *what is said*, not *how* it is said – and to think too much about the former, blinds us to the latter. To become preoccupied with a writer's style is therefore a waste of time. You should just take the style for granted: it's like a skill in sport – either writers have it, in which case you read on, or they haven't, in which case you simply read no further.

5. I think too much of what we have read in this chapter is over-fastidious about style – encouraging us to write in an upper-class elitist way. I like to write just as I speak. And I think this is the honest way, instead of dressing up my thoughts in a so-called 'fine' style.

6. There is so much waffle talked about the style of writing. I think all you really need is to follow a few simple technical rules. The ones I always like to bear in mind are those Harold Evans, the famous newspaper editor, lists in his bible for journalists, *Newsman's English* (1972).

(a) Don't use no double negatives.
(b) Make each pronoun agree with their antecedent.
(c) When dangling, watch your participles.
(d) Don't use commas, which aren't necessary.
(e) Verbs has to agree with their subjects.
(f) About those sentence fragments.
(g) Try to not ever split infinitives.
(h) Its important to use apostrophe's correctly.
(i) Always read what you have written to see if you any words out.
(j) Correct spelling is esential.

Ten commandments wittily put – and if you memorize them and carry them out, you can forget about good style.

7. It is a great mistake to attempt to study diction as though it were separable from the shape and movement of sentences. To ignore the place words occupy and the shifts in their value in relation to the rhythms of sentences is to falsify our response to prose.

3

Metaphorical language

In the previous chapter we indicated the difference between the literal and the metaphorical meaning of words and defined simile and metaphor. If you remain uncertain of the difference between literal and metaphorical language, you should reread pages 19–22 before venturing further, for in this chapter we intend to define in greater depth some of the functions of metaphorical language.

Louis Untermeyer, in the light-hearted passage we quoted on page 21, is reminding us that we are for ever using metaphorical language in everyday speech, to such an extent that many of the metaphorical expressions we use have become clichés. We do so because we often wish to describe an object or a feeling by saying that certain qualities of the object or feeling we have in mind can be compared with certain qualities of the metaphorical word(s) we select. So, to use an example given in the Untermeyer passage, when we wish to describe our feelings about the excellent quality of our last night's sleep, we can say that we 'slept like a log' – using the word 'log' in a metaphorical sense to indicate something deep, motionless and undisturbed. Here is another example, from *North and South* (1855) by Elizabeth Gaskell: 'her cares were all blown away as lightly as thistledown'. That the character in the novel has certain feelings about her 'cares' – they are unimportant and can be easily dismissed – is made clearer to the reader and to the character herself by transferring the qualities of thistledown in the wind (its lightness and the ease with which the wind can move it) to the cares.

In literary criticism, we call this first element in the comparison – that is, the object or feeling we are writing about – the *tenor*, while we classify the metaphorical medium as the *vehicle*. (This terminology comes from I. A. Richards's influential book, *Principles of Literary Criticism*, 1925, which you should consult.) So in the two examples we have cited here, the tenor in the first is our sleeping and in the second 'her cares', while the vehicle in the first is 'a log' and in the second 'blown away as lightly as thistledown'.

Which is tenor and which vehicle in the following examples?

(a) Outside the cemetery the air was soaked pale yellow, like a low cloud of poison, the effect of the sodium lamps.

Paul Theroux: *The Family Arsenal* (1976)

(b) They were as naive and immature in the expression of their love as a pair of children.

Jack London: *Martin Eden* (1909)

(c) Angling may be said to be so like mathematics that it can never be fully learnt.

Izaak Walton: *The Compleat Angler* (1653)

(d) Coffee should be as black as Hell, strong as death, and sweet as Love.

Turkish Proverb

The repeated, everyday use of comparisons can make us forget the idea which first generated the metaphor or simile. If I say 'my hands are like ice' or 'my heart is light as a feather', these similes are so hackneyed that you are unlikely to *imagine* the coldness of ice or a feather floating in the air. When we read of 'the long arm of the law' it would be surprising if we actually saw in our mind's eye an arm which sweeps across continents to apprehend some criminal. These are examples of dead metaphorical language, and in the kind of prose with which this book is principally concerned, we can assume that generally writers will attempt to draw on fresher and more expressive sources of metaphor.

This is not to say that in prose we must always look for the original and new-minted kind of language which poets often search for and which is so central to their work. In much prose of a discursive type, indeed, it is usually desirable that a comparison should not draw too much attention to itself: it is generally present as a means to an end – illustration or perhaps clarification – rather than an end in itself. In some kinds of imaginative prose, however, we may find the use of comparison aiming for the intensity and complexity of poetic metaphor. In what follows in this section, we wish to consider metaphorical or figurative language from its most superficial usage to its most profound, and we will attempt to pinpoint some of its functions.

TO ILLUSTRATE AND TO MAKE CONCRETE

Earlier we asked you to comment on a number of comparisons (see page 22), one of which (example a) involved comparing the questions you might ask when faced with a passage of prose (tenor) with 'helpful signposts' (vehicle). To dignify the comparison with this literary terminology is a shade absurd: you probably found that the originality and force of the comparison was less than striking. And so it is; but we did not intend our comparison to draw attention to itself and ask to be praised for its inventiveness and dramatic impact. This would clearly have been absurd, as the point of using such a comparison was to try to make our argument clearer to the reader by keeping the abstract concepts with which we are dealing in touch with what is familiar to the reader – that is, 'signposts'. This is a crucial element in the use of metaphorical language: the way that, like guy lines attached to an air balloon, it can ground the general in the particular and keep the abstract in relation with more immediate experience. (Now comment on the last simile we have used, and say how effective you think it is!)

In each of the following three passages, how successfully do the comparisons help to clarify the argument of the authors?

A. Since justice demands that all individuals be entitled to a minimum of freedom, all other individuals were of necessity to be restrained, if need be by force, from depriving anyone of it. Indeed, the whole function of law was the prevention of such collisions: the state was reduced to what (has been described) as the functions of a nightwatchman or traffic-   5
policeman.

> Sir Isaiah Berlin: 'Two Concepts of Liberty' (1958) taken from *Four Essays on Liberty* (1975)

B. We believe that the way schools are currently conducted does very little, and quite probably nothing, to enhance our chances of . . . survival; that is, to help us solve any or even some of the problems we have mentioned. One way of representing the present condition of our educational system is as follows: it is as if we are driving a multi-million-   5
dollar sports car, screaming, "Faster! Faster!" while peering fixedly into the rear view mirror. It is an awkward way to tell us where we are, much less where we are going, and it has been sheer dumb luck that we have not smashed ourselves to bits so far. We have paid almost exclusive attention to the car, equipping it with all sorts of fantastic gadgets and an engine   10
that will propel it at ever increasing speeds, but we seem to have forgotten where we wanted to go in it.

> Postman & Weingartner: *Teaching as a Subversive Activity* (1969)

C. Yet still the nicest and most delicate touches of Satire consist in fine Raillery . . . But how hard to make a Man appear a Fool, a Blockhead, or a Knave, without using any of those opprobrious terms! To spare the grossness of the Names, and to do the thing yet more severely, is to draw a full Face, and to make the Nose and Cheeks stand out, and yet not to   5
employ any depth of Shadowing. This is the Mystery of that Noble Trade, which yet no Master can teach to his Apprentice; He may give the Rules, but the Scholar is never the nearer in his practice. Neither is it true, that this fineness of Raillery is offensive. A witty Man is tickl'd while he is hurt in this manner, and a Fool feels it not. The occasion of an   10
Offence may possibly be given, but he cannot take it. If it be granted that in effect this way does more Mischief; that a Man is secretly wounded, and though he be not sensible himself, yet the malicious World will find it for him: yet there is still a vast difference betwixt the slovenly Butchering of a Man, and the fineness of a stroke that separates the Head from the   15
Body, and leaves it standing in its place. A man may be capable, as Jack Ketch's[1] Wife said of his Servant, of a plain piece of Work, a bare

---

[1] Jack Ketch was an official executioner.

Hanging; but to make a malefactor die sweetly was only belonging to her Husband.

Dryden: 'A Discourse Concerning the Original and Progress of
Satire' (1693)

TO CLARIFY, TO EXPLICATE OR TO MAKE ACCESSIBLE WHAT IS UNFAMILIAR OR UNKNOWN

In many ways this categorization is simply an extension of the previous one. It is a question here, perhaps, of metaphorical language working at a more profound level – possibly to help us understand what is involved in a complex idea or to come to grips with what is beyond our own experience. A science teacher, for example, may well begin to explain Einstein's Theory of Relativity with reference to some mundane starting-point, perhaps using a comparison in the same way in which parable or analogy work.

To take a more dramatic example: have you ever been shot? Probably not. Orwell had this experience, fighting in the Civil War in Spain.

The whole experience of being hit by a bullet is very interesting and I think it is worth describing in detail.

It was at the corner of the parapet, at five o'clock in the morning. This was always a dangerous time, because we had the dawn at our backs, and if you stuck your head above the parapet it was clearly outlined against the sky. I   5
was talking to the sentries preparatory to changing the guard. Suddenly, in the very middle of saying something, I felt – it is very hard to describe what I felt, though I remember it with the utmost vividness.

Roughly speaking it was the sensation of being at the centre of an explosion. There seemed to be a loud bang and a blinding flash of light all   10
round me, and I felt a tremendous shock – no pain, only a violent shock, such as you get from an electric terminal; with it a sense of utter weakness, a feeling of being stricken and shrivelled up to nothing. The sand-bags in front of me receded into immense distance. I fancy you would feel much the same if you were struck by lightning. I knew immediately that I was hit, but   15
because of the seeming bang and flash I thought it was a rifle nearby that had gone off accidentally and shot me. All this happened in a space of time much less than a second. The next moment my knees crumpled up and I was falling, my head hitting the ground with a violent bang which, to my relief, did not hurt. I had a numb, dazed feeling, a consciousness of being very   20
badly hurt, but no pain in the ordinary sense.

Homage to Catalonia (1938)

With clinical understatement Orwell records what was involved. He asks us to imagine what it must be like to be 'at the centre of an explosion' or to be 'struck by lightning'. These are offered as analogous experiences. He felt 'shrivelled up to nothing' and then 'numb'. As a point of contact with the reader – a possible shared experience which may convey something of what it is like to be shot – he compares the sensation with 'a violent shock, such as you get from an electric terminal'. It is through these comparisons that Orwell hopes we may get some inkling of an experience which is, fortunately, fairly unusual and very difficult to describe.

As well as making apparently inaccessible sensations available to the reader, metaphorical language can also help us to form pictures of objects and scenes we have never witnessed. Indeed, the literary term 'imagery', though it is admittedly slightly woolly at the edges, refers principally to the way in which the language of comparison renders sensory experience alive to the reader's imagination.

This next passage shows the writer using comparison in a systematic picture-making way – and the various parts of the picture are formed out of materials which are intimately familiar and close to hand.

Lewis is describing the place where he grew up in the second decade of this century.

Here is the recipe for imagining it. Take a number of medium-sized potatoes and lay them down (one layer of them only) in a flat-bottomed tin basin. Now shake loose earth over them till the potatoes themselves, but not the shape of them, is hidden; and of course the crevices between them will now be depressions of earth. Now magnify the whole thing till those crevices are   5
large enough to conceal each its stream and its huddle of trees. And then, for colouring, change your brown earth into the chequered pattern of fields, always small fields (a couple of acres each), with all their normal variety of crop, grass, and plough. You have now got a picture of the 'plain' of Down, which is a plain only in the sense that if you were a very large giant you   10
would regard it as level but very ill to walk on – like cobbles. And now remember that every cottage is white. The whole expanse laughs with these little white dots; it is like nothing so much as the assembly of white foam-caps when a fresh breeze is on a summer sea. And the roads are white too; there is no tarmac yet. And because the whole country is a turbulent   15
democracy of little hills, these roads shoot in every direction, disappearing and reappearing. But you must not spread over this landscape your hard English sunlight; make it paler, make it softer, blur the edges of the white cumuli, cover it with watery gleams, deepening it, making all unsubstantial. And beyond all this, so remote that they seem fantastically abrupt, at the   20
very limit of your vision, imagine the mountains. They are no stragglers. They are steep and compact and pointed and toothed and jagged. They seem to have nothing to do with the little hills and cottages that divide you from them. And sometimes they are blue, sometimes violet; but quite often they look transparent – as if huge sheets of gauze had been cut out into   25
mountainous shapes and hung up there, so that you could see through them the light of the invisible sea at their backs.

I number it among my blessings that my father had no car, while yet most of my friends had, and sometimes took me for a drive. This meant that all these distant objects could be visited just enough to clothe them with   30
memories and not impossible desires, while yet they remained ordinarily as

inaccessible as the Moon. The deadly power of rushing about wherever I pleased had not been given me. I measured distances by the standard of man, man walking on his two feet, not by the standard of the internal combustion engine.

35

C. S. Lewis: *Surprised by Joy* (1955)

What are the 'intimately familiar' materials that Lewis uses as the vehicles for his metaphors when describing the Down landscape? Choose three examples of his use of metaphorical language and show what connotations these have.

ILLUSTRATIVE AND ORGANIC METAPHORS
Towards the end of the passage by C. S. Lewis, the author wrote:

This [the lack of ease of transport] meant that all these distant objects could be visited just enough to clothe them with memories and not impossible desires, while yet they remained ordinarily as inaccessible as the Moon.

Take first the metaphor, 'clothe'. The essential idea is, of course, that these distant objects were 'dressed' or overlaid with memories – from the infrequent occasions on which they were visited; there is the suggestion of a romantic aura hanging over them. It is the adolescent Lewis who, through his imagination, provides this emotional investment – the 'garment' of his own reaction, if you like. The metaphor conveys this well enough. Yet one can imagine all kinds of different ways in which the same idea might be adequately stated. A down-to-earth reader might even suggest that there is something faintly ludicrous about adding clothing to an expanse of Irish countryside; but the image is familiar enough: we often speak of hills being 'clothed' with sunshine or heather; and simply to state the idea in a literal form would probably be to lose the faintly mysterious emotional quality Lewis requires here.

The simile which ends this sentence – 'as inaccessible as the Moon' – is a clearer example of what we will define as purely illustrative imagery. Time has, of course, caught up with Lewis and the moon is no longer quite inaccessible. But that is not really the point. If Lewis were to write, in place of the simile, the literal 'completely' or 'totally inaccessible', would we really be losing all that much? Are the connotations of the moon – its remoteness, mystery and romantic aura – indispensable here? Could we provide another simile – as inaccessible as 'Samarkand' or 'outer space' – which would perform much the same function?

If, on the whole, your answer to these questions is a guarded 'yes', then this simile is largely illustrative. To use Lewis's first image, it is a 'dressing up' of the thought, an apt illustration; it is not integral to what is being said.

Metaphorical language can, however, operate at a much higher *organic* level. The clearest example of what we mean by a kind of organic metaphor may be found when we turn to great poetry – when, for instance, Lady Macbeth, in an attempt to re-awaken her husband's ambitions for the crown, says:

> Was the hope drunk,
> Wherein you dress'd yourself? Hath it slept since?
> And wakes it now, to look so green and pale
> At what it did so freely?

It is virtually impossible to separate the metaphors from what is being said; vehicle and tenor are bound tightly together. One can imagine no other way in which the full complexity of the statement could be conveyed. Introduce other metaphors and you are bound to change the meaning radically. State the idea in some elaborate literal paraphrase and you are left with a pale shadow. There is no sense of a dressing up of a statement, or of metaphor as an ornament. The more you examine the statement, the more you see the connections between the various ideas and feelings this language embodies metaphorically.

Now in prose we are rarely going to come across organic figurative language of this unity and intensity. But, as we will see later, some prose can approach this in its general tendency, and you may find the distinction we have made between 'illustrative' and 'organic' metaphor a useful one. The exact point at which comparisons from the first category enter the second is, perhaps, largely arbitrary – the demarcation line will often be blurred. Opinions might differ, for example, as to whether the imagery Lewis uses in the first paragraph is completely organic or largely illustrative. What do you think? Locate specific details of the imagery and present an argument for their falling into one category or the other.

The following passages have been chosen to illustrate some of the functions of comparative language we have already discussed and to introduce some new ones. If you are working in a class, divide into groups and discuss each passage. Answer the following question: what use does each author make of metaphorical language? Report back and share your findings with the whole class. Finally, you may wish to look at the jottings we made on the first two extracts.

A. There, absolutely stilled with fear beneath his glance, crouched a very big locust. What an amusing face the thing had! A lugubrious long face, that somehow suggested a bald head, and such a glum mouth. It looked like some little person out of a Disney cartoon. It moved slightly, still looking up fearfully at him. Strange body, encased in a sort of old-fashioned creaky armour. He had never realised before what ridiculous-looking insects locusts were! Well, naturally not, they occur to one collectively, as a pest – one doesn't go around looking at their faces.
   The face was certainly curiously human and even expressive, but looking at the body, he decided that the body couldn't really be called a body at all. With the face, the creature's kinship with humans ended. The body was flimsy paper stretched over a frame of matchstick, like a small

boy's homemade aeroplane. And those could not be thought of as legs –
the great saw-toothed back ones were like the parts of an old crane, and
the front ones – like one of her hairpins, bent in two. At that moment the   15
creature slowly lifted up one of the front legs, and passed it tremblingly
over its head, stroking the left antenna down. Just as a man might take
out a handkerchief and pass it over his brow.

> Nadine Gordimer: 'The Soft Voice of the Serpent' (from *No Place
> Like*, 1975)

B. My conscience now was sore, and would smart at every touch; I could
not now tell how to speak my words, for fear I should misplace them. Oh,
how gingerly did I then go in all I did or said! I found myself as on a miry
bog that shook if I did but stir; and was there left both of God and Christ,
and the Spirit, and all good things.   5
   But, I observe, though I was such a great sinner before conversion, yet
God never much charged the guilt of the sins of my ignorance upon me;
only he showed me I was lost if I had not Christ, because I had been a
sinner; I saw that I wanted a perfect righteousness to present me without
fault before God, and this righteousness was nowhere to be found, but in   10
the person of Jesus Christ.
   But my original and inward pollution, that, that was my plague and
my affliction; that, I say, at a dreadful rate, always putting forth itself
within me; that I had the guilt of, to amazement; by reason of that, I was
more loathsome in my own eyes than was a toad; and I thought I was so   15
in God's eyes too; sin and corruption, I said, would as naturally bubble
out of my heart, as water would bubble out of a fountain. I thought now
that everyone had a better heart than I had; I could have changed heart
with anybody; I thought none but the devil himself could equalise me for
inward wickedness and pollution of mind. I fell, therefore, at the sight of   20
my own vileness, deeply into despair; for I concluded that this condition
that I was in could not stand with a state of grace. Sure, thought I, I am
forsaken of God; sure I am given up to the devil, and to a reprobate
mind; and thus I continued a long while, even for some years together.

> John Bunyan: *Grace Abounding to the Chief of Sinners* (1666)

A drive down the main street of a town in the Southern States of America.

C. The Ford having been excited into a sort of restless resentful life Clark
and Sally Carrol rolled and rattled down Valley Avenue into Jefferson
Street, where the dust road became a pavement; along opiate Millicent
Place, where there were half a dozen prosperous substantial mansions;
and on into the down-town section. Driving was perilous here, for it was   5
shopping time; the population idled casually across the streets and a
drove of low-moaning oxen were being urged along in front of a placid
street-car; even the shops seemed only yawning their doors and blinking
their windows in the sunshine before retiring into a state of utter and
finite coma.   10

> F. Scott Fitzgerald: 'The Ice Palace' (1919)

An African scene at sunset – from the opening of a story.

   D. The veranda, which was lifted on stone pillars, jutted forward over the
garden like a box in the theatre. Below were luxuriant masses of
flowering shrubs, and creepers whose shiny leaves, like sequins, reflected
light from a sky stained scarlet and purple and apple-green. This
splendiferous sunset filled one half of the sky, fading gently through   5
shades of mauve to a calm expanse of ruffling grey, blown over by tinted
cloudlets; and in this still evening sky, just above a clump of darkening
conifers, hung a small crystal moon.
   There sat Major Gale and his wife, as they did every evening at this
hour, side by side trimly in deck chairs, their sundowners on small tables 10
at their elbows, critically watching, like connoisseurs, the pageant
presented for them.
   Major Gale said, with satisfaction: 'Good sunset tonight,' and they
both turned their eyes to the vanquishing moon. The dusk drew veils
across sky and garden; and punctually, as she did every day, Mrs Gale   15
shook off nostalgia like a terrier shaking off water and rose, saying:
'Mosquitoes!' She drew her deck chair to the wall, where she neatly
folded and stacked it.

Doris Lessing: 'The De Wets Come to Kloof Grange' (from *This was
the Old Chief's Country*, 1951)

A. Imagery used in a close-up fashion – to convey a vivid picture and
some feelings towards the locust. Difference between head and body:
head given human quality, an absurd yet endearing impression ('like
some little person out of a Disney cartoon'); it's almost as if he thinks of it
as some ageing, ungainly, frail, old man (see simile in last sentence). The
body does not suggest human analogies – but objects. Use of familiar
things – 'flimsy paper . . . a frame of matchstick'; 'the parts of an old
crane'; 'hairpins' – to convey what it looks like. Fragility; unwieldiness –
'creaky armour'. Some of the imagery is almost like the raw material for a
poem? Certainly conveys the impression of a creature which is being
looked at with attention for the first time.

B. Comparisons used to enforce strong feeling – sense of overwhelming
sin which makes salvation seem impossible. Element of self-loathing –
'inward pollution'; 'plague'; 'more loathsome . . . than was a toad'.
Powerless to escape sin, it seems – image of it bubbling out of his heart
like water from a fountain. Is he over-dramatizing? All this thrashing
around with his fallen nature – only the devil his equal etc. Image of 'miry
bog' suggests his precarious spiritual state – almost in an allegorical way.
Strongly influenced by language and imagery of the Bible.

HOW MANY MEANINGS?

When you were discussing the metaphor of the theatre in the extract from
the story by Doris Lessing, it is possible that there was some disagreement

about how much meaning could be read into this extended comparison. In the light of your discussion, how justified do you consider the following two comments to be?

(i) The Gales are clearly people in exile clinging rather incongrously to old habits of thought. They are also passive and detached.
(ii) In superimposing theatrical artifice on the African landscape, the author is suggesting that the Gales are complacent, superficial people: we are meant to see the egoism of imagining that the lighting effects of the sunset are part of a special performance mounted for their benefit.

To allow any part of these statements as *possible* interpretations may cause some anxiety to the student who wishes to pin down meaning as objectively as possible. Perhaps they prompt the accusation that 'meanings are being foisted on the passage which the author never intended.'

One response to a charge of this kind is to emphasize that the text itself must be the final authority of 'what the author intends'. After all, what other real authority is there? Even if we are able to ask authors to recall what they had in mind at the moment of composition, is it not likely that the memory of their initial intention would be hazy and imprecise? Moreover, the process of imaginative writing is inherently mysterious. So is it not possible that what the author has achieved does not necessarily match his or her conscious intention? Most wise authors are finally content to be simply readers of their own work rather than a court of final appeal.

How, then, are we to *know* how much meaning we are entitled to unpack from a particular image or sentence? Simply to answer that it is a matter of common sense or a literary tact which develops from a wide experience of reading will not answer the problem. We must agree – not 'admit', for this fact is one of the joys of literary criticism – that our response to imaginative prose *is* subjective and will therefore vary from one person to the next. (Hence the value of sharing our views in discussion and reading criticism, in order to enhance our own response). This subjective variation of response is not infinite, of course; otherwise we could never agree on any kind of shared judgement. The variation must operate within the limits which the text defines. There are, obviously, interpretations of the comparison from the Doris Lessing story we began by discussing which would be *wrong*. Somebody who argued that the comparison 'made us think of excited children at a pantomime who are so carried away by the performance that they forget to thank their parents for paying for the seats' would be missing the point. Neither the comparison itself, nor the context in which it operates, suggests this interpretation.

The importance of context in controlling our response to a word or image cannot be over-emphasized. To take the simplest example, drawn from a metaphor which we have already decided is virtually 'dead' (see page 53):

> He came into the house, shook the snow from his boots, and took off his gloves. His hands were ice.

You will recognize immediately that the vehicle (ice) is related to the tenor (hands) to suggest the idea of 'coldness'. The context makes it clear that it is not the hardness, the texture or the strictly scientific properties of ice that are relevant.

There is no complexity here! In the simpler kind of comparison that is frequently used in prose we can often say that the metaphor or simile is used in an almost algebraic way: hands = ice (because of their coldness). The comparison embodies one central point of contact. But the comparison we were discussing earlier is not of this kind. It is not simply illustrating one point: 'a' is like 'b' for a variety of reasons. (This is often a feature of the organic sort of comparison: refer back to our earlier distinction on page 57). Remember too, that the Doris Lessing passage was taken from the *beginning* of a story. The comparison of the Gales' response to the African sunset with the idea of people in a theatre watching a performance or of spectators at a pageant, is clearly intended to plant a number of possible meanings in the reader's mind: some may grow into importance; others may not even take root. This will depend, of course, on the wider context as we read further into the story.

When we are dealing with a concentrated comparison of this sort, there is a virtue in keeping a sensitive openness to many suggestions, and holding the final judgement in abeyance. In this area, it is a mistake to think of meaning as if it were the contents of a Christmas cracker: you pull both ends and out drops your simple motto and little party hat. Some readers, unfortunately, limit their response to complex prose by seeking for one clear 'message' – a dangerous term to use because of its reductive connotations. If we are hunting for images to convey what the search for meaning in imaginative prose is like, perhaps we do better to think of a critically close interpretation as the peeling away of the many layers of an onion.

It is not being unduly extravagant to say that some rich centres of metaphor in a highly wrought novel may only be *fully* understood in the context of the whole novel. And here we confront a difficulty which is implicit in the kind of study we are undertaking, for most of the prose you will be called upon to consider in this book or in an examination in Practical Criticism is not self-contained, like a lyric poem. It is rather a bleeding gobbet torn from the body of an essay, a short story or a novel. Faced with the interpretation of a complex comparison, therefore, sometimes one simply has to offer the fullest response one can within the limits of the given context.

As an exercise in the interpretation of a comparison in relation to the context provided, we want you to read the following passage carefully and then focus on the simile which we have italicized at the end of the extract.

[The door] at the far end of the landing had a little notice on it. I read, in large letters, *Props Room*, and underneath in smaller letters, *Miss Quentin*. I closed my eyes for a moment and stilled my breathing. Then I knocked.

The sound echoed strangely. Then a husky voice said: 'Come in.'

I stepped into the room. It was a long narrow room with large windows   5
opening in to the river, and it was filled to overflowing with a sort of multicoloured chaos which I couldn't at the first moment take in. In the midst of this Anna sat writing at a desk with her back to me. I shut the door behind me as she turned slowly. For a long moment we looked at each other in silence. Like a filling glass I felt my soul rise into my eyes; and in the   10
intense equilibrium of the meeting we both experienced almost a moment of contemplation. Anna got up and said 'Jake!' Then I saw her.

She was plumper and had not defended herself against time. There was about her a sort of wrecked look which was infinitely touching. Her face, which I remembered as round and smooth as an apricot, was become just a   15
little tense and drawn, and her neck now revealed her age. The great brown eyes, which once opened so blandly upon the world, seemed narrowed, and where Anna had used to draw a dark line upward at their corners the years had sketched in a little sheaf of wrinkles. Tresses of hair which had escaped from the complex coronet curled about her neck, and I could see streaks of   20
grey. I looked upon the face that I had known so well and now that for the first time I saw its beauty as mortal I felt that I had never loved it so dearly. Anna took in my glance, and then with an instinctive gesture she took refuge behind her hands.

'What brings you here, Jake?' said Anna.   25

The spell was broken. 'I wanted to see you,' I said; and now I was anxious just to avoid looking at her and to collect my wits. I looked around the room. An astonishing medley of objects lay about in piles which in places reached up to the ceiling. The contents of the room had a sort of strange cohesion and homogeneity, and they seemed to adhere to the walls like the   30
contents of a half-empty jam jar. Yet here was every kind of thing. It was like a vast toy shop that had been hit by a bomb. In my first glance I noticed a French horn, a rocking-horse, a set of red-striped tin trumpets, some Chinese silk robes, a couple of rifles, Paisley shawls, teddy bears, glass balls, tangles of necklaces and other jewellery, a convex mirror, a stuffed snake,   35
countless toy animals, and a number of tin trunks out of which multi-coloured costumes trailed. Exquisite and expensive playthings lay enlaced with the gimcrack contents of Christmas crackers. I sat down on the nearest seat, which happened to be the back of the rocking-horse, and surveyed the scene.   40

'What is this extraordinary place?' I said. 'What are you doing these days, Anna?'

'Oh, this and that,' said Anna. She had always used to say this when she didn't want to tell me something. I could see she was nervous, and as she talked she kept picking things up, now a piece of ribbon, or now a ball or a   45
long band of Brussels lace . . .

'You look just the same, Jake,' said Anna. It was true. I still looked much
as I did when I was twenty-four.

She added, 'I wish I did!'

'You look lovely,' I said.   50

Anna laughed, and picked up a wreath of artificial flowers.

'What a mess this place is!' she said. 'I keep meaning to tidy it.'

'It's lovely too,' I said.

'Well, if you call *this* lovely!' said Anna.

All this time she avoided my eye. In a moment we should be talking   55
soberly like two old acquaintances. I wasn't going to allow this. I looked at
her, and amid the enchanting chaos of silks and animals and improbable
objects that seemed to rise almost to her waist *she looked like a very wise
mermaid* rising out of a motley coloured sea; but in a moment she would
have escaped me.   60

Iris Murdoch: *Under the Net* (1954)

Decide which of the following ten comments on the italicized simile are
justified by the general context of the passage. It might help if you class
each of the comments under one of the following three headings:

   (i) unquestionably relevant to the material presented in the passage;
  (ii) possibly suggestive, but we would have to read on to be certain;
 (iii) completely out of the question.

1. The simile operates at its primary level as a visual image: the lower
   half of Anna's body is hidden under 'the sea' of objects in which she
   seems to swim; she is, as it were, only a visible woman above the
   waist.

2. Mermaids are noted for their singing and swimming, so we can
   expect these to be among Anna's abilities.

3. Anna's presence and the stunning impact of the room cast, for
   Jake, a kind of magical spell. At first he is not sure about what he is
   seeing, as if bewitched. The mermaid image therefore underlines
   this effect and connects with diction such as 'enchanting' and
   'improbable'.

4. The ancestors of mermaids were the Sirens, and in fable and song
   mermaids were supposed to lure men to their doom. Jake has
   clearly had an earlier relationship with Anna, and she would
   appear to be about to return to his life as a *femme fatale*.

5. To Jake, Anna represents an idealized type of womanhood which
   the mermaid comparison, with its supernatural overtones, embodies. Jake finds in Anna a supremely attractive woman whose
   beauty is beyond the power of years to change; she is sensuous
   (note her 'husky' voice) and yet totally unattainable and remote.

6. Mermaids in fable are reputed to sit on rocks all day combing their
   hair. The comparison must suggest that Anna is a lazy, vain

woman who is totally preoccupied with the impression she makes on men.

7. The room seems to be the Properties Room of a theatrical company. Its medley of objects suggests both the artifice of the stage and a lost world of childhood and the fantastic. To call the presiding creature of this setting a mermaid has, therefore, its appropriateness.

8. The comparison implies that Anna is a kind of hybrid; she spends only half her existence in the real world; the rest of her time is taken up with escapism and unreality.

9. A mermaid is a cynosure – she attracts the eye with a magnetic appeal; she compels Jake's undivided attention.

10. The epithet 'very wise' qualifies many of the connotations of 'mermaid', suggesting that the description is primarily ironic or even mocking. You would normally think of mermaids as types of flighty, superficial womanhood; but to add the adjective 'wise' undercuts all these associations.

After such an exclusive concentration on one aspect of this passage, we would like to direct your attention to another area of interest. Bearing in mind that this is a narrative written in the first person and everything is described from Jake's point of view, what is your opinion of Jake's credentials as a narrator? Take as a starting-point the view that he 'combines an intellectual's striving after emotional intensity with occasionally disturbing touches of a Mills and Boon manner'.

Finally in this section there follow two passages which reveal quite a dense and complex use of metaphorical language. Having located the important elements of the metaphorical language, decide on the functions, the breadth and appropriateness of its use. Then answer the questions.

Hurtle Duffield, a painter, has retreated from civilization and built himself a crude shack in the Australian outback.

However crude and basic the house or shack on the edge of the gorge, it was the artifact he had made. Helped by its primitive nature it soon settled into the ironstone and eucalypt landscape. The rocks might have been fired on a primordial occasion before it was decided to disguise the cleft of the gorge with its austere fringes of vegetation. It remained an oven in summer. Not 5 surprisingly, trees sown in rocky crevices had taken the colour of smoke, of ash, their leaves narrow and listless, but tough. Even now, smoke would unravel without warning, its pungent strands threading through the bush. The whole of one night he stood by his unfinished house and watched the gorge snap and gnash at its own flames, as the trees went up in a clatter of 10 fiery blinds. In the first light he himself felt ashen, not to say emotionally charred, while he still waited with a hacked-off branch to protect, if

necessary, his timber skeleton of a house. It continued standing. The half-
empty water-tank glittered as the morning clapped its eye on the unpainted
iron corrugations.   15
   The bush never died, it seemed, though regular torture by fire and
drought might bring it to the verge of death. Its limbs were soon putting on
ghostly flesh: of hopeful green, as opposed to the ashtones of a disillusioned
maturity: the most deformed and havocked shrubs were sharpening lance
and spike against the future.   20
   He liked to scramble down the face of the gorge through the evening light,
chocking his boots against rock, clinging to the hairy trunks of trees, his
fingers slithering over the slippery, fleshier ones. Once he caught his mouth
trying out the response of one of the pinker, smoother torsoes. He was never
so happy as in the communicative silence of the evening light. Sometimes he 25
remembered he had been a painter before growing physically exhausted:
musclebound, wooden-headed, contented.

Patrick White: The Vivisector (1970)

(i) What impressions of this landscape are conveyed through the
    imagery?
(ii) 'Sometimes he remembered he had been a painter . . .' (lines 25–
     26). In what ways is the landscape described as it might strike an
     artist?

*Milton's 'Areopagitica' (1644) is one of the great defences of the freedom to
express opinion without the fear of censorship. Here Milton expresses his
belief in the importance of the individual conscience being left to make its
own choices, and in the second part of the passage he writes of his hopes for
the future after religious reformation has been completed.*

Good and evil we know in the field of this World grow up together almost
inseparably; and the knowledge of good is so involv'd and interwoven with
the knowledge of evill, and in so many cunning resemblances hardly to be
discern'd, that those confused seeds which were impos'd on *Psyche* as an
incessant labour to cull out, and sort asunder, were not more intermixt. It   5
was from out the rinde of one apple tasted, that the knowledge of good and
evill as two twins cleaving together leapt forth into the World. And perhaps
this is that doom which *Adam* fell into of knowing good and evill, that is to
say of knowing good by evill. As theretofore the state of man now is; what
wisdome can there be to choose, what continence to forbeare without the   10
knowledge of evill? He that can apprehend and consider vice with all her
baits and seeming pleasures, and yet abstain, and yet distinguish, and yet
prefer that which is truly better, he is the true warfaring Christian. I cannot
praise a fugitive and cloister'd vertue, unexercis'd and unbreath'd, that
never sallies out and sees her adversary, but slinks out of the race, where   15
that immortall garland is to be run for, not without dust and heat.
Assuredly we bring not innocence into the World, we bring impurity much
rather: that which purifies us is triall and triall is by what is contrary. That
vertue therefore which is but a youngling in the contemplation of evill, and
knows not the utmost that vice promises to her followers, and rejects it, is   20
but a blank vertue, not a pure; her whitenesse is but an excrementall
whitenesse; Which was the reason why our sage and serious Poet *Spencer*,

whom I dare be known to think a better teacher than *Scotus* or *Aquinas*, describing true temperance under the person of *Guion*, brings him in with his palmer through the cave of Mammon, and the bowr of earthly blisse that   25
he might see and know, and yet abstain.

[A ferment of widespread debate in England] is a lively and cherfull presage of our happy successe and victory. For as in a body, when the blood is fresh, the spirits pure and vigorous, not only to vital, but to rationall faculties, and those in the acutest, and the pertest operations of wit and suttlety, it argues   30
in what good plight and constitution the body is, so when the cherfulnesse of the people is so sprightly up, as that it has, not only wherewith to guard well its own freedom and safety, but to spare, and to bestow upon the solidest and sublimest points of controversie, and new invention, it betok'ns us not degenerated, nor drooping to a fatall decay, but casting off the old   35
and wrincl'd skin of corruption to outlive these pangs and wax young again, entring the glorious waies of Truth and prosperous vertue destin'd to become great and honourable in these latter ages. Methinks I see in my mind a noble and puissant Nation rousing herself like a strong man after sleep, and shaking her invincible locks: Methinks I see her as an Eagle   40
muing her mighty youth, and kindling her undazl'd eyes at the full midday beam; purging and unscaling her long abused sight at the fountain itself of heav'nly radiance; while the whole noise of timorous and flocking birds, with those also that love the twilight, flutter about, amaz'd at what she means, and in their envious gabble would prognosticat a year of sects and   45
schisms.

What should ye doe then, should ye suppresse all this flowry crop of knowledge and new light sprung up and yet springing daily in this City, should ye set an *Oligarchy* of twenty ingrossers over it, to bring a famin upon the minds again, when we shall know nothing but what is measur'd to   50
us by their bushel? Beleeve it, Lords and Commons, they who counsell ye to such a suppressing, doe as good as bid ye suppresse yourselves.

(i) Drawing on the material presented in the first eighteen lines, explain, why Milton 'cannot praise a fugitive and cloistered vertue' (line 14).

(ii) Where do we find imagery used: (a) to explain or clarify ideas; (b) to inspire and arouse strong feeling?
Comment, with close reference to specific examples, on the effectiveness of each kind of imagery.

(iii) Two important elements in the passage, apart from the imagery, are (a) the rhetorical structuring of sentences, and (b) the polemical, combative tone of public utterance.
Write a paragraph on the contribution each of these elements make to the total effect of the passage.

EXTENDED METAPHOR

A metaphor or simile can be used in a quick-fire fashion, to illustrate or point up a correspondence, or it can be developed and extended at some length. We have already seen examples of this second type in the passages by

C. S. Lewis and Milton. Sometimes the underlying metaphor of a passage
may be the principal unifying factor. Read the following description of a
tea party.

> The party went off as such parties do. There were fat old ladies, in fine silk
> dresses, and slim young ladies, in gauzy muslin frocks; old gentlemen stood
> up with their backs to the empty fireplace, looking by no means so
> comfortable as they would have done in their own armchairs at home; and
> young gentlemen, rather stiff about the neck, clustered near the door, not as   5
> yet sufficiently in courage to attack the muslin frocks, who awaited the
> battle, drawn up in a semi-circular array. The warden endeavoured to
> induce a charge, but failed signally, not having the tact of a general; his
> daughter did what she could to comfort the forces under her command, who
> took in refreshing rations of cake and tea, and patiently looked for the   10
> coming engagement: but she herself, Eleanor, had no spirit for the work; the
> only enemy whose lance she cared to encounter was not there, and she and
> others were somewhat dull.
>
> Anthony Trollope: *The Warden* (1855)

(i) What is the nature of the extended metaphor?
(ii) Given that what is being described is a polite tea party held by a
    church warden in a cathedral city, what is meant to be our reaction
    to this metaphor?
    Link your answer with your view of the 'tone' of the passage.

The metaphor in the previous passage signals its presence very clearly:
there is a sense in which Trollope enjoys extending and exploring its
possibilities with a certain display of literary panache. Metaphors,
however, can still be powerfully operative even when they do not lie so
obviously on the surface of a piece of prose. They can be 'buried' or even
implicit. To see how this can work in an extended form, look closely at the
metaphorical language and diction of the following passage.

*A young boy, Oliver, accompanied by his mother, is taken for his first music
lesson with Bounce.*

> Halfway along the righthand side of the dark brown hall was a dark brown
> door with a dark brown settle beside it. After I had put my hat, my gloves,
> my muffler and my coat on the settle, we three went through the dark brown
> door into a darkness without any brown in it. All I could detect were two
> disparate eyes of faint light; one, a dull red spot low down, the other a blue   5
> bud, high up. Bounce's face approached the bud and turned it into an
> incandescence which illuminated the darkness without removing it. There
> was no pink or white in her face, only pale yellow, which combined with her
> high cheek bones, lashless eyes and hairless brows, gave her an appearance
> Chinese rather than European, indeterminate rather than female. At that   10
> time I thought of people as male or female by the nature of the clothes they
> wore, and the only thing definably female about Bounce was her skirt. Even
> her mousey hair, pulled back and pinned into a bun, was no positive
> evidence, since the bun was so flat as to be all but invisible from my level.

But while I examined her mutely I heard the soft closing of the door behind 15
me. I gazed at the glimmering bow window and heard my mother's step
across the cobbles. When I looked back at Bounce I found she was doing
something serious with a sort of rack that hung on the wall, so I started to
examine the room instead. The darkness still crouched everywhere behind
the hissing gaslight; but – as I was to discover through the years – even 20
daylight could do no more than filter through curtains of yellowing muslin.
Had there been no curtains, daylight could still only penetrate halfway
down the room; for it was interrupted by an enormous grand piano that
grinned savagely at the curtains as if it would gnaw them, given the chance.
It had an attachment I have seen nowhere else – a complete set of organ 25
pedals and the appropriate long, smooth seat. The lid was piled almost to
the ceiling with tattered music, broken strings, a violin, books, dust,
curious, unidentifiable objects, and the teetering bust of a bearded
gentleman I later knew as Brahms. In the darkness beyond the piano was
the red spot of the fire that smoked almost as much as Bounce. For while I 30
had been examining the room she had selected and filled one of a dozen
pipes. She sat at the organ seat and lighted the pipe; she drew, puffed,
expelled long coils of smoke which joined an air already laden with dust and
must. I looked away again at the rack, and then above the rack to the large,
brown photograph of a lady in a cap and gown, and the large, brown 35
photograph of a man who stared bleakly across the room above my head. I
looked back at Bounce, because she began to talk a little between puffs.
'There's – nothing – quite – as satisfying – as a pipe.'

William Golding: The Pyramid (1967)

(i) Decide first what predominant impression of the room and its
contents is conveyed through the key words, and then identify
three important metaphors or images, all of which revolve around
the same essential idea.

(ii) Explain briefly exactly what is being referred to in the case of each
metaphor you have selected.

(iii) Show how these metaphors help to convey the feelings of young
Oliver.

Sometimes you will encounter a prose style which revels high-spiritedly
in the metaphorical life of language – a prose full of word play and verbal
fireworks. Dickens, for example, is very fond of the metaphorical *tour de
force*.

In fact, Doctor Blimber's establishment was a great hot-house, in which
there was a forcing-apparatus incessantly at work. All the boys blew before
their time. Mental green-peas were produced at Christmas, and intellectual
asparagus all the year round. Mathematical gooseberries (very sour ones
too) were common at untimely seasons, and from mere sprouts of bushes, 5
under Doctor Blimber's cultivation. Every description of Greek and Latin
vegetable was got off the driest twigs of boys, under the frostiest
circumstances. Nature was of no consequence at all. No matter what a

young gentleman was intended to bear, Doctor Blimber made him bear to
pattern somehow or other.   10

Dombey and Son (1848)

Writers of our own period tend to avoid the 'purple patch', perhaps;
but here is a fairly recent example of the kind of prose which delights in
the rich extension of a metaphor, exploring, with some elements of
parody, as many possibilities as most imaginations could conceive of. It
will help us if we know that Adam, the central figure here, is in a state of
constant anxiety about the possibility of his wife becoming pregnant
again; and that he is working in the Reading Room of the British Museum
on a thesis concerning the modern novel, his current pre-occupation
being the work of D. H. Lawrence.

How successful do you find this passage as an elaborate set-piece of
metaphorical extension? Are you amused?

He passed through the narrow vaginal passage, and entered the huge womb
of the Reading Room. Across the floor, dispersed along the radiating desks,
scholars curled, foetus-like, over their books, little buds of intellectual life
thrown off by some gigantic act of generation performed upon that nest of
knowledge, those inexhaustible ovaries of learning, the concentric inner   5
rings of the catalogue shelves.

The circular wall of the Reading Room wrapped the scholars in a
protective layer of books, while above them arched the vast, distended belly
of the dome. Little daylight entered through the grimy glass at the top. No
sounds of traffic or other human business penetrated to that warm, airless   10
space. The dome looked down on the scholars, and the scholars looked
down on their books; and the scholars loved their books, stroking the pages
with soft pale fingers. The pages responded to the fingers' touch, and yielded
their knowledge gladly to the scholars, who collected it in little boxes of file-
cards. When the scholars raised their eyes from their desks they saw nothing   15
to distract them, nothing out of harmony with their books, only the smooth,
curved lining of the womb. Wherever the eye travelled, it met no arrest, no
angle, no parallel lines receding into infinity, no pointed arch striving
towards the unattainable: all was curved, rounded, self-sufficient, complete.
And the scholars dropped their eyes to their books again, fortified and   20
consoled. They curled themselves more tightly over their books, for they did
not want to leave the warm womb, where they fed upon electric light and
inhaled the musty odour of yellowing pages.

But the women who waited outside felt differently. From their dingy flats
in Islington and cramped semis in Bexleyheath, they looked out through the   25
windows at the life of the world, at the motor-cars and the advertisements
and the clothes in the shops, and they found them good. And they resented
the warm womb of the Museum which made them poor and lonely, which
swallowed up their men every day and sapped them of their vital spirits and
made them silent and abstracted mates even when they were at home. And   30
the women sighed for the day when their men would be expelled from the
womb for the last time, and they looked at their children whimpering at their

feet, and they clasped their hands, coarsened with detergent, and vowed that these children would never be scholars.

Lawrence, thought Adam. It's time I got on to Lawrence.   35

> David Lodge: *The British Museum is Falling Down* (1965)

We suggested in the Introduction (pages 00–00) that the writing of parodies can be a rewarding way of studying an author's style. If you want to see the original which David Lodge clearly has in mind here, read the opening pages of D. H. Lawrence's *The Rainbow* (1915).

PERSONIFICATION

Much of the sparkle of the previous passage derives from 'personification': the kind of figurative language which endows an inanimate object or an abstract concept with human attributes or feeling. To illustrate this, notice how in 'the dome looked down on the scholars', the dome of the Reading Room is being endowed by David Lodge with the human ability to look down, or how, in 'the warm womb of the Museum', the inanimate Museum has been given the human female attribute of a womb. You will probably be able to recall examples of personification from passages earlier in this section. Remember how Fitzgerald described the shops in the sleepy Southern town as *yawning their doors and blinking their windows* or C. S. Lewis's suggestion that *the whole expanse [of the plain] laughs with these little white dots [of cottages]*. Incidentally, this last example also illustrates the 'pathetic fallacy', a term coined by Ruskin in the nineteenth century to describe the tendency of writers and painters to credit nature with human feelings: for example, 'the smiling fields of corn' or 'the cruel sea'.

In the following extract, L. P. Hartley is describing a little boy's fear and fascination when, for the first time, he sees a large deadly nightshade. To make these feelings more vivid, the author describes him as imagining the plant to be alive and ready to eat him.

> I felt that the plant could poison me, even if I didn't touch it, and that if I didn't eat it, it would eat me, it looked so hungry, in spite of all the nourishment it was getting.

> *The Go-Between* (1951)

In the next two short extracts decide what the authors are personifying and what effect is intended.

(a) The stove was cold. Papa shook the grates, and raised an ashen dust. The grates grumbled and squealed.

> Saul Bellow: *Herzog* (1964)

(b) Plantations[1] are amongst ancient, primitive, and heroical works. When

---

[1] *Plantations*: settlements of people in new lands; colonies.

the world was young, it begat more children; but now it is old, it begets
fewer: for I may justly account new plantations to be the children of
former kingdoms.

Francis Bacon. 'Essay of Plantations' (1625)

Our final example of personification is a somewhat longer one.

Read the passage and discuss what is contributed by the personifications. One point you should consider is the part the personifications in
the second paragraph play in the change of tone which occurs further on
in the passage. Comment on the emotional impact the author intends
these personifications to have on the reader.

This town of Marney was a metropolis of agricultural labour, for the
proprietors of the neighbourhood having for the last half-century acted on
the system of destroying the cottages on their estates, in order to become
exempted from the maintenance of the population, the expelled people had
flocked to Marney, where, during the war, a manufactory had afforded them   5
some relief, though its wheels had long ceased to disturb the waters of the
Mar.

Deprived of this resource, they had again gradually spread themselves
over that land which had, as it were, rejected them; and obtained from its
churlish breast a niggardly subsistence. Their re-entrance into the surround-   10
ing parishes was viewed with great suspicion; their renewed settlement
opposed by every ingenious contrivance; those who availed themselves of
their labour were careful that they should not become dwellers on the soil;
and though, from the excessive competition there were few districts in the
kingdom where the rate of wages was more depressed, those who were   15
fortunate enough to obtain the scant remuneration, had, in addition to their
toil, to endure, each morn and even, a weary journey before they could reach
the scene of their labour, or return to the squalid hovel which profaned the
name of home. To that home, over which malaria hovered, and round whose
shivering hearth were clustered other guests beside the exhausted family of   20
toil – Fever, in every form, pale Consumption, exhausting Synochus,[1] and
trembling Ague, – returned after cultivating the broad fields of merry
England, the bold British peasant, returned to encounter the worst diseases,
with a frame the least qualified to oppose them; a frame that, subdued by
toil, was never sustained by animal food; drenched by the tempest, could not   25
change its dripping rags; and was indebted for its scanty fuel to the windfalls
of the woods.

Benjamin Disraeli: *Sybil* (1845)

There are other figures of speech besides the essential ones of metaphor,
simile and personification, such as 'metonymy' and 'synecdoche', and, if
you wish, you can look these up in any glossary of literary terms. There is
no real justification, however, in a simple labelling of parts, and the
danger is that some students are tempted to use these terms simply to

---

[1] *Synochus*: a debilitating fever.

impress, like bringing a favourite son forward to give him a pat on the head. Unless the use of the terminology is supported by close analysis, it is sterile: we have already discussed some of the dangers into which the misuse of jargon can lead us. If, however, the correct critical vocabulary is used as a kind of shorthand which is immediately followed by a discussion of *how* the particular device works, then it is valuable. Remember this if you ever find yourself writing baldly that 'The author uses a lot of similes' – and leaving it at that!

JUDGEMENTS ON THE EFFECTIVENESS OF METAPHORICAL LANGUAGE

When you are asked to consider the *effectiveness* of a comparison, the essential starting-point is its appropriateness or aptness. We need to ask first, what are the links between vehicle and tenor? (Refer back to page 52 if you are unsure of these terms). After considering why the two elements in the comparison have been brought into contact, we need to discuss whether this conjunction is illuminating and convincing.

Elementary mistakes can be made in the selection of comparisons, such as the use of dead or hackneyed metaphorical language or the mixing of metaphors that shows confusion of thought (see example (d) on page 22). Vague and unfocused comparisons should also be avoided (remember the one we commented on, page 48), and it is usually important to ensure that metaphorical language fits in with the particular purpose and tone of the context. For example, it is generally undesirable for a series of flashy explosions of metaphor to break into discursive prose which has been moving along in a quiet and unostentatious manner.

Yet, having said all this, opinions about the effectiveness of comparisons in a passage will often vary, with both sides in the disagreement claiming that they can justify their response by close analysis of the text. To demonstrate this we conclude with two passages which, when they were discussed by one class, produced strong disagreement.

We have summarized the disagreement about the first passage as follows: one faction claimed that the comparisons were 'used in an eye-catching and witty way, so that a sense of individuality and originality was added to a kind of writing which all too often was no more than a stringing together of the same old sports writer's clichés'. The others argued that the comparisons were a 'mish-mash of bad taste and exhibitionism, made all the more repugnant by the fact that the writer was so obviously applauding her own supposed lively ingenuity.' What do you think?

When a manager has sampled 32 years in football and his experiences are as varied as a sub-section of Roget's *Thesaurus*, you would expect him to give retirement from duty the sort of reception Aix laid on for the trio from Ghent. You would have got Alec Stock rather wrong. Preventing Stock from working is like keeping dandelions out of your garden and when he   5

joined Bournemouth nineteen days ago he must have galloped to the
starting gate more times than Red Rum.

'Sheer boredom,' he said, drove him back to the game after he bowed out
with honour from Fulham in 1977. 'So when someone from Bournemouth
said "Would you?" I couldn't think of anything better. Strike a blow for the   10
over 60s. Show everyone you're not debris at 60. Had to be good, hm?
Bournemouth in the spring. Not like Scunthorpe.'

It has to be good, indeed, even though spring is a somewhat imaginative
term for Bournemouth's current climatic conditions and frost sticks to its
generous training pitch like toothpaste round the side of a wash-basin.   15
Stock's return to employment is a comforting reward for a man who once
feared that experience ultimately counted for nothing, bought nothing
except a ticket on the slow train to the wilderness.

He hit the jackpot right away, too. Stock's courageous satisfaction in
taking on and succeeding with struggling clubs would daunt a younger   20
member of his trade. Not that this marvellously sharp and likeable man
shows any sign of incipient decrepitude. Under the pancake of a cap his eyes
gleam with enthusiasm and mischief and the whacking great sports car in the
club car park belongs not to some young sprig on the playing staff but to
him.   25

Julie Welch: *Observer*, 18.2.79.

Again opinions varied about the use of metaphorical language in this
second passage: on the one hand, it was claimed that the way comparison
was used was 'perfectly in keeping with the writer's own rapt, almost
religious intensity of feeling and that the imagery enabled us to see
through to the heart of the mystery that was unfolded.' On the other
hand, it was alleged that 'the imagery of the passage was overblown and
emotionally indulgent and that its pseudo-religious puerility and hector-
ing assertiveness produced resistance in the reader, mingled with a degree
of embarrassment on the writer's behalf.' Which side of the argument are
you on?

So the sun in the seed, and the earthly one in the seed take hands, and laugh,
and begin to dance. And their dancing is like a fire kindled, a bonfire with
leaping flame. And the treading of their feet is like the running of little
streams, down into the earth. So from the dance of the sun-in-the-seed with
the earthy death-returner, green little flames of leaves shoot up, and hard   5
little trickles of roots strike down. And the host laughs, and says: '*I am being
lifted up! Dance harder! Oh wrestle, you two, like wonderful wrestlers, neither
of which can win.*' So sun-in-the-seed and the death-returner, who is earthy,
dance faster and faster and the leaves rising greener begin to dance in a ring
above-ground, fiercely overwhelming any outsider, in a whirl of swords and   10
lions' teeth. And the earthy one wrestles, wrestles with the sun-in-the-seed,
so the long roots reach down like arms of a fighter gripping the power of
earth, and strangles all intruders, strangling any intruder mercilessly. Till
the two fall in one strange embrace, and from the centre the long flower-stem
lifts like a phallus, budded with a bud. And out of the bud the voice of the   15
Holy Ghost is heard crying: '*I am lifted up! Lo! I am lifted up! I am here!*' So

the bud opens, and there is the flower poised in the very middle of the universe, with a ring of green swords below, to guard it, and the octopus, arms deep in earth, drinking and threatening. So the Holy Ghost, being a dandelion flower, looks round, and says: '*Lo! I am yellow! I believe the sun* 20 *has lent me his body! Lo! I am sappy with golden, bitter blood! I believe death out of the damp black earth has lent me his blood! I am incarnate! I like my incarnation! But this is not all. I will keep this incarnation. It is good! But oh! if I can win to another incarnation, who knows how wonderful it will be! This one will have to give place. This one can help to create the next.*' 25

So the Holy Ghost leaves the clue of himself behind, in the seed, and wanders forth in the comparative chaos of our universe, seeking another incarnation.

And this will go on for ever. Man, as yet, is less than half grown. Even his flower-stem has not appeared yet. He is all leaves and roots, without any clue 30 put forth. No sign of bud anywhere.

Either he will have to start budding, or he will be forsaken of the Holy Ghost: abandoned as a failure in creation, as the ichthyosaurus was abandoned. Being abandoned means losing his vitality. The sun and the earth-dark will cease rushing together in him. Already it is ceasing. To men, 35 the sun is becoming stale, and the earth sterile. But the sun itself will never become stale, nor the earth barren. It is only that the *clue* is missing inside men. They are like flowerless, seedless fat cabbages, nothing inside.

D. H. Lawrence: 'Reflections on the Death of a Porcupine' (from *Selected Essays*, 1925)

4

Rhythm

INTRODUCTION

Perhaps a short indication of what people mean when they speak of rhythm in prose would be useful at this stage. An examination of prose rhythms is concerned with the ordering of words and the patterning of sound – the movement, tone and emphasis of words and phrases and clauses within sentences, and the subsequent patterning of sentences within a paragraph. To help you start thinking in these terms, here are six short passages in which the writers have paid particular attention to the effect of certain clear rhythmical devices. Consider these examples and try to discover (i) what the effect of the passage is, and (ii) how the writers used rhythm to achieve their ends.

(a) When I was a child, I spoke as a child, I understood as a child, I thought as a child; but when I became a man, I put away childish things.

St Paul: 1 Corinthians, 13

(b) 'Now, what I want is, Facts. Teach these boys and girls nothing but Facts. Facts alone are wanted in life. Plant nothing else, and root-out everything else. You can only form the minds of reasoning animals upon Facts: nothing else will even be of any service to them. This is the principle on which I bring up my own children, and this is the principle on which I bring up these children. Stick to Facts, sir!'

Charles Dickens: *Hard Times* (1854)

(c) Listen. It is night in the chill, squat chapel, hymning in bonnet and brooch and bombazine black, butterfly chocker and bootlace bow, coughing like nannygoats, sucking mintoes, fortywinking hallelujah.

Dylan Thomas: *Under Milk Wood* (1954)

(d) Friends, Romans, Countrymen, lend me your ears. I come to bury Caesar, not to praise him.

Shakespeare: *Julius Caesar* (1599)

(e) I leaned down in the scrum, watched the ball come in, go out. I stood up. The whistle went. Half-time. The men sprawled and collapsed onto the massage table and the bench. Belching and groaning.

D. Storey: *This Sporting Life* (1960)

(f) There is in the Midlands a single-line tramway system which boldly leaves the country-town and plunges off into the black, industrial countryside, up hill and down dale, through the long ugly villages of workmen's houses, over canals and railways, past churches perched high and nobly over the smoke and shadows, through stark grimy cold little market places, tilting away in a rush past cinemas and shops down to the hollows where the collieries are, then up again, past a little rural church, under the ash trees, on in a rush to the terminus, the last little ugly place of industry, the cold little town that shivers on the edge of the wild, gloomy country beyond.

D. H. Lawrence: 'Tickets, Please' (1922)

We hope that your discussion brought out some of the following 'rhythmic techniques' that the authors put to effective use. For instance:

(i) the repetition of a key word (*facts*) or phrase (*as a child*) for emphasis;
(ii) the accumulation and balancing of phrases and clauses within a sentence to produce a climax or an anti-climax: for example in passages (a), (b) and (c);
(iii) the effect of pauses: for instance in passages (b) and (e);
(iv) the ways in which the structure of sentences creates differing effects: for example, the length and pace of the tram journey, example (f), or the brief, abrupt rhythms of example (e), conveying the exhaustion felt by rugby players nearing half-time.

Of course, this by no means exhausts all there is to say about the use of prose rhythms in these extracts, and we will need to define shortly exactly what we mean by such terms as 'sentence', 'clause' or 'balance'; but we hope that your preliminary discussions have at least shown you the importance of rhythm to writers of prose, and how they can use it to vary effects.

Warning! We have not played entirely fair with you in our examples because one of them is taken not from prose, but from verse. Can you tell which one? We have done this in order to remind you that there can be some overlap in the rhythmic techniques of prose and verse writers, especially in the more heavily patterned pieces of prose, but we would not suggest, of course, that prose is usually rhythmical in the same way as a sonnet or piece of blank verse. In a poem we will often find that there is a basic metre, a pattern of stressed and unstressed syllables, but in prose we will seldom find such a disciplined and conscious use of rhythm. (Passages (a) and (c) could almost be termed 'poetic' in this respect. Do you agree?) For this reason, analysis of prose rhythms cannot be approached in a dogmatic or rigid way; they are often illusive and different readers may 'feel' different patterns.

All spoken and written language has its rhythms; they derive from the natural syntax of the language itself. And, to a greater or a lesser extent, all writers must concern themselves with the pattern and balance of the words they use and the shaping of the sentences they form. Can the prose of everyday books, such as this one, have a rhythm in the sense that our six opening examples can be said to be 'rhythmic'? In this type of writing you may feel that the writer is concerned not so much with the creation of special rhythmic effects as with the pressing need to make good sense. You may even suggest that, in this context, if the flag of rhythmic emphasis is flourished too insistently, the reader's attention can easily be diverted from what is actually being said. Of course, if this does happen, the writing is certainly open to criticism: rhythm in prose should be an aid to communication and not an end in itself. When the aim of a passage of prose is simply that of plain exposition, it may well be that the limit of the writer's concern with rhythm is to ensure that there is a variety of constructions which regulate the movement of the prose and prevent monotony.

However, you will remember that in our introductory chapter we decided that prose has many other functions besides mere exposition, and the rest of this section will be concerned with the writing of imaginative or emotionally persuasive prose in which the full range of the rhythmic resources of the language are used. Remember, however, that in speaking of rhythm, we are not suggesting that it is something that works independently from the meaning of the passage. It is *not* a kind of literary cosmetic which writers cleverly smear over the surface of their prose. When rhythm is used to any significant and successful effect, it is always as an integral part of the whole texture of the language.

THE SENTENCE

When we begin to think of the patterns that prose can form, it is to the basic unit of the sentence that we must turn our attention. In the kinds of prose we are interested in, the balance and shape of a sentence can be crucial. To illustrate this, let us look at four different versions of one sentence:

(i) Before he had been in Brighton three hours, Hale knew that they meant to murder him.
(ii) Hale knew that they meant to murder him before he had been in Brighton three hours.
(iii) Hale knew, before he had been in Brighton three hours, that they meant to murder him.
(iv) That they meant to murder him, Hale knew, before he had been in Brighton three hours.

In each of these versions the pattern and the rhythm of the sentences vary and the effect obtained by the writer is slightly different. A discussion of these questions should help to bring this out:

(i) Do any seem awkward or stilted?

(ii) Do they all express their meaning clearly? Point out any ambiguities.

(iii) Do any seem to express tension better than others?

(iv) Which would you choose as the one most likely to capture your attention at the very start of a novel? (You can see if you were right by looking at Graham Greene's *Brighton Rock* (1938). One of our sentences is its opening.)

(v) Why would a writer using English reject this version: 'To murder him, Hale knew they meant before in Brighton three hours he had been'?

Presumably in answer to this last question you will have said it was unacceptable (though not meaningless) because it does not conform to the conventions of normal English word order. In fact, you may feel that it reads like a clumsy translation from a foreign language or the utterence of someone unfamiliar with English. So, you will see that, though pattern and rhythm within individual sentences can be deliberately varied to create different effects and emphases, as you will have noticed in examples (i) to (iv), they cannot be infinitely varied, as example (v) illustrates. Our sentences must be written with reference to the grid-iron of English grammar and syntax. *The word-order of a sentence vitally affects not only the emphasis, but sometimes also its meaning.*

Sentences come in many shapes and sizes. The *simple sentence* has as its basic unit what is often classified grammatically as a *subject* and a *predicate*. The term 'subject' is virtually self-explanatory: it is a noun or a pronoun, with perhaps an adjective or a phrase attached, which tells us what we are to read about. The 'predicate' adds to this what we are going to be told about the subject. So, in this simple sentence, 'They meant to murder him', we would classify 'They' as the subject and 'meant to murder him' as the predicate.

Before we proceed to more sophisticated kinds of sentence, we should first define what we generally mean by a sentence. It is a topic which grammarians have split hairs over, but for our purposes, a sentence can be defined fairly straightforwardly as a unit of words which makes complete sense in its own right and possesses a finite verb. If you were to read, for instance, 'meaning to murder him' or 'to murder him', you should sense the fragmentary nature of these half-statements: both examples are *phrases* because they do not contain a finite verb – that is, a verb which expresses a clear, limited action or state of being. ('Meaning' is a present participle; 'to murder' is the infinitive of the verb.)

The simple sentence we quoted – 'They meant to murder him' – could be built up into a longer, more complex sentence by adding to it other *clauses*, a clause being a *part* of a sentence with a subject and predicate. In a *compound sentence* we add a subordinate (or dependent) clause to a main clause:

They meant to murder him *before he had been in Brighton three hours.*

The italicized part of the sentence is a subordinate clause: it requires the main clause to complete its sense. Of course, we can add a whole string of subordinate clauses to a single main clause. In our original example, from Greene's *Brighton Rock*, there are two subordinate clauses:

> Hale knew, before he had been in Brighton three hours, that they meant to murder him.

What is the main clause? (A clue: do not put off if it seems a very short one, in this example.)

What are the two subordinate clauses? Is it possible to say what grammatical function each clause has?

Clause analysis used to be a regular drill for most students of English language. It has tended to fall out of fashion in recent years as the work of many modern linguists has suggested that this kind of analysis is a simplification, or even a distortion, of much more complex patterns and structures in language. However, up to our own period, it is certainly the case that most writers of English believed that they were writing prose in accordance with the kind of ground rules we have briefly sketched in, and this traditional approach does have the virtue of enabling readers to detect simple underlying patterns in prose fairly easily. The terminology we have introduced is often used in criticism as a convenient shorthand, for when we are considering sentence structure, we need to be aware that the patterning of sentences should not be an arbitrary matter. A series of loosely constructed simple sentences, perhaps connected by the use of a string of conjunctions, can suggest, for example, the kind of spontaneity we associate with the speaking voice. On the other hand, tightly knit complex sentences, full of balanced clauses, antitheses and qualifying subordinate clauses, will create a measured, premeditated effect. Students need some basic tools in order to be able to examine in detail the design of an English sentence.

However, as the structure of a sentence is virtually inseparable from its meaning, there is little use in discussing in the abstract the shapes sentences make. We have chosen a number of short extracts, many of which are not longer than a single sentence. We suggest that you work on them in small groups, each group taking a number of sentences and reporting back on their answers to the following questions:

(i)   Does the syntax (that is, the order of words in the sentence) lead to any special stress?

(ii) Is the arrangement of words the order we expect or are we surprised by any unusual pattern?

(iii) Is the sentence structure loose or carefully controlled? (Remember what we have briefly discussed about the tools of clause analysis.)

(iv) Is the punctuation used to any significant effect?

(v)   In what precise ways is the sentence structure related to the writer's (a) intention, (b) subject matter and (c) tone?

(a) Undulating through the market, who so gay as Ibrahim? He, in crepitating silk, hair-clips holding curls in place, basket swinging, fist clutched tightly round two crumpled dollar notes, went to do the morning's shopping.

Anthony Burgess: *Time for a Tiger* (1956)

(b) *Description of a deserted house*
Once only a board sprang on the landing; once in the middle of the night with a roar, with a rupture, as after centuries of quiescence, a rock rends itself from the mountain and hurtles crashing into the valley, one fold of the shawl loosened and swung to and fro.

Virginia Woolf: *To the Lighthouse* (1927)

(c) As Sir Roger is Landlord to the whole Congregation, he keeps them in very good Order, and will suffer no Body to sleep in it besides himself; for if by Chance he has been surprized into a short Nap at Sermon, upon recovering out of it he stands up and looks about him, and if he sees any Body else nodding, either wakes them himself, or sends his Servants to them.

Addison: *The Spectator*, No. 112 (1711)

(d) *A French man-of-war anchored off the coast of Africa*
There wasn't even a shed there, and she was shelling the bush. It appears the French had one of their wars going on thereabouts. Her ensign dropped limp like a rag; the muzzles of the long six-inch guns stuck out all over the low hull; the greasy, slimy swell swung her up lazily and let her down, swaying her thin masts. In the empty immensity of earth, sky, and water, there she was, incomprehensible, firing into a continent. Pop, would go one of the six-inch guns; a small flame would dart and vanish, a little white smoke would disappear, a tiny projectile would give a feeble screech – and nothing happened. Nothing could happen.

Joseph Conrad: *Heart of Darkness* (1902)

(e) Thus the mind itself is bowed to the yoke; even in what people do for pleasure, conforming is the first thing thought of; *they like crowds*; they exercise choice only among things commonly done; peculiarity of taste, eccentricity of conduct, are shunned equally with crimes; until by dint of not following their own nature they have no nature to follow; their human capacities are withered and starved.

J. S. Mill: *On Liberty* (1859)

(f) *Lady Bracknell to the young man seeking her daughter's hand*
To lose one parent, Mr Worthing, may be regarded as a misfortune; to lose both looks like carelessness.

Oscar Wilde: *The Importance of Being Earnest* (1895)

(g) Although Bertha Young was thirty she still had moments like this when she wanted to run instead of walk, to take dancing steps on and off the pavement, to bowl a hoop, to throw something up in the air and catch it again, or to stand still and laugh at – nothing – at nothing, simply.

Katherine Mansfield: 'Bliss' (1920)

(h) *En route*, to his taciturn, and, not to put too fine a point on it, not yet perfectly sober companion, Mr Bloom, who at all events, was in complete possession of his faculties, never more so, in fact disgustingly sober, spoke a word of caution *re* the dangers of nighttown, women of ill fame and swell mobsmen, which, barely permissible once in a while, though not as a habitual practice, was of the nature of a regular deathtrap for young fellows of his age particularly if they had acquired drinking habits under the influence of liquor unless you knew a little jujitsu for every contingency as even a fellow on the broad of his back could administer a nasty kick if you didn't look out.

James Joyce: *Ulysses* (1922)

(i) The schoolboy whips his taxed top – the beardless youth manages his taxed horse, with a taxed bridle, on a taxed road; – and the dying Englishman, pouring his medicine, which had paid seven per cent, into a spoon that had paid fifteen per cent – flings himself back upon his chintz bed, which has paid twenty-two per cent – and expires in the arms of an apothecary who has paid a licence of a hundred pounds for the privilege of putting him to death.

Sydney Smith (1771–1845): Review of Seybert's *Statistical Annals of the United States*

(j) The landscape softens where the border line on the map begins, and the grizzled faces of Afghans, whose heads are sloppily swathed in white turbans, are replaced by the angular beakiness of Pakistanis, who wear narrow slippers and have the thin scornful mustaches of magicians and movie villains.

Paul Theroux: *The Great Railway Bazaar* (1975)

(k) About seven rose again to dress myself, and there looked out at the window, and saw the fire not so much as it was and further off. So to my closett to set things to rights after yesterday's cleaning. By and by Jane comes and tells me that she hears that above 300 houses have been burned down tonight by the fire we saw, and that it is now burning down all Fish-Street, by London Bridge. So I made myself ready presently, and walked to the Tower, and there got up upon one of the high places . . . and there did I see the houses at that end of the bridge all on fire, and an infinite great fire on this and the other side the end of the bridge.

Pepys's *Diary*, 2nd September, 1666

(l) He who first shortened the labour of copyists by device of *Movable Types* was disbanding hired armies, and cashiering most Kings and Senates, and creating a whole new democratic world: he had invented the art of printing.

Carlyle: *Sartor Resartus* (1833–34)

(m) He felt the prefect of studies touch [his hand] for a moment at the fingers to straighten it and then the swish of the sleeve of the soutane as the pandybat was lifted to strike. A hot burning stinging tingling blow like the loud crack of a broken stick made his trembling hand crumple together like a leaf in the fire: and at the sound and the pain scalding tears were driven into his eyes.

James Joyce: *A Portrait of the Artist as a Young Man* (1916)

(n) What is character but the determination of incident? What is incident but the illustration of character?

Henry James: *Prefaces* (1909)

(o) It was raining. The rain dripped from the palm trees. Water stood in pools on the gravel paths. The sea broke in a long line in the rain and slipped back down the beach to come up and break again in a long line in the rain.

Hemingway: 'Cat in the Rain' (1939)

(p) You must go on, I can't go on, I'll go on.

Beckett: *The Unnameable* (1959)

(q) *Anna Livia Plurabelle = the river Liffey.*
In the name of Annah the Allmaziful, the Everliving, the Bringer of Plurabilities, haloed be her eve, her singtime sung, her rill be run, unhemmed as it is uneven!

James Joyce: *Finnegans Wake* (1939)

(r) It is only through an unremitting never-discouraged care for the shape and ring of sentences that an approach can be made to plasticity, to colour, and that the light of magic suggestiveness may be brought to play for an evanescent instant over the commonplace surface of words: of the old, old words, worn thin, defaced by ages of careless usage.

Joseph Conrad: Preface to *The Nigger of the Narcissus* (1897)

If you are interested in taking your study of sentence structure to a more advanced level, we suggest you consult *Designs in Prose* by Walter Nash (Longman, 1980).

SOME PRACTICAL ANALYSIS

We should be ready now to consider sentence structure as a part of a wider context. We will begin by looking at the way sentences are constructed in the opening passages of two eighteenth-century novels. The first passage is taken from Defoe's *Colonel Jack* (1722). We suggest that you read it through twice: the first time, concentrate on what is being said; the second time, look carefully at the shapes of the sentences and then jot down in the form of rough notes anything that strikes you as interesting.

A. My original may be as high as any Bodies for ought I know, for my
Mother kept very good Company, but that part belongs to her Story,
more than to mine; all I know of it, is by oral tradition thus; my Nurse
told me my Mother was a Gentlewoman, that my Father was a Man of
Quality, and she (my Nurse) had a good piece of Money given her to take   5
me off his Hands, and deliver him and my Mother from the
Importunities that usually attend the Misfortune, of having a Child to
keep that should not be seen or heard of.

My Father it seems gave my Nurse something more than was agreed
for at my Mother's request, upon her solemn Promise that she would use   10
me well, and let me be put to school, and charg'd her that if I liv'd to
come to any bigness, capable to understand the meaning of it, she should
always take care to bid me remember, *that I was a Gentleman*, and this he
said was all the Education he would desire of her for me, for he did not
doubt, he said, but that sometime or other the very hint would inspire me   15
with thoughts suitable to my Birth, and that I would certainly act like a
Gentleman, if I believed myself to be so.

But my Disasters were not directed to end as soon as they began; 'tis
very seldom that the Unfortunate are so but for a Day, as the Great rise
by degrees of Greatness to the Pitch of Glory, in which they shine, so the   20
Miserable sink to the depth of their Misery by a continu'd Series of
Disaster, and are long in the Tortures and Agonies of their distress'd
Circumstances before a Turn of Fortune, if ever such a thing happens to
them, gives them a prospect of Deliverance.

My Nurse was as honest to the Engagement she had enter'd into, as   25
cou'd be expected from one of her Employment, and particularly as
honest as her Circumstances would give her leave to be; for she Bred me
up very carefully with her own Son, and with another Son of shame *like
me*, who she had taken upon the same terms.

The making of an immediate note of your first impressions of a passage is a method we have recommended before as a useful way of beginning to formulate your ideas. Compare your notes with the following jottings:

Sentence Structure: first two paragraphs consist of loosely constructed sentences; strings of simple conjunctions are used – for example in the second paragraph ('that . . . and . . . and . . .that . . .' etc.). Slightly clumsy repetition of 'for' (line I) and again (line 14); a parenthesis is hastily slipped in (line 5) to make the pronoun 'she' unambiguous. *Pace*: sentences rush along with a reckless life of their own – in the

natural speech rhythms of the narrator. *Punctuation* aids this effect –
lots of commas stitch the rather long, straggling sentences together in
the most basic way. Placing of comma at line 7 – a pause for breath? or
to make a special emphasis?

It is important to stress that this is written in the *first person*. Something
of the *narrator's character* is conveyed immediately through his style –
a garrulous, breathless narrative manner. He is certainly no poised,
conscious stylist! *Tone* suggests a man of the world – full of racy
dispatch.

Change in sentence construction in the third paragraph is quite marked;
there is almost an air of contrivance here? The clause 'as the great . . . '
obviously balanced by 'so the miserable . . . ' This antithesis signals a
change in the *purpose* of the prose as the narrator moves from his
narrative manner to a more mannered style which is meant to enforce a
(rather trite?) moral. This done, he returns at once to his earlier, looser
construction until the end of the extract.

Do you find yourself in broad agreement?

Now read this extract from Smollett's *Peregrine Pickle* (1751). In the
questions which follow you will be asked to make certain comparisons
with the passage from Defoe.

B. In a certain county of England, bounded on one side by the sea, and at
the distance of one hundred miles from the metropolis, lived Gamaliel
Pickle Esq; the father of that hero whose adventures we propose to
record. He was the son of a merchant in London, who (like Rome) from
small beginnings, had raised himself to the highest honours of the city,   5
and acquired a plentiful fortune, tho', to his infinite regret, he died before
it amounted to a Plum,[1] conjuring his son, as he respected the last
injunction of a parent, to imitate his industry and adhere to his maxims,
until he should have made up the deficiency, which was a sum
considerably less than fifteen thousand pounds.   10

This pathetic remonstrance had the desired effect upon this representative, who spared no pains to fulfil the request of the deceased; but
exerted all the capacity with which nature had endowed him, in a series
of efforts, which, however, did not succeed; for, by that time he had been
fifteen years in trade, he found himself five thousand pounds worse than 15
he was when he first took possession of his father's effects: a circumstance that affected him so nearly, as to detach his inclinations from
business, and to induce him to retire from the world, to some place where
he might at leisure deplore his misfortune, and, by frugality, secure
himself from want, and the apprehensions of a jail, with which his   20
imagination was incessantly haunted. In short, his talents were not
naturally active, and there was a sort of inconsistency in his character;
for, with all the desire of amassing which any citizen could possibly
entertain, he was encumbered by a certain indolence and sluggishness

---

[1] *Plum*: a slang term for £100,000.

that prevailed over every interested consideration, and even hindered   25
him from profiting by that singleness of apprehension, and moderation
of appetites, which have so frequently conduced to the acquisition of
immense fortunes, and which he possessed in a very remarkable degree.
Nature, in all probability, had mixed little or nothing inflammable in his
composition; or, whatever seeds of excess she might have sown within   30
him, were effectually stifled and destroyed by the austerity of his
education.

(i) Compare the first paragraph of passages A. and B. How would
you define the difference(s) in the way each author constructed
sentences? Does the movement of the prose differ significantly?

(ii) With close reference to passage B., write on the effect of:
(a) Smollett's use of balanced and parallel constructions. Locate
specific examples and comment on their effect. Did you notice that
Smollett also often uses words in pairs? Why?
(b) Smollett's punctuation. How does it differ from Defoe's?
Would you say that Smollett tends to use more or less punctuation
than a modern writer?

(iii) Decide what you think is Smollett's attitude to the character he is
describing, and then say whether you think the movement of the
sentences contributes anything to the expression of this attitude.
Would the same question be relevant to Defoe?

(iv) Does the fact that passage (A.) is written in the first person and
passage (B.) in the third person affect the sentence construction of
each passage? Or is the determining factor the method of
characterization adopted by each author? (This is a complex
question: we will be discussing the use of different narrative
viewpoints in a later chapter. At this stage we would simply like
you to consider the relative influence the demands of a certain
viewpoint and method of characterization have on the rhythms of
language. You may decide that these two elements are not
separable.)

(v) Which of the following would you accept as accurate in describing
the general nature of Smollett's sentence construction as compared with Defoe's?
(a) 'more controlled and complex'.
(b) 'lacks the immediate presence of a speaking voice'.
(c) 'more cultured and polished'.
(d) 'stiff and contrivedly pompous'.
(e) 'better prose'.

PATTERNING AND PARALLELISM

You will remember that we have already noted how *antithesis* (see page
85), a device whereby one group of words is balanced in a parallel
structure against a contrasting following group, can be used in an attempt

to impart a succinct clarity and memorability to a statement. So when Dr Johnson writes: 'Marriage has many pains, but celibacy has no pleasures', the pithy, balanced way the statement is made catches the eye. This kind of parallelism within sentences lends itself to writing which strives after aphoristic or epigrammatic effect, the balancing of the syntactic units providing something of the concentration of language into a memorable unit which rhyme and metre produce in poetry.

You might find it interesting to look through any dictionary of quotations and note down perhaps a dozen examples in prose of an obvious patterning effect which gives the statement its force. In each case, give a brief comment on the elements of syntax and balance which are at work.

It is possible that while you may admire the artistry of some of the quotations you have selected for your own list, others may strike you as forced and contrived. For example, how do you react to a statement like Burke's 'Kings will be tyrants from policy when subjects are rebels from principle'? You may feel that this is no more than a facile jingle; the very neatness of the construction pulls our attention away from *what* is being said, to *how* it is being said. (There is room for disagreement here!)

To consolidate the points we have covered in this section, we would like you to examine closely three passages which exhibit a high degree of patterning in their sentence construction.

Studies serve for delight, for ornament, and for ability. Their chief use for delight, is in privateness and retiring; for ornament, is in discourse; and for ability, is in the judgement and disposition of business. For expert men can execute, and perhaps judge of particulars, one by one; but the general counsels, and the plots and marshalling of affairs, come best from those that are learned. To spend too much time in studies is sloth; to use them too much for ornament is affectation; to make judgement wholly by their rules, is the humour of a scholar. They perfect nature, and are perfected by experience; for natural abilities are like natural plants, that need pruning by study; and studies themselves do give forth directions too much at large, except they be bounded in by experience. Crafty men condemn studies, simple men admire them, and wise men use them; for they teach not their own use; but that is a wisdom without them, and above them, won by observation. Read not to contradict and confute; nor to believe and take for granted; nor to find talk and discourse; but to weigh and consider.   5   10   15

Bacon: 'Of Studies' (1625)

Bacon's writing here has a clipped, concentrated power. What is the device at work in the construction of the sentences that produces this effect?

Here De Quincey is describing some of the images from the bad dreams he had under the influence of opium.

All the feet of the tables, sofas, &c., soon became instinct with life: the abominable head of the crocodile, and his leering eyes, looked out at me,

multiplied into ten thousand repetitions; and I stood loathing and
fascinated. So often did this hideous reptile haunt my dreams, that many
times the very same dream was broken up in the very same way: I heard   5
gentle voices speaking to me (I hear everything when I am sleeping), and
instantly I awoke; it was broad noon, and my children were standing, hand
in hand, at my bedside, come to show me their coloured shoes, or new
frocks, or to let me see them dressed for going out. No experience was so
awful to me, and at the same time so pathetic, as this abrupt translation from   10
the darkness of the infinite to the gaudy summer air of highest noon, and
from the unutterable abortions of miscreated gigantic vermin to the sight of
infancy, and innocent *human* natures.

Confessions of an English Opium-Eater (1822)

What is the precise effect of the final sentence of the above passage, and
how is it achieved?

The education bestowed on Flora Poste by her parents had been expensive,
athletic and prolonged; and when they died within a few weeks of one
another during the annual epidemic of the influenza or Spanish Plague
which occurred in her twentieth year, she was discovered to possess every art
and grace save that of earning her own living.   5

Her father had always been spoken of as a wealthy man, but on his death
his executors were disconcerted to find him a poor one. After death duties
had been paid and the demands of the creditors satisfied, his child was left
with an income of one hundred pounds a year, and no property.

Flora inherited, however, from her father a strong will and from her   10
mother a slender ankle. The one had not been impaired by always having her
own way nor the other by the violent athletic sports in which she had been
compelled to take part, but she realised that neither was adequate as an
equipment for earning her keep.

She decided, therefore, to stay with a friend, a Mrs Smiling, at her house in   15
Lambeth until she could decide where to bestow herself and her hundred
pounds a year.

Stella Gibbons, *Cold Comfort Farm* (1932)

The witty turning of a sentence is a device which can be used to create
humour. Locate three or four examples from the passage, and comment
on their effectiveness.

DOES IT HAVE TO BE IN SENTENCES?

You can regard this section as something of an interlude. You may find it
challenges some of the assumptions we have led you into making, for the
answer to our opening question may be that a writer does not have to
write in sentences – if we define a sentence as a grammatical unit which
contains a finite verb and makes sense in its own right. Many writers in
our own century have experimented with various styles which loosen, or
even fragment the generally accepted conventions of English syntax.

When we are confronted, for example, with strings of 'verbless sentences' or an unpunctuated 'stream of consciousness', it is important to recognize that the effect achieved is generally a result of a playing off of innovatory style against the reader's awareness of what the underlying, yet severely dislocated, pattern is.

See what you make of the following extract. Do not be worried if at first you find it difficult. The first question you should ask yourself is: why has Joyce chosen to write in this way?

Here we are given the thoughts of Mr Bloom as he is just about to leave a cemetery in Dublin, having attended the funeral of a friend, Paddy Dignam.

How many! All these here once walked round Dublin. Faithful departed. As you are now so once were we.

Besides how could you remember everybody? Eyes, walk, voice. Well, the voice, yes: gramophone. Have a gramophone in every grave or keep it in the house. After dinner on a Sunday. Put on poor old greatgrand-   5
father Kraahraark! Hellohellohello amawfullyglad kraark awfully glada-seeragain hellohello amarawf kopthsth. Remind you of the voice like the photograph reminds you of the face. Otherwise you couldn't remember the face after fifteen years, say.

Rtststr! A rattle of pebbles. Wait. Stop.   10

He looked down intently into a stone crypt. Some animal. Wait. There he goes.

An obese grey rat toddled along the side of the crypt, moving the pebbles. An old stager: greatgrandfather: he knows the ropes. The grey alive crushed itself in under the plinth, wriggled itself in under it. Good hidingplace for   15
treasure . . . Making his rounds.

Tail gone now.

One of those chaps would make short work of a fellow. Pick the bones clean no matter who it was. Ordinary meat for them. A corpse is meat gone bad. Well and what's cheese. Corpse of milk. I read in that *Voyages of China*   20
that the Chinese say a white man smells like a corpse. Cremation better. Priests dead against it. Devilling for the other firm. Wholesale burners and Dutch oven dealers. Time of the plague. Quicklime fever pits to eat them. Lethal chamber. Ashes to ashes. Or bury at sea. Where is that Parsee tower of silence? Eaten by birds. Earth, fire, water. Drowning they say is the   25
pleasantest. See your whole life in a flash. But being brought back to life no. Can't bury in the air however. Out of a flying machine. Wonder does the news go about whenever a fresh one is let down. Underground communi-cation. We learned that from them. Wouldn't be surprised. Regular square feed for them. Flies come well before he's dead. Got wind of Dignam. They   30
wouldn't care about the smell of it. Saltwhite crumbling mush of corpse: smell, taste like raw white turnips.

The gates glimmered in front: still open. Back to the world again. Enough of this place. Brings you a bit nearer every time.

Joyce, *Ulysses* (1922)

We hope you realized that Joyce has adopted this kind of sentence structure because he wants us to share in the shifting impressions and feelings of Mr Bloom. The movement of his prose is an instrument for registering the flux of Mr Bloom's mind.

The following questions are designed to help you understand the general nature of Bloom's thoughts and his transitions from one stage to the next.

(i)   What is the link in ideas between the opening paragraph and the second? Write down the key words from paragraph one which prepare us for this transition.

(ii)   What is going on in lines 5–7? How would you answer somebody who said this was gibberish? What about 'kopthsth'? Can you find a pun here?

(iii)   Why the four very short sentences (?) in line 10?

(iv)   What has 'cheese' (line 20) to do with Bloom's immediate thoughts? Is Joyce being irrelevant? Or is it impossible to be irrelevant in this kind of writing?

(v)   How would you describe the movement of his language from lines 20 to 27? What does this tells us about the nature of Bloom's thoughts?

(vi)   Why do you think there is an abrupt shift in Bloom's thoughts after 'Out of a flying machine' (line 27) and again after ' . . . taste like raw white turnips' (line 32)?

The next questions on the passage will, we hope, prompt you to general discussion on some of the wider issues raised by this style of writing.

(vii)   How did you react to the techniques of this kind of writing?

(viii)   Did the extract give you a strong impression of a mind at work?

(ix)   Does this style make any special demands of a reader?

(x)   What are the advantages and disadvantages of this approach?

(xi)   How would you answer the objection to this kind of stream of consciousness writing that 'People do not think in words'?

Our second example is taken from the opening of Mark Twain's *The Adventures of Huckleberry Finn* (1884). It is apparently more straightforward than the passage from *Ulysses*, but again it raises the question of in what circumstances, and for what reasons, a writer may depart from conventional sentence structure.

You don't know about me, without you have read a book by the name of *The Adventures of Tom Sawyer*, but that ain't no matter. That book was made by Mr Mark Twain, and he told the truth, mainly. There was things which he stretched, but mainly he told the truth. That is nothing. I never seen anybody but lied, one time or another, without it was Aunt Polly, or the   5
widow, or maybe Mary. Aunt Polly – Tom's Aunt Polly, she is – and Mary, and the Widow Douglas, is all told about in that book – which is mostly a true book; with some stretchers, as I said before.

Now the way that the book winds up, is this: Tom and me found the money that the robbers hid in the cave, and it made us rich. We got six   10

thousand dollars apiece – all gold. It was an awful sight of money when it
was piled up. Well, Judge Thatcher, he took it and put it out at interest, and
it fetched us a dollar a day apiece, all the year round – more than a body
could tell what to do with. The Widow Douglas, she took me for her son,
and allowed she would sivilize me; but it was rough living in the house all the   15
time, considering how dismal regular and decent the widow was in all her
ways; and so when I couldn't stand it no longer, I lit out. I got into my old
rags, and my sugar-hogshead again, and was free and satisfied. But Tom
Sawyer, he hunted me up and said he was going to start a band of robbers,
and I might join if I would go back to the widow and be respectable. So I   20
went back.

Discuss the following criticism of this passage:
As well as the slang, which is slovenly and imprecise, the writer's
construction of sentences is very poor. Has Twain never been taught how to
write proper English? Just look at the two sentences in lines 4 to 8, for
example: clauses are not connected together properly and the sentences
stumble on in a totally ungrammatical way. I would want to rewrite the
opening sentence, too, so it was at least literate. It should read something
like this: 'Unless you have read a novel entitled *The Adventures of Tom
Sawyer*, you will not know my character, but that is really of no concern.'

FROM SENTENCES INTO PARAGRAPHS

In most kinds of prose, especially where the writer is concerned with the
exposition of an argument, the underlying principle is the achievement of
clarity and a carefully controlled continuity. Each sentence should lead to
the next and the reader should not have to make the transitions between
sentences necessitated by a careless author. In this way, the sentences
should build up into well-constructed paragraphs. In the following
extract, George Orwell is arguing that 'the English language is in a bad
way' and we suggest that you try to see how he has linked his sentences
together and whether he has achieved clarity in his arguments.

Now, it is clear that the decline of a language must ultimately have political
and economic causes: it is not due simply to the bad influence of this or that
individual writer. But an effect can become a cause, reinforcing the original
cause and producing the same effect in an intensified form, and so on
indefinitely. A man may take to drink because he feels himself to be a failure,   5
and then fail all the more completely because he drinks. It is rather the same
thing that is happening to the English language. It becomes ugly and
inaccurate because our thoughts are foolish, but the slovenliness of our
language makes it easier for us to have foolish thoughts. The point is that the
process is reversible. Modern English, especially written English, is full of   10
bad habits which spread by imitation and which can be avoided if one is
willing to take the necessary trouble.

'Politics and the English Language' (1946)

These few questions may help to guide your discussion:

(i) Which words or phrases signal Orwell's steps in his argument?

(ii) Why do you think he introduces the comparison with drinking in the third sentence?

(iii) Is this comparison linked in any way to what precedes and what succeeds it?

(iv) Do you find Orwell's argument easy to follow? Why (not)?

The next two passages will also help you to see the ways that writers make sentences and ideas follow on from each other. You may also like to consider the difference of pace at which arguments are unfolded. These passages are more difficult and you will need to read them carefully. You will see that we have made a number of comments about the extracts, some of which are true and some false. We suggest that you discuss our comments and try to see into which category they fall.

As for those wingy Mysteries in Divinity, and airy subtleties in Religion, which have unhing'd the brains of better heads, they never stretched the *Pia Mater* of mine. Methinks there be not impossibilities enough in Religion for an active faith; the deepest Mysteries ours contains have not only been illustrated, but maintained, by Syllogism and the rule of Reason. I love to   5
lose myself in a mystery, to pursue my Reason to an O altitudo! 'Tis my solitary recreation to pose my apprehension with those involved Ænigmas and riddles of the Trinity, with Incarnation, and Resurrection. I can answer all the Objections of Satan and my rebellious reason with that odd resolution I learned of Tertullian, *Certum est, quia impossible est.* I desire to   10
exercise my faith in the difficultest point; for to credit ordinary and visible objects is not faith, but persuasion. Some believe the better for seeing CHRIST'S Sepulchre; and, when they have seen the Red Sea, doubt not of the Miracle. Now, contrarily, I bless my self and am thankful that I lived not in the days of Miracles, that I never saw CHRIST nor His Disciples. I would   15
not have been one of those Israelites that pass'd the Red Sea, nor one of CHRIST'S patients on whom He wrought His wonders; then had my faith been thrust upon me, nor should I enjoy that greater blessing pronounced to all that believe and saw not. 'Tis an easie and necessary belief, to credit what our eye and sense hath examined.   20

Sir Thomas Browne: *Religio Medici* (1643)

When Christianity appeared in the world, even these faint and imperfect impressions [of pagan superstitious belief] had lost much of their original power. Human reason, which by its unassisted strength is incapable of perceiving the mysteries of faith, had already obtained an easy triumph over   5
the folly of Paganism; and when Tertullian or Lactantius employ their labours in exposing its falsehood and extravagance, they are obliged to transcribe the eloquence of Cicero or the wit of Lucian. The contagion of these sceptical writings had been diffused far beyond the number of their readers. The fashion of incredulity was communicated from the philosopher   10
to the man of pleasure or business, from the noble to the plebeian, and from the master to the menial slave who waited at his table, and who eagerly listened to the freedom of his conversation. On public occasions the philosophic part of mankind affected to treat with respect and decency the

religious institutions of their country, but their secret contempt penetrated
through to the thin and awkward disguise; and even the people, when they 15
discovered that their deities were rejected and derided by those whose rank
or understanding they were accustomed to reverence, were filled with doubts
and apprehensions concerning the truth of those doctrines to which they
had yielded the most implicit belief. The decline of ancient prejudice exposed
a very numerous portion of human kind to the danger of a painful and 20
comfortless situation. A state of scepticism and suspense may amuse a few
inquisitive minds. But the practice of superstition is so congenial to the
multitude that, if they are forcibly awakened, they still regret the loss of their
pleasing vision. Their love of the marvellous and supernatural, their
curiosity with regard to future events, and their strong propensity to extend 25
their hopes and fears beyond the limits of the visible world, were the
principal causes which favoured the establishment of Polytheism. So urgent
on the vulgar is the necessity of believing, that the fall of any system of
mythology will most probably be succeeded by the introduction of some
other mode of superstition. Some deities of a more recent and fashionable 30
cast might soon have occupied the deserted temples of Jupiter and Apollo,
if, in the decisive moment, the wisdom of Providence had not interposed a
genuine revelation fitted to inspire the most rational esteem and conviction,
whilst, at the same time, it was adorned with all that could attract the
curiosity, the wonder, and the veneration of the people. In their actual 35
disposition, as many were almost disengaged from their artificial prejudices,
but equally susceptible and desirous of a devout attachment, an object much
less deserving would have been sufficient to fill the vacant place in their
hearts, and to gratify the uncertain eagerness of their passions. Those who
are inclined to pursue this reflection, instead of viewing with astonishment 40
the rapid progress of Christianity, will perhaps be surprised that its success
was not still more rapid and still more universal.

Edward Gibbon: *The Decline and Fall of the Roman Empire* (1776–88).

(i)   Thomas Browne's opening sentences are slightly abrupt. They
seem to stand as single declarative units.

(ii)   These opening sentences are only connected in so far as each one
illuminates a slightly different aspect of what is virtually the same
reiterated idea.

(iii)   Browne continues in this style throughout the passage; nowhere
do we find any formal linking of ideas contained in sentences.

(iv)   The effect of reading Thomas Browne is to be challenged to agree
or disagree with him, because he is such an assertive and
dogmatic writer.

(v)   The same is true of the tone of Edward Gibbon's writing. He
does not try to persuade us to his point of view, but like Browne,
directly asserts it.

(vi)   Gibbon is a writer whose argument unfolds with a careful
balance between summary, exposition and general statement.

(vii)   He moves quickly from point to point.

(viii)   Both writers agree in their attitude towards religion.

Though the pace at which the material was unfolded and the movement from one sentence to the next presented something of a contrast between the methods of Sir Thomas Browne and Gibbon, we find in both passages a central topic elaborated within a clearly defined paragraph structure. Both paragraphs fulfil our expectation that the writer intends to guide us good-manneredly towards a definite goal, the speed of the journey and the route taken being an expression of the writer's own personality and peculiar habit of mind.

There will, of course, sometimes be good reasons for departing from a paragraph structure of steady organic growth. Read the following paragraph which opens a chapter from Christopher Isherwood's *Goodbye to Berlin* (1939), and then answer the questions which follow.

I wake early and go out to sit on the verandah in my pyjamas. The wood casts long shadows over the fields. Birds call with sudden uncanny violence, like alarm-clocks going off. The birch-trees hang down laden over the rutted, sandy earth of the country road. A soft bar of cloud is moving up from the line of trees along the lake. A man with a bicycle is watching his   5
horse graze on a patch of grass by the path; he wants to disentangle the horse's hoof from its tether-rope. He pushes the horse with both hands, but it won't budge. And now an old woman in a shawl comes walking with a little boy. The boy wears a dark sailor suit; he is very pale and his neck is bandaged. They soon turn back. A man passes on a bicycle and shouts   10
something to the man with the horse. His voice rings out, quite clear yet unintelligible, in the morning stillness. A cock crows. The creak of the bicycle going past. The dew on the white table and chairs in the garden arbour, and dripping from the heavy lilac. Another cock crows, much louder and nearer. And I think I can hear the sea, or very distant bells.   15

  (i) Where do we find sentences which are 'unrelated'? Where in the paragraph is this effect most pronounced?

 (ii) What effect is Isherwood attempting to create through the relation of one sentence to the next? (Don't overlook the *tense* he adopts here.)

Now consider this second passage, from Evelyn Waugh's novel *Scoop* (1938). This paragraph introduces us for the first time to Julia Stitch, as seen through the eyes of John Boot who has just been ushered into her bedroom.

What effect does this sequence of sentences produce in the reader?

As her husband had told him, she was still in bed although it was past eleven o'clock. Her normally mobile face encased in clay was rigid and menacing as an Aztec mask. But she was not resting. Her secretary, Miss Holloway, sat at her side with account books, bills, and correspondence. With one hand Mrs Stitch was signing cheques; with the other she held the telephone to which, at   5
the moment, she was dictating details of the costumes for a charity ballet. An elegant young man at the top of a step ladder was painting ruined castles on the ceiling. Josephine, the eight-year-old Stitch prodigy, sat on the foot of

the bed construing her day's passage of Virgil. Mrs Stitch's maid, Brittling, was reading her the clues of the morning crossword. She had been hard at it 10 since half past seven.

While the general principle of good prose may be that of a steadily unfolding sequence, we must note – not for the first time – that not all prose conveniently follows set rules. In the paragraph by Waugh there is a marked sense of *discontinuity*, particularly towards its end. This is precisely what the author intends: his sentence movement mirrors John Boot's slightly bemused reaction to the seeming incoherence and eccentricity of the scene in the bedroom; each item is locked within its sentence; John Boot, understandably, fails to connect these disparate phenomena.

What if a writer wants to create an even more extreme sense of confused, apparently unrelated experience? Since 'good style' is the matching of subject matter and manner, the prose itself may lack obvious continuity and logical progression – though this is not to say that all the writer has to do to create confusion is to be confused. There is a great deal of *art* in the creating of the *effect* we observe in the opening passage of James Joyce's *Portrait of the Artist as a Young Man* (1916). We quote only the first section. You may want to read what follows for yourself: the way Joyce develops his style from this opening repays close study.

Once upon a time and a very good time it was there was a moocow coming down along the road and this moocow that was coming down along the road met a nicens little boy named baby tuckoo . . .

His father told him that story: his father looked at him through a glass: he had a hairy face. 5

He was baby tuckoo. The moocow came down the road where Betty Byrne lived: she sold lemon platt.

O, the wild rose blossoms
On the little green place.

He sang that song. That was his song. 10

O, the green wothe botheth.

When you wet the bed first it is warm then it gets cold. His mother put on the oilsheet. That had the queer smell.

SENTENCE LENGTH AND MOVEMENT

When we describe sentence lengths, 'long' and 'short' are relative terms. (How long is a piece of string?) However, in this section, we want to look not only at the sheer length or shortness of sentences, but also, more closely, at the effects which the 'movement' of a sentence creates. We will start with an example which is indubitably a long sentence.

But the dentist had only walked once over to the nurse before he was back again prodding, this time nonchalantly, without asking what was felt, and before Pemberton could speak or even make his delaying noise, a deep groaned gutteral vowel, a hand was over his mouth concealing – kind conjuror! – the wink of a bright instrument, a white arm was braced dark 5

against the sky, he heard inside his ears a crunching, felt nothing, saw the
arm arc swiftly back to place something on the tray, then instantly brace
back again, brace, crunch, arc, brace, crunch, arc, five times, and so expertly
that Pemberton could make no sound, his mouth in any case immobilised
wide, and then his head was gently pushed forward and the dentist, with the   10
grave, knowing smile reserved to his calling, was saying: 'Would you spit,
please?' and out of his mouth into the glass bowl with its little circular hiss of
water he saw his blood drop, not with horror, but with a beautiful relief. He
had felt nothing. Condemned, he had been reprieved. He looked up at the
dentist with worship of such dexterity, with love. This passed quickly to a   15
sensation of personal bravery. 'I got through.' 'It was nothing.' He felt like a
man who has pulled somebody from the Thames and slips anonymous away
from his congratulations.

> William Sansom: 'A Visit to the Dentist' taken from *Among the
> Dahlias and Other Stories* (1957)

You will have noticed that lines 1 to 13 are all one sentence, and the
obvious question is, 'why'? It should be clear that the writer here wishes to
convey the idea of a quick, continuous, dextrous series of movements.
The movement of the sentence mirrors the speed of the actions – at one
place quite blatantly (' . . . then instantly brace back again, brace,
crunch . . . ' etc.) and underlines 'He had felt nothing.' The shorter
sentences which follow gain much of their effect by contrast to what has
gone before: Pemberton now has time for reflection – and self-
congratulation. The sentences move accordingly. In what way do the tone
and structure of the sentence 'Condemned, he had been reprieved'
prepare us exactly for the way we are meant to react to the concluding
simile of the passage?

We have selected the following three passages because in all of them, the
movement and length of the sentences clearly have an important part to
play in creating the overall effect that the writers wish to achieve. Each
passage is followed by short notes made after discussion with students.

He went. In a few moments, she blew the light out. The rain was falling
steadily and the night was a black gulf. All was intensely still. Geoffrey
listened everywhere: no sound save the rain. He stood between the stacks,
but only heard the trickle of water, and the light swish of rain. Everything
was lost in blackness. He imagined death was like that, many things   5
dissolved in silence and darkness, blotted out, but existing. In the dense
blackness he felt himself almost extinguished. He was afraid he might not
find things the same. Almost frantically, he stumbled, feeling his way, till his
hand touched the wet metal. He had been looking for a gleam of light.

> D. H. Lawrence: *Love Among the Haystacks* (1930)

(Short sentences. Abrupt staccato movement. Reader held up at heavy
pauses. Steady beat conveys tension; this matches tension within
Geoffrey's mind. He is apprehensive, alert, feels vulnerable. Repetition of
'he' at start of sentences reflects breathlessness.)

We began at Oslo. Early morning. A great black monster of a steam train. An empty carriage with cushions of carmine velvet. And throughout the day mounted through long Norway, from slush to snow, from snow to deeper snow, proceeding both up the map and on to higher ground. Which together makes for a most pleasing sensation.

> William Sansom: 'A World of Glass' (from *The Stories of William Sansom*, 1963)

(Opening three sentences have casual 'shorthand' rhythm of diary. Feeling of spontaneity. Impressionistic. Fifth sentence longer, recurrent use of prepositions (suggesting stages of a journey?); balancing of 'from slush to snow' against 'from snow to deeper snow' contrasts with opening. Fifth sentence suggests deliberate and consecutive movement. Long vowel sounds in this sentence. Why full stop after ground?)

But there were trim, cheerful villages too, with a neat or handsome parsonage and grey church set in the midst; there was the pleasant tinkle of the blacksmith anvil, the patient cart horses waiting at his door; the basket-maker peeling his willow wands in the sunshine; the wheelwright putting the last touch to a blue cart with red wheels; here and there a cottage with bright   5
transparent windows showing pots full of blooming balsams or geraniums, and little gardens in front all double daisies or dark wallflowers; at the well, clean and comely women carrying yoked buckets, and towards the free school small Britons dawdling on, and handling their marbles in the pockets of unpatched corduroys adorned with brass buttons.   10

> George Eliot: *Felix Holt* (1866)

(Slow, relaxed movement – 'legato' effect. The paragraph is all of a piece – almost like the opening of a film with the camera panning smoothly from image to image; careful, balanced punctuation and the attachment of abundant adjectives to nouns enhances feeling of tranquillity. Contrast Isherwood description, page 94, where we found almost an arbitrary sense of objects striking the viewer's perception. Everything here is planned, premeditated – like a conducted tour.)

From time to time in this book, we have suggested that, as here, you make notes of your initial impressions of a passage (or of one aspect of it) before turning them into a more polished piece of writing. As an example of what we mean, here is the way in which one writer used these notes on the extract from *Felix Holt* to produce a short essay:

The effect of reading this description of a scene in a mid-nineteenth century English village is like being taken on a guided tour by a knowledgeable and confident host. The reader is introduced to the blacksmith, the basket-maker and the wheelwright; the cottages and gardens are indicated, as are the women and children of the village. The author's description could easily   5
be transformed into the opening of a film, setting the scene and mood, with the camera panning smoothly and leisurely from image to image, and the whole mood created by the writing is one of relaxed, unified tranquillity.

This unity is achieved by the paragraph's being one sentence; yet within
this sentence the author ensures that there is a careful balance between the   10
various units. For instance, the rhythmic weight of 'the basket-maker
peeling his willow wands in the sunshine' is equivalent to the weight of 'the
wheelwright putting the last touch to a blue cart with red wheels'; moreover,
the repeated use of the present participle in this section of the extract
conveys a sense of activities proceeding in an unhurried fashion. The   15
beginnings of clauses or phrases direct the reader's inner eye – 'there
were . . . there was . . . here and there . . . at the well . . . towards the free
school . . . ' – and each section of the sentence is clearly separated either by
commas, or when there is a change of focus, by semi-colons. The feeling of
ease and tranquillity in this idealized portrait of a village where the reader is   20
invited to discover that everything is very much as he would expect to find it,
is also enhanced by George Eliot's abundant attachment of adjectives to
nouns throughout the paragraph: for example, the 'parsonage' is 'neat or
handsome', the cart-horses are 'patient' and the women are 'clean and
comely'.   25

This passage can also be usefully compared with the description by
Christopher Isherwood (page 94) in which there is an almost arbitrary
sense of objects striking the viewer's perception; we move from clouds to a
man with a bicycle to a horse to an old woman in a shawl. With George
Eliot, however, the reader is given a sense that there is an order to this
series of perceptions and that the author is in firm and sympathetic
control.

The following passages appear without any comment. Write your own
assessment of the part sentence length and movement have to play.

The crowd was thinning out. If she saw me first so obviously sitting on my
saddle in the gutter and waiting, the game would be up. Had to be an
accident, I had to be riding when she saw me; so I pushed off and balanced
along with circus slowness, half-hoping now that the crisis was at hand that
she would not come out and my misbehaving heart would be able to settle   5
again, wobble wobble heart and bike and she appeared with two others,
turned and walked away without seeing me. But I had rehearsed this too
often in my bed for my heart and swelling hands to let me down. The whole
thing was mechanical, fruit of terrible concentrated thought and repetition.
I rode casually, one hand in my pocket and the other on my hip, look no   10
hands, swaying this way and that. She was past and behind me. Startled I
looked back, grabbed the handlebars, braked and skidded to a stop by the
pavement, looked back brazenly as she approached, grinned brazenly in
immense surprise –
'Why, if it isn't Beatrice Ifor!'   15
So they stopped all three while my rehearsed prattle left her no chance of
moving off without being rude; 'was just cycling past – never dreamed – so
this is where the training college is, is it? I come along this road a lot or shall
do in the future – Look. I was just going to have a cup of tea before I ride the
rest – how – oh, but you must! One doesn't meet – Yes I can leave the bike –'   20

William Golding: *Free Fall* (1959)

Thomas Gradgrind, sir. A man of realities. A man of facts and calculations. A man who proceeds upon the principle that two and two are four, and nothing over, and who is not to be talked into allowing for anything over. Thomas Gradgrind, sir – peremptorily Thomas – Thomas Gradgrind. With a rule and a pair of scales, and the multiplication table always in his pockets, sir, ready to weigh and measure any parcel of human nature, and tell you exactly what it comes to.   25

Charles Dickens: Hard Times (1854)

She lectured on temperance and the rights of women; the ends she laboured   30
for were to give the ballot to every woman in the country and to take the flowing bowl from every man. She was held to have a very fine manner, and to embody the domestic virtues and the graces of the drawing room; to be a shining proof, in short, that the forum, for ladies, is not necessarily hostile to the fireside. She had a husband, and his name was Amariah.   35

Henry James: The Bostonians (1886)

In the extracts we have discussed so far we have seen, and possibly heard, how the movement of prose can mirror the action that is being described, help to sustain a particular mood, or even, in its inflexions, suggest something of the nature and thought-processes of a character.

At this point, you may want to put into practice some of the lessons you have learnt by producing some writing of your own. First, try to construct a long sentence which describes a series of quick, continuous movements. We leave it to you to select subject matter which lends itself to this treatment. (Return to the passage by Sansom on page 95 to see how the writer did this.) Next, perhaps you could attempt to write a piece of prose which uses short units of sense and omits the more customary linking words, definite articles, prepositions etc. which we generally use to produce smoothly flowing sentences. Look again at the short, descriptive passage by Sansom on page 97. What are the advantages of this approach? What subjects and moods are most appropriate for this technique? Does this approach have any pitfalls?

PATTERNS WRIT LARGE

When we are analyzing a piece of prose, the comments we make on the use of rhythm may be local and small-scale. We may want to point out, for example, the way a sentence is shaped so as to emphasize a word or phrase, or the effect of parallelism in different parts of a sentence. However, there are occasions when we will find that the plan of attack of a piece of prose is so clearly formulated in terms of a unifying rhythmic pattern that it virtually forces itself on our attention. In this case we need to show awareness of the rhythmic pattern simply to read the passage properly.

We would like you to consider two important devices which may predominate in this fashion, and for convenience we have labelled them 'repetition' and 'accumulation'.

Repetition

The following passage is the second paragraph from the opening of Dickens's novel Bleak House *(1852–3).*

Fog everywhere. Fog up the river, where it flows among green aits and meadows; fog down the river, where it rolls defiled among the tiers of shipping, and the waterside pollutions of a great (and dirty) city. Fog on the Essex marches, fog on the Kentish heights. Fog creeping into the cabooses of collier-brigs, fog lying out on the yards, and hovering in the rigging of   5
great ships; fog dropping on the gunwhales of barges and small boats. Fog in the eyes and throats of ancient Greenwich pensioners, wheezing by the firesides of their wards; fog in the stem and bowl of the afternoon pipe of the wrathful skipper, down in his close cabin; fog cruelly pinching the toes and fingers of his shivering little 'prentice boy on deck. Chance people on the   10
bridges peering over the parapets into a nether sky of fog, with fog all round them, as if they were up in a balloon, and hanging in the misty clouds.

You may find it useful to read this passage aloud to yourself, which is often a good way of testing for rhythm. Now answer the following questions.

(i)   What is the precise effect produced by the repetition of the key word 'fog'? Try to link your comments with the *mood* you feel Dickens creates here.

(ii) Comment on the effect of the repetition of similarly constructed syntactic units. For example:

(a) 'Fog *up the river, where it flows* . . .' juxtaposed against 'fog *down the river, where it rolls* . . . ' (lines 1–2)

(b) Lines 4–6, where we find the key word followed by a string of present participles.

(iii) What kind of change is there in the rhythm of the last sentence of the passage? Account for the change.

(iv) Finally, how would you answer this comment: 'Dickens is indulging in mere word-spinning. He should simply have written 'London was enveloped in fog', left it at that and got on with the story'?

Now have a look at the next passage which comes from the opening of the Gospel According to St John. Consider how repetition is used to create an effect of magisterial and weighty solemnity. Is there any other important rhythmic device at work here?

In the beginning was the Word, and the Word was with God, and the Word was God. The same was in the beginning with God. All things were made by him; and without him was not anything made that was made. In him was life; and the life was the light of men. And the light shineth in darkness; and the darkness comprehended it not.   5
    There was a man sent from God, whose name was John. The same came for a witness, to bear witness of the Light, that all men through him might

believe. He was not that Light, but was sent to bear witness of that Light. That was the true Light, which lighteth every man that cometh into the world. He was in the world, and the world was made by him, and the world 10 knew him not. He came unto his own, and his own received him not. But as many as received him, to them gave he the power to become the sons of God, even to them that believe on his name; which were born, not of blood, nor of the will of the flesh, nor of the will of man, but of God. And the Word was made flesh, and dwelt among us, (and we beheld his glory, the glory as of the 15 only begotten of the Father,) full of grace and truth.

Compare the passage you have just read from the Authorized Version, which appeared in 1611, with this modern translation of *The New English Bible* (1961).

When all things began, the Word already was. The Word dwelt with God, and what God was, the Word was. The Word, then, was with God at the beginning, and through him all things came to be; no single thing was created without him. All that came to be was alive with his life, and that life was the light of men. The light shines on in the dark, and the darkness has 5 never mastered it.

There appeared a man named John, sent from God; he came as a witness to testify to the light, that all might become believers through him. He was not himself the light; he came to bear witness to the light. The real light which enlightens every man was even then coming into the world. 10

He was in the world, but the world, though it owed its being to him, did not recognize him. He entered his own realm, and his own would not receive him. But to all who did receive him, to those who have yielded him their allegiance, he gave the right to become children of God, not born of any human stock, or by the fleshly desire of a human father, but the offspring of 15 God himself. So the Word became flesh; he came to dwell among us, and we saw his glory, such glory as befits the Father's only Son, full of grace and truth.

Are there any important differences in the use of repetition? Make as many *specific* comparisons as you can.

Is one version more clearly rhythmical than other? Which version do you personally prefer? Why?

Finally, we want you to consider the use of repetition in this passage from James Joyce's *Portrait of the Artist as a Young Man* (1916).

The hero, Stephen Dedalus, has faced a number of crises which make him question his attitude to his domestic circumstances, his native country, Ireland, and his religion. Now he decides that his role in life must be that of the artist, and his immediate destiny will be to travel abroad.

He started up nervously from the stoneblock, for he could no longer quench the flame in his blood. He felt his cheeks aflame and his throat throbbing with song. There was a lust of wandering in his feet that burned to set out for the ends of the earth. On! On! his heart seemed to cry. Evening would deepen above the sea, night fall upon the plains, dawn glimmer before the 5 wanderer and show him strange fields and hills and faces. Where?

He looked northward towards Howth. The sea had fallen below the line
of seawrack on the shallow side of the breakwater and already the tide was
running out fast along the foreshore. Already the long oval bank of sand lay
warm and dry amid the wavelets. Here and there warm isles of sand gleamed   10
above the shallow tide, and about the isles and around the long bank and
amid the shallow currents of the beach were lightclad figures, wading and
delving.

In a few moments he was barefoot, his stockings folded in his pockets and
his canvas shoes dangling by their knotted laces over his shoulders and,   15
picking a pointed salteaten stick out of the jetsam among the rocks, he
clambered down the slope of the breakwater.

There was a long rivulet in the strand and, as he waded slowly up its
course, he wondered at the endless drift of seaweed. Emerald and black and
russet and olive, it moved beneath the current, swaying and turning. The   20
water of the rivulet was dark with endless drift and mirrored the highdrifting
clouds. The clouds were drifting above him silently, and silently the
seatangle was drifting below him and the warm grey air was still and a new
wild life was singing in his veins.

Where was his boyhood now? Where was the soul that had hung back   25
from her destiny, to brood alone upon the shame of her wounds and in her
house of squalor and subterfuge to queen it in faded cerements and in
wreaths that withered at the touch? Or where was he?

He was alone. He was unheeded, happy and near to the wild heart of life.
He was alone and young and wilful and wildhearted, alone amid a waste of   30
wild air and brackish waters and the seaharvest of shells and tangle and
veiled grey sunlight and gayclad, lightclad figures of children and girls and
voices childish and girlish in the air.

(i)   First establish what you feel is Stephen's emotional state in this
      passage. You should try to define the connection between
      Stephen's feelings and the landscape which surrounds him.
(ii) Locate particular examples of repetition, and define their effect.
      Why is it that repetition plays such a dominant part?
(iii) What is the purpose of the exclamations and questions in
      paragraphs 1 and 5?
(iv) Comment on the effect of the *sound* of words in the passage. (Begin
      by examining lines 18 to 24 and 29 to 33.)
(v)   What kind of diction accompanies the strong rhythms here?
(vi) Comment on these two observations:

      (a) 'The writing is too obviously a 'purple passage' – far too
           artificial, too cleverly constructed.'
      (b) 'This is not a passage to take out of its context in the novel:
           without knowing what has led up to it, the language seems
           strained and emotionally indulgent.'

Accumulation

By accumulation we mean the careful construction of a syntactic pattern
in which there is the effect of a 'piling up' of phrases, clauses or sentences,

so that the prose is given a strong momentum. Often, in this kind of cumulative construction, the prose will move to a definite climax or anti-climax.

For example, here we have a series of rhetorical questions from *The Letters of Junius* (1769–71) addressed to George III.

> With a great military, and the greatest naval power in the known world, have not foreign nations repeatedly insulted you with impunity? Are you a prince of the House of Hanover, and do you exclude all the leading Whig families from your councils? Are you so infatuated as to take sense of your people from the representation of ministers, or from the shouts of a mob,   5
> notoriously hired to surround your coach, or stationed at a theatre?

This is clearly polemical prose. You might even want to call it propaganda. Its effect is produced by the controlled, insistent pressing of one question after another. Just one question left to stand on its own would not be nearly so destructively effective as this rapid accumulation.

Now read this extract from a letter written by Dr Johnson in 1755 to the Earl of Chesterfield who, after promising help with Johnson's great pioneering Dictionary, had delayed his assistance until Johnson felt it was no longer required.

> Seven years, My Lord have now passed since I waited in your outward Rooms or was repulsed from your Door, during which time I have been pushing on my work through difficulties of which it is useless to complain, and have brought it at last to the verge of Publication without one Act of assistance, one word of encouragement, or one smile of favour. Such   5
> treatment I did not expect, for I never had a Patron before.
>   Is not a Patron, My Lord, one who looks with unconcern on a Man struggling for Life in the Water and when he has reached ground encumbers him with help? The notice which you have been pleased to take of my Labours, had it been early, had been kind; but it has been delayed till I am   10
> indifferent and cannot enjoy it, till I am solitary and cannot impart it, till I am known and do not want it.

You should be able to locate two examples of accumulation. What is the effect of each one? What do they contribute to the expression of a certain tone in Johnson's remarks?

We move now to a more complex example in which the whole of the passage exhibits the most powerful kind of accumulation. The effect of the extract depends to a large extent on your awareness of the relationship between main and subordinate clauses. You might find it helpful to remind yourself what we mean by these terms (pages 79–80). Then read the passage and make some notes of your own before you read our short analysis.

Burke is lamenting the effects of the French Revolution.

> Indeed, when I consider the face of the kingdom of France; the multitude and opulence of her cities; the useful magnificence of her spacious high roads

and bridges; the opportunity of her artificial canals and navigations opening
the conveniences of maritime communication through a solid continent of
so immense an extent; when I turn my eyes to the stupendous works of her   5
ports and harbours, and to her whole naval apparatus, whether for war or
trade; when I bring before my view the number of her fortifications,
constructed with so bold and masterly a skill, and made and maintained at
so prodigious a charge, presenting an armed front and impenetrable barrier
to her enemies upon every side; when I recollect how very small a part of that   10
extensive region is without cultivation, and to what complete perfection the
culture of many of the best productions of the earth have been brought in
France; when I reflect on the excellence of her manufactures and fabrics,
second to none but ours, and in some particulars not second; when I
contemplate the ground foundations of charity, public and private, when I   15
survey the state of all the arts that beautify and polish life; when I reckon the
men she has bred for extending her fame in war, her able statesmen, the
multitude of her profound lawyers and theologians, her philosophers, her
critics, her historians and antiquaries, her poets and her orators, sacred and
profane; I behold in all this something which awes and commands the   20
imagination, which checks the mind on the brink of precipitate and
indiscriminate censure, and which demands that we should very seriously
examine, what and how great are the latent vices that could authorize us at
once to level so spacious a fabric with the ground. I do not recognize in this
view of things, the despotism of Turkey. Nor do I discern the character of a   25
government, that has been on the whole, so oppressive, or so corrupt, or so
negligent, as to be utterly unfit *for all reformation*. I must think such a
government well deserved to have its excellencies heightened, its faults
corrected, and its capacities improved into a British constitution.

Reflections on the Revolution in France (1790)

As you read through Burke's first sentence here, you probably felt the
deliberate setting up of a rhythm which runs counter to your normal
expectation concerning the relation between main and subordinate
clauses. A whole series of subordinate clauses makes the reader strain for
the concluding final clause, which is delayed to an extraordinary degree.
This rhythm inevitably produces a driving motion which builds towards a
climax that is, perhaps, anticipated by the reader as a blazing finale. In
fact, when the climax comes (lines 20 f.), Burke's use of language is
surprisingly restrained and controlled. His power has been generated earlier,
so in the last sentence, he can even afford to understate his case. Within this
general structure, you should be able to find many minor but contributory
examples of rhythmic balance of word and phrase. It is also worth noting
Burke's resourcefulness in varying his choice of verb at the beginning of
each of those insistent 'when' clauses in the first sentence: for example,
'when I consider . . . '; 'when I turn my eyes' etc.

This is clearly an example of rhythm which derives from a most
carefully orchestrated accumulation and balancing of clauses.

Incidentally, we call this kind of structure, in which the main clause is
saved up or delayed until after the subordinate clause(s) a 'periodic

sentence'. Such sentences do not always have to be as long as our example, of course.

RHETORIC

By rhetoric we generally mean the various technical devices a writer or an orator uses to *persuade* his reader or audience of the truth of his case.

We could say that the last passage you read by Burke has a most carefully considered rhetorical structure, and you will probably not be surprised to learn that Burke was one of the most notable parliamentarians of his day. His prose gains much from being read aloud: its tone and rhythms suggest public utterance clearly, and Burke does not scruple to utilize both the emotive use of language and the compelling rhythm of the orator.

The mechanics of rhetoric include such devices as rhetorical questions, apostrophe, hyperbole, understatement and antithesis. Prose like Burke's, which is full of figures of this kind, may strike the modern reader as being too contrived. Modern English sentence structure has tended to move away from the ornate periods and highly wrought syntax which distinguishes a traditional rhetoric. We may prefer more loosely constructed sentences, even in a public speech, because these favour a greater sense of spontaneity; for as soon as you begin to construct sentences which have the rhetorical force of Burke's, you give the impression of careful premeditation. It should also be said that the techniques Burke develops to a high pitch to convey a sense of magisterial authority can easily, in less able hands, descend to the merely ponderous. Yet you will not have to look very far to find in our political speeches and debates, newspaper editorials and in strongly polemical prose, a continuation of the traditional arts of rhetoric. It seems almost as if we have been conditioned to use repeated patterns of syntax and rhetorical devices when we are in the grip of strong feeling and wish to present our case forcefully. Read, for example, this extract from an article written for the *Observer* in 1977 by the modern writer, John Le Carré.

All my adult life I have watched, you see, in the institutions that I have served – whether they were educational or administrative or, as now, artistic – the same sourceless, unled bigotry at work that characterised the bedlam of my childhood. I have watched how it poisons the natural communication between British men and women who, in their own spheres, 5 possess marvellous good will. I have watched the white comedy of George Orwell denying his Eton education and Evelyn Waugh, too late, doing his damnedest to acquire one.

I have watched, and watch still, how the minute, cellular distinctions of our society can entirely insulate the decision-makers from those whose 10 destinies they are shaping; and how the knotted shadows of our childhood become the very snares with which we trip our own children. I have seen the greatest (and first) trade union movement in the world disintegrate into a sectarian brawling shop, as laden with outdated notions as any English public

school. I have seen the Mother of Parliaments turn herself into a body   15
without a shred of public respect, and a supposedly Socialist party cutting
public spending on education welfare and the hospital service while
maintaining virtually unchanged the vast army of bureaucrats who made
these very services so costly in the first place. To rule the whole of India and a
third of the world to boot, we never needed half of this impossible, self-   20
consuming structure. *The Times* thunders drearily on about the need for a
party of the centre. But in England, ever since I can remember, the centre has
ruled through thick and thin. For the centre is finally the complicity between
the sergeant and his master.

(i) Does Le Carré make use of any of the devices of repetition or
accumulation we discussed in the last section? How does his
style compare with Burke's?

(ii) To what extent would you say this kind of rhetorical structure
goes hand in hand with the use of emotive language? Locate and
comment on particular examples of his diction.

(iii) What sort of *feeling* is communicated here? How effective do
you find this passage as a piece of persuasive prose?

To help further define your feelings about the place of rhetoric in prose,
we would like you to turn back to the chapter on diction. Reread the
extract from Churchill's wartime speech (page 34) in conjunction with
this second example of Churchill's oratory, written at the time of Dunkirk
when Great Britain was facing the possibility of the destruction of the
army.

I have, myself, full confidence that if all do their duty, if nothing is neglected,
and if the best arrangements are made, as they are being made, we shall
prove ourselves once again able to defend our island home, to ride out the
storm of war, and to outlive the menace of tyranny, if necessary for years, if
necessary alone. At any rate, that is what we are going to try to do. That is   5
the resolve of His Majesty's Government – every man of them. That is the
will of Parliament and the nation. The British Empire and the French
Republic, linked together in their cause and in their need, will defend to the
death their native soil, aiding each other like good comrades to the utmost of
their strength. Even though large tracts of Europe and many old and famous   10
States have fallen or may fall into the grip of the Gestapo and all the odious
apparatus of Nazi rule, we shall not flag or fail. We shall go on to the end, we
shall fight in France, we shall fight on the seas and oceans, we shall fight with
growing confidence and growing strength in the air, we shall defend our
island whatever the cost may be, we shall fight on the beaches, we shall fight   15
on the landing grounds, we shall fight in the fields and in the streets, we shall
fight in the hills; we shall never surrender, and even if, which I do not for a
moment believe, this island or a large part of it were subjugated and
starving, then our Empire beyond the seas, armed and guarded by the
British Fleet, would carry on the struggle, until, in God's good time, the new   20
world, with all its power and might, steps forth to the rescue and the
liberation of the old.

Decide where either repetition or accumulation, or other rhetorical devices, lead to a heightening of the movement of the prose. One minor point you may have overlooked is the way Churchill often uses words in pairs. Why does he do this?

The Churchill passages have raised some strong objections among students and these were voiced in the following comments. Discuss them and see how far you agree with them.

1. This kind of rhetoric sickens and embarrasses me: it's so obviously contrived and false.
2. Possibly that is so at our safe distance from the time of Dunkirk. To appreciate the galvanizing force of Churchill's prose you've got to use a little bit of historical imagination and put yourself back in the time he is writing about.
3. The rhythms are *so* insistent, you stop listening to what is being said: the language just washes over your head like a series of big waves. It's all sound and fury – just noise.
4. It's not so much the construction of his prose I object to as the dangerous use of emotive language.
5. You must remember that these were written as speeches: they were not intended to be analyzed as prose.

Now that you have had some experience of rhetorical writing, you should feel able to answer these two general points, which raise important issues about rhetoric.

(i) Look up the word 'rhetoric' in your dictionary and you will find that one of its definitions is 'language which is showy, false, artificial'. How do you think the term acquired this meaning?
(ii) Are we right to be suspicious of rhetoric? Of *all* rhetoric? Do you agree with the person who said: 'Rhetoric is evil: it attempts to manipulate people's feelings and make them believe false things.'

Finally, to show that the techniques we have discussed in *Patterns Writ Large* and *Rhetoric* are not confined solely to persuasive prose, we will conclude with two examples of different kinds of prose. The first is what we might call 'anecdotal' and the second is descriptive. Both passages have a rhythmic pattern writ large. Both also have a rhetorical structure in the widest sense of using language to heighten a recollected moment, in one case, and to persuade the reader to share in a powerfully imagined scene in the other.

This extract is taken from Peter Ustinov's autobiography Dear Me *(1977). He is writing about working on the film* 'Spartacus' *with Lord Olivier.*

One of my first scenes with Larry Olivier consisted in my rushing up to his horse as it cavorted among a huge mass of prisoners-of-war, grabbing its bridle, and gazing up at its immaculate rider: 'If I identify Spartacus for you,

Divinity, will you give me the women and children?' I said, in the character
of the sleazy slave dealer.   5
   There followed the most enormous pause while Larry let his eyes
disappear upwards under his half-open lids, licked his lips, pushing at his
cheeks from within with his tongue, let his head drop with a kind of comic
irony at the quirks of destiny, hardened once again into the mould of mortal
divinity, looked away into the unknown as his profile softened from brutal   10
nobility into subtlety. 'Spartacus!' he suddenly cried, as though slashing the
sky with a razor, and then hissed, 'You have found him?'
   I was so absolutely staggered at the extent of the pause that I expressed
precisely the surprise I felt. Now I gazed over the prisoners with a closed
expression, giving nothing away. Then I let a furtive smile play on my lips for   15
a moment at some private thought, chasing it away, and seemed about to say
something, but changed my mind. I ran the gamut of impertinence, of
servility, and of insincerity as he had of vanity, power, and menace. At long
last, when he least expected it, I let a practically inaudible 'Yes' slip from my
mouth.   20
   'Dear boy,' said Larry, in a business-like voice which ill-concealed a
dawning annoyance, 'D'you think you could come in a little quicker with
your Yes?'
   'No,' I said politely.
   We both looked at each other straight in the eye, and smiled at the same   25
moment.

How does Ustinov cleverly achieve a kind of rhythmic balance here?
What makes the climax of the anecdote effective?

Now read through the following descriptive passage and look closely at
the use of rhythmic accumulation.

This piece comes from one of Dylan Thomas's short stories, The Followers
published in A Prospect of the Sea and Other Stories *(1955)*

The peeling, liver-coloured room might never have been drunk in at all.
Here, commercials told jokes and had Scotches and sodas with happy, dyed,
port-and-lemon women; dejected regulars grew grand and muzzy in the
corners, inventing their pasts, being rich, important, and loved; reprobate
grannies in dustbin black cackled and nipped; influential nobodies revised   5
the earth; a party, with earrings, called 'Frilly Willy' played the crippled
piano, which sounded like a hurdy-gurdy playing under water, until the
publican's nosy wife said, 'No.' Strangers came and went, but mostly went.
Men from the valleys dropped in for nine or ten; sometimes there were
fights; and always there was something doing, some argie-bargie, giggle and   10
bluster, horror or folly, affection, explosion, nonsense, peace, some wild-
goose flying in the boozy air of that comfortless, humdrum nowhere in the
dizzy, ditchwater town at the end of the railway lines. But that evening it was
the saddest room I had ever known.

Comment on the movement of the prose and the effects it creates.
Where does the language move quickly? Where slowly? What kind of
atmosphere is created through these rhythms?
   Is the *sound* of the language important?

THE SOUND MUSIC OF PROSE

We hope that you observed how Dylan Thomas frequently used 'sound effects'. Words chime and ring one against the other to create the noise and activity of the Swansea public house: 'some argie-bargie, giggle and bluster, horror and folly . . . ' You may also have noticed that his slower, emphatic ending of the penultimate sentence – after the pace of the frequently paired words which have previously been reeled off so rapidly – is in part sustained by the heavy alliteration in 'the *di*zzy *di*tchwater town' and the rhyming effect of 'air' set off against the second syllable of 'nowhere'. Throughout the passage the sound quality of words like 'muzzy' and the onomatopoeic 'cackled' is an important mood-creating element. In fact, you may have decided that this prose is close to poetry.

In this respect, of course, the passage is untypical of prose in general. It is 'a poet's prose'. However, it is worth paying some attention to this specialized kind of prose which sets out to utilize the sound of words and, in some cases, to create a kind of word music. The effect need not be nearly as concentrated as we found it to be in Dylan Thomas's prose. Sometimes it may simply be the occasional use of long vowel sounds or harsh consonants to create a particular effect.

We sometimes draw on musical analogies when we want to define sentence movement. You may recall our earlier use of the terms 'staccato' and 'legato' when we were discussing passages by Lawrence and George Eliot (pages 96–97). Do you also remember this sentence from the same section? It is William Sansom's description of the movement of a train through Norway:

> And throughout the day [the train] mounted through long Norway, from slush to snow, from snow to deeper snow.

Would it be entirely fanciful to suggest that there is something in the sound of the long vowels – linked to the way the punctuation and the balancing of 'from slush to snow' and 'from snow to deeper snow' holds up the reader – which helps to underline the nature of the slow climb through '*long* Norway'? If you accept this point, we may have in this passage an example of the way sound in prose can be used locally and less obtrusively than the way Dylan Thomas uses it.

In what other passages in this section could you argue that the sound of words had a significant part to play? Locate particular examples.

We will leave you with three passages which, in varying degrees, show what may be contributed to meaning by the sounds of words. If you are working through the book with other people, this might be a good point to split up into groups. Each member of the group should prepare a reading of one of the passages. (You may wish to refer to the hints and advice we gave about this in our Introduction on page 8). When the passage is read aloud, other people in the group should offer their comments and their own alternative readings.

One final word of warning: remember that in prose, as a general rule, sense comes before sound, so do not feel that you have to strain to pick up purely imaginary word music.

[She] said to William Bankes: 'It suddenly gets cold. The sun seems to give less heat,' she said, looking about her, for it was bright enough, the grass still a soft deep green, the house starred in its greenery with purple passion flowers, and rooks dropping cool cries from the high blue. But something moved, flashed, turned a silver wing in the air. It was September after all, the   5 middle of September, and past six in the evening. So off they strolled down the garden in the usual direction, past the tennis lawn, past the pampas grass, to that break in the thick hedge, guarded by red-hot pokers like braziers of clear burning coal, between which the blue waters of the bay looked bluer than ever.   10

They came there regularly every morning drawn by some need. It was as if the water floated off and set sailing thoughts which had grown stagnant on dry land, and gave to their bodies even some sort of physical relief. First, the pulse of colour flooded the bay with blue, and the heart expanded with it and the body swam, only the next instant to be checked and chilled by the prickly   15 blackness on the ruffled waves. Then, up behind the great black rock, almost every evening spurted irregularly, so that one had to watch for it and it was a delight when it came, a fountain of white water; and then, while one waited for that, one watched, on the pale semi-circular beach, wave after wave shedding again and again smoothly a film of mother-of-pearl.   20

They both smiled, standing there. They both felt a common hilarity, excited by the moving waves; and then by the swift cutting race of a sailing boat, which, having sliced a curve in the bay, stopped; shivered; let its sail drop down; and then, with a natural instinct to complete the picture, after this swift movement, both of them looked at the dunes far away, and instead   25 of merriment felt come over them some sadness – because the thing was completed partly, and partly because distant views seem to outlast by a million years (Lily thought) the gazer and to be communing already with a sky which beholds an earth entirely at rest.

Virginia Woolf: *To the Lighthouse* (1927)

It was Miss Murdstone who was arrived, and a gloomy-looking lady she was: dark, like her brother, whom she greatly resembled in face and voice, and with very heavy eyebrows, nearly meeting over her large nose, as if, being disabled by the wrongs of her sex from wearing whiskers, she had carried them to that account. She brought with her two uncompromising   5 hard black boxes, with her initials on the lids in hard brass nails. When she paid the coachman she took her money out of a hard steel purse, and she kept the purse in a very jail of a bag which hung upon her arm by a heavy chain, and shut up like a bite. I had never, at that time, seen such a metallic lady altogether as Miss Murdstone was.   10

Dickens: *David Copperfield* (1850)

I was set down from the carrier's cart at the age of three; and there with a sense of bewilderment and terror my life in the village began.

The June grass, amongst which I stood, was taller than I was, and I wept. I had never been so close to grass before. It towered above me and all around me, each blade tatooed with tiger-skins of sunlight. It was knife-edged, dark 5 and wicked green, thick as a forest and alive with grasshoppers that chirped and chattered and leapt through the air like monkeys.

I was lost and didn't know where to move. A tropic heat oozed up from the ground, rank with sharp odours of roots and nettles. Snow-clouds of elder-blossom banked in the sky, showering upon me the fumes and flakes of 10 their sweet and giddy suffocation. High overhead ran frenzied larks, screaming, as though the sky were tearing apart.

For the first time in my life I was out of the sight of humans. For the first time in my life I was alone in the world whose behaviour I could neither predict nor fathom: a world of birds that squealed, of plants that stank, of 15 insects that sprang along without warning. I was lost and I did not expect to be found again. I put back my head and howled, and the sun hit me smartly on the face like a bully.

From this daylight nightmare I was wakened, as from many another, by the appearance of my sisters. They came scrambling and calling up the steep 20 rough bank, and parting the long grass found me. Faces of rose, familiar, living; huge shining faces hung up like shields between me and the sky; faces with grins and white teeth (some broken) to be conjured up like genii with a howl, brushing off terror with their broad scoldings and affection. They leaned over me – one, two, three – their mouths smeared with red currants 25 and their hands dripping with juice.

"There, there, it's all right, don't you wail any more. Come down 'ome and we'll stuff you with currants."

And Marjorie, the eldest, lifted me into her long brown hair, and ran me jogging down the path and through the steep rose-filled garden, and set me 30 down on the cottage doorstep, which was our home, though I couldn't believe it.

That was the day we came to the village, in the summer of the last year of the First World War.

Laurie Lee: *Cider with Rosie* (1959)

5

Point of view

WHAT WAS THE GOAL LIKE?

A. An undistinguished end of season game flared briefly into life during its
dying stages when a finely-created winning goal in the 85th minute at
Burnden Park virtually secured Manchester City's future in the First
Division. Bolton Wanderers had been mounting considerable pressure
on the City goal for most of the second half, but just as the game seemed   5
destined to remain goalless, largely as the result of Trautmann's sterling
work in goal, Leivers played a long, telling ball from outside his own
penalty area to find Sambrook unmarked on the left wing. As the skilful
City winger bore down on goal, Hayes made a run into the near post
which pulled the Wanderers' defence to the left, leaving Sambrook to   10
chip a calculated, delicate cross over a statuesque Wanderers' defence.
With pinpoint accuracy the ball came to Neyam, the City centre-forward
who, finding himself in oceans of space, probably could hardly believe
his good fortune. In what amounted to virtually his sole contribution to
the game, he volleyed an easy chance firmly into the open net from close   15
range.

B. I'm working away, but having no luck. Service from mid-field is non-
existent and our defence is under the cosh. But then there's a break on –
the bench is screaming at me to go down the middle, but Higgins has
been playing inside my shirt all afternoon, so I pulls out wide on the right
side of the park. Don't remember much about the build-up, though   5
Sammy told me after that it was him who crossed it – without looking,
he was just hoping there'd be somebody there. Well, the ball comes to me
at a difficult height over a ruck of white shirts, so I don't see it till the last
moment and I'm thinking 'This one could end up in the back of the stand
if I'm not careful' and wondering 'Should I head it?' Anyhow, I swivel   10
and keeps my head down – hits it just right, so it goes off my left peg like
greased lightning. Well . . . I was over the moon. I've always got a nose
for the half-chance that will nick the game – that's why the lads call me
Sniffer.

These are, of course, two accounts of the same incident – one from the
press box and one from the field of play. As you would expect, both see
and judge what happened from a different perspective, and this is
reflected in what they describe and the manner in which they describe it. Is
one account more valuable or more totally accurate than the other? You
will certainly have noticed at least two major discrepancies between these

two versions, yet both accounts remain essentially valid: they simply provide different types of information and response. If you want a fairly detached and more complete picture, you will probably turn to passage (A); if, however, you want an insider's view and a sense of immediacy, you will perhaps favour passage (B).

To help you consider further the difference in perspective of the two accounts, answer the following questions.

(i) What are the two major discrepancies to which we referred? How do you account for them?

(ii) We have used the terms 'detachment' and 'immediacy' to characterize an essential difference between the two accounts. What specific elements in the language used – for example, diction, syntax, the tense of verbs etc. – create this contrast?

POINT OF VIEW

What we have referred to in the previous section as the 'perspective' of the writer or speaker is in a literary context often described as 'point of view'. By this term we do not mean the opinion or argument expressed by a writer, but the angle of vision, the viewpoint, from which characters, events and settings are observed and presented. The essential questions involved here, put at their simplest, are (i) Who is doing the narrating or describing?; and (ii) Where is this person standing? Is a piece of writing, for example, in the form of a first person narration with the 'I' involved at the centre of the action? Or, at the other extreme, do we have an all-seeing narrator who uses the third person ('he', 'she' and 'they') and switches between several different points of view? To continue our example of the football match, an account might be written by one player, or it could draw on the viewpoints of members of both teams, the referee, managers, directors, fanatical and disinterested spectators, the wife of a player, and so on.

You will see that once a writer has decided on what point(s) of view to use, a number of related decisions are involved about the selection of material and the way events are placed in a time sequence. The writer's adoption of a certain point of view will also lead in the direction of a certain kind of diction, syntax, tone and attitude to the reader. So, not for the first time, we find ourselves recognizing that the elements which we often separate for the purpose of literary criticism are, in fact, all vitally interdependent.

Sometimes in the matter of choosing a point of view, writers will know at once from whose perspective to tell the story or describe the scene. On other occasions it will be a question to which they will give a lot of thought, perhaps starting one draft only to realize that a different perspective is required. Indeed, in some narratives the way in which the story is told *is* the story. (We will return later to explore further that enigmatic thought.)

We would like to consider a sort of case history of the way in which the conception of a story leads to the selection of a particular point of view.

E. M. Forster tells us in the Introduction to his *Collected Short Stories* (1947) that, after completing a couple of successful stories, he was struck with an idea which he thought must be an 'instant winner'. He comments:

> Here [at the Gurnard's Head in Cornwall] . . . a story met me . . . and I embraced it as a masterpiece. It was about a man who was saved from drowning by some fishermen, and knew not how to reward them. What is your life worth? £5? £5,000? He ended by giving nothing, he lived among them, hated and despised. As the theme swarmed over me, I put my hand 5 into my purse, drew out a golden sovereign – they existed then – and inserted it into a collecting-box of the Royal Lifeboat Institution which had been erected upon the Gurnard's Head for such situations as this. I could well afford it. I was bound to make the money over and again. Calm sea, flat submerged rock whereon my hero was to cling and stagger, village whence 10 his rescuers should sally – I carried off the lot, and only had to improvise his wife, a very understanding woman.

There we have the genesis of the story. As you read the story itself, pay particular attention to the point of view at work.

The Rock

We had been talking for some time and she was so full of kindness and of insight that at last I ventured to ask about her husband.

'Did you ever question him? I hope so,' she added, seeing that I hesitated.

'I went down to see him last month. We went for a sail.'

'Did he charge you anything?'   5

'I did pay him a little.'

'And I suppose you talked to the people?'

'The excitement is over. They resent him no longer. They – I won't say understand, for nobody could understand. But they have accepted him.'

'I hoped for that,' she said gravely. 'They are simple and manly again, and he 10 will be one of them. You saw the rock?'

'Oh yes. He showed me the rock.'

On the north coast of Cornwall there is a promontory, high and fantastic, stretching for a half mile into the sea. In places it is crowned with broad boulders, in places its backbone is so narrow that one can see the water on 15 either side, foaming against precipices that are polished black. Great moors are behind it, full of cairns and stone circles and the chimneys of deserted mines. Nearer at hand lies the farmers' country, a fertile strip that follows the indentations of the cliff. And close under the promontory itself is a little fishing village, so that many types of civilization, fruitful and fruitless, can 20 be encompassed in a single gaze.

The rock of which she was speaking is hidden from all of them, for it lies very low in the water. It is some two hundred yards from the extreme point and resembles a square brown desk, with a slope towards the land. A wave will break on the high part, seethe down the slope, and then be merged in the 25 surrounding blue, to break yet again at the foot of the promontory. One day, during their holidays, he sailed too near this rock, capsized, and was washed up onto it. There he lay, face downwards, with the rising tide frothing over him. She was up on the headland, and ran to the village for help. A boat put out at once. They rowed manfully – they were splendid fellows – and they reached him just as his hands relaxed and he was sliding head foremost into death. So much is known to all of us, and it was the crisis of his life. But in a story about his life, it is not the crisis. 30

She began to speak, but waited a moment for the maid to clear away the tea. In the waning light her room seemed gentle and gray, and there hung about it an odour (I do not write '*the* odour') of Roman Catholicism, which is assuredly among the gracious things of the world. It was the room of a woman who had found time to be good to herself as well as to others; who had brought forth fruit, spiritual and temporal; who had borne a mysterious tragedy not only with patience but actually with joy. 35

'When he got to land,' she said, 'he would not even shake hands with them. He kept on saying, 'I don't know what to do. I can't think. I shall come to you again,' and they replied, 'Oh that'll be all right, sir.' You can imagine the scene, and it was not till the evening that I realised his difficulty. You – how much would you give for your life?' 45

I stared blankly.

'I hope that you will never have to decide. May you always have your life as a right. Most of us do. But now and then a life is saved – as one might save a vase from breaking – and then the proprietor must think what is it worth.' 50

'Is there not a tariff for rescues?' said I, inclined to be irritable and dense.

'In calm weather – it was quite calm and they did not run the slightest danger – the tariff appears to be fifteen shillings a rescuer. For two pounds five my husband could have been clear of all obligation. We neither of us felt two pounds five enough. Next morning we left, full of promises. I think they still believed in us, but I am not sure.' 55

She paused, and I ventured to say: 'But a sum that was great to *them* – that was the point. The question is purely practical.'

'So all our friends said. One suggested a hundred pounds, another the present of a new boat, another that, every Christmas, I should knit each man a comforter. You see, there are no such things as purely practical questions. Every question springs straight out of the infinite, and until you acknowledge that you will never answer it.' 60

'Then what did *you* suggest?'

'I suggested that I should settle that bill myself, and never show him the receipt. But he refused and, I think, rightly. Nor do I know what I should have done.' 65

'But what did those three men want?' I persisted. 'You cannot drive me from it; that's the point.'

'They would have accepted anything: they were in want of nothing. Until we tourists came they were happy and independent. We taught them the craving for money – money obtained by rowing half a mile upon the tranquil sea. The minister, with whom we corresponded, implored us to be quick. He said that the whole village was anxious and greedy, and that the men were posing as heroes. And there were we, finding the world more glorious every day, the air more delicate, music sweeter, birds, sky, the sun – everything transfigured because he had been saved. And our love – we had 70 75 been married five years, but now it never seemed to have been love before. Can you tell me what these things are worth?'

I was silent. I told myself that this was fluid, unsubstantial stuff. But in my   80
heart I knew that she and all that she said was a rock in the tideway.

'For a time he was merely interested. He was amused at the problem, and the sensations it aroused in him. But at last he only cared for the solution. He found it one evening in this little room, when a sunset, more glorious than today's was flaming under the wych-elm. He asked me, as I ask you, what   85
such things were worth, and gave the answer: "Nothing; and nothing is my reward to the men who saved me." I said: "It is the only possible reward. But they will never understand it." "I shall make them understand it in time," he told me, "for my gift of nothing shall be all that I have in the world."'

Again the story becomes common property. He sold up his goods –   ·90
everything – every cherished trifle that he had – and gave the value of them to the poor. Some money was settled on her, and that he could not touch, but he gave away the rest. Then he went down to that village penniless and asked for charity from his rescuers.

His sufferings had been terrible. He drew out all their disappointment and   95
pettiness and cruelty; she covered her face when she spoke of it. I was glad to tell her that this had passed; they had come to treat him as an idiot and then as a good fellow, and now he was working for one of them. As I moved from her room I said, 'No one but you will ever understand it.' But her eyes filled with tears and she cried: 'Don't – don't praise me for that. For if I had not   100
understood, he might be with us now.'

This conversation taught me that some of us can meet reality on this side of the grave. I do not envy them. Such adventures may profit the disembodied soul, but as long as I have flesh and blood I pray that my grossness preserve me. Our lower nature had its dreams. Mine is of a certain   105
farm, windy but fruitful, halfway between the deserted moorland and the uninhabitable sea. Hither, at rare intervals, she should descend and he ascend, to shatter their spiritual communion by one caress.

1. The story has elements of a fable, the meaning of which emerges in the last paragraph.

    (a) Write in your own words what conclusion the narrator comes to.

    (b) Forster tells us (see the introductory comments) that he only had 'to improvise' the wife in the story. In fact, he had also to invent a narrator endowed with certain characteristics. What are these 'characteristics' and what use does Forster make of his narrator's general outlook? (A good starting-point might be to consider what the narrator means by the admission of his 'grossness'.)

2. Give reasons (a) why Forster has chosen a narrator who is known to the two major figures in the story, and yet is himself on the fringe of the essential events, and (b) why the narrative is given a 'retrospective' quality – that is, its major episodes are set back in time and commented on by two characters in conversation.

3. Would any of the following narrative techniques be acceptable, bearing in mind the effect you think Forster wishes to achieve?

   (a) An account in the first person, in the form of a diary written by the husband, taking in all the events from the time of his rescue.

   (b) A description, using dialogue and the third person, of the fishermen, some of whom were 'posing as heroes', discussing the recent arrival among them of the man whose life they had saved.

   (c) Epistolary form: the wife writes a letter to her husband at the time she learns he has just begun to be accepted by the villagers.

   (d) A conversation between the village priest and the narrator Forster uses at the time of the narrator's visit.

   (e) An account in the third person in *three* separate scenes. First episode: a dramatic account of his rescue. Second: conversation between husband and wife some time later about what must be done. Third: an account of the husband's gradual acceptance by the fishermen once he has gone to live among them.

   You might like to try adopting one of these points of view and producing your own version of the story, or perhaps you can think of other narrative points of view which will offer interesting possibilities.

4. Finally, you may be interested to learn that Forster's own later judgement on his story was that he had produced 'a complete flop'. He comments, 'My inspiration had been genuine but worthless, like so much inspiration . . .'; he chose not to include 'The Rock' in his *Collected Short Stories*. Would you go along with Forster's judgement? Give reasons for your judgement, paying particular attention to a final view of the success/failure of the point of view technique used in the story. You might also like to consider how successfully Forster makes use of symbolism.

FIRST-PERSON AND THIRD PERSON NARRATIVES

As our previous section should have made clear, there are many possible different points of view available to an author, and if you want to see a number of them at work, we suggest you consult Wallace Hildick's *Thirteen Types of Narrative* (1968). In his book, Hildick ingeniously applies various narrative methods to the same plot in turn, and so illustrates their characteristic strengths and limitations. However, we should begin any serious consideration of point of view with the elementary, but essential, distinction between the use of the first and the third person.

To begin a narrative 'Let me tell you what happened when I . . . .' may sound unoriginal, and yet it is the most natural opening in the world. This point of view, using the first person singular, generally has the advantages of immediacy and spontaneity: we are at once presented with a narrator with whom we may identify; what is to be written can be given the pressure and warmth of personal utterance; and the character of the narrator may be conveyed and developed not only through what he or she observes but also as a product of the individual nuances of his or her language. (Remember, for example, how Mark Twain characterizes Huck Finn on pages 41 and 90). These potential advantages of the portrayal of vivid, first-hand experience are counterbalanced, however, by the limitation put upon the first person point of view: it is necessarily restricted to one particular experience and locked into one dominating consciousness. Two rather silly examples will demonstrate how this can operate at the lowest level:

(a) The party was getting into full swing, and old Tom Gizand began this amazingly scurrilous story about my former wife, Gladys; but unfortunately, just at that moment, Mary called me into the kitchen to make some more rum punch . . .
(b) Two masked figures rushed into the petrol station office as I was   5
standing by the till. One of them coshed me over the head . . .

The third-person point of view, while possibly lacking in the immediate capacity for vividness that the first-person technique bestows, does give the writer the opportunity of moving from one mind to the next: this approach therefore tends to be more detached and probably broader and more comprehensive in its potential. In the widely used convention of the 'omniscient narrator', the reader accepts that Authors are in the god-like position of 'knowing all': they are given a free hand in switching the narrative focus from one person to the next; they can tell us what every character is thinking or feeling; and they can take us from one setting to the next as they feel necessary.

A little experiment may help to give you the sense of the nature of the shift from the first to the third-person point of view. Imagine that you wish to write about a deeply personal, possibly even embarrassing experience. You begin: 'I had been told by Liz that the High School Dance was to be in fancy dress, and so I turned up in my Mahatma Gandhi outfit with a gallon of real Boddington's ale in a flagon. You can appreciate my horror when the headmistress . . . .' It is possible that at this point, winces of embarrassment and self-consciousness may ensue – and prevent you from writing further. But now change to 'he' or 'she' – 'He had been told . . . etc.' – and you may discover a new ease of composition. Before, you were in a sense *too* close to your material to write uninhibitedly about it; now your new point of view enables your very feelings to remain more detached and distanced from the original experience. The move may be sensed as one from a *subjective* to a more *objective* stance.

In the comments we have made so far, there is a dangerous element of generalization. The reader must take nothing for granted and judge the actual effect of the use of a particular point of view as it works in practice. For instance, it is perfectly possible for a first-person narrator to maintain a clinical tone of detachment; and in the use of the third-person, an author may surrender large areas of possible omniscience by concentrating exclusively on just one or two points of view, or may indeed present a scene almost like a dramatist by giving the reader dialogue and action, but no special rights of inner access to the feelings and motivations of characters involved. (In different ways Ivy Compton–Burnett and Hemingway often adopt this approach in their writing.) You need to bear in mind, too, that some narratives in the third person may present one character's viewpoint in such a dominating and detailed way that this central character takes on for the reader something of the vividness we generally associate with first person narratives. Henry James often used one character as a 'centre of consciousness' in his novels: the reader is made to look through the eyes – and identify with the feelings – of this presiding point of view. It should be added, however, that in a James novel such as *The Ambassadors* (1903), there will always be a degree of detachment: the Author, of course, knows more than the central character through whose consciousness the novel is filtered.

You should find that the *general* distinctions we have made between narratives written in the first- and the third-person are exemplified in the following passages. Both extracts concern the reactions of characters who are newly arrived in France, and both occur at the beginning of the narratives from which they are taken.

– They order, said I, this matter better in France –
– You have been in France? said my gentleman, turning quick upon me with the most civil triumph in the world. – Strange! quoth I, debating the matter with myself, That one and twenty miles sailing, for 'tis absolutely no further from Dover to Calais, should give a man these rights – I'll look into   5
them: so giving up the argument – I went straight to my lodgings, put up half a dozen shirts and a black pair of silk breeches – 'the coat I have on,' said I, looking at the sleeve, 'will do' – took a place in the Dover stage; and the packet sailing at nine the next morning – by three I had got sat down to my dinner upon a fricaseed chicken so incontestably in France, that had I died   10
that night of an indigestion, the whole world could not have suspended the effects of the *Droits d'aubaine*[1] – my shirts, and black pair of silk breeches – portmanteau and all must have gone to the King of France – even the little picture which I have so long worn, and so often have told thee, Eliza, I would carry with me into my grave, would have been torn from my neck. –   15
Ungenerous! – to seize upon the wreck of an unwary passenger, whom your subjects had beckon'd to their coast – by heaven! SIRE, it is not well done; and much does it grieve me, 'tis the monarch of a people so civilized and courteous, and so renowned for sentiment and fine feelings, that I have to reason with –   20
But I have scarce set foot in your dominions –

Laurence Sterne: *A Sentimental Journey* (1768)

---

[1] *All the effects of strangers (Swiss and Scotch excepted) dying in France, are seized by virtue of this law, though the heir be upon the spot – the profit of these contingencies being farmed, there is no redress. (Author's note.)*

On a brilliant day in May, in the year 1868, a gentleman was reclining at his ease on the great circular divan which at that period occupied the centre of the Salon Carré, in the Museum of the Louvre. This commodious ottoman has since been removed, to the extreme regret of all weak-kneed lovers of the fine arts; but the gentleman in question had taken serene possession of its 5 softest spot, and, with his head thrown back and his legs outstretched, was staring at Murillo's beautiful moon-borne Madonna in profound enjoyment of his posture. He had removed his hat, and flung down beside him a little red guide-book and an opera-glass. The day was warm; he was heated with walking, and he repeatedly passed his handkerchief over his forehead, 10 with a somewhat wearied gesture. And yet he was evidently not a man to whom fatigue was familiar; long, lean, and muscular, he suggested the sort of vigor that is commonly known as 'toughness'. But his exertions on this particular day had been of an unwonted sort, and he had often performed great physical feats which left him less jaded than his tranquil stroll through 15 the Louvre. He had looked out all the pictures to which an asterisk was affixed in those formidable pages of fine print in his Baedeker;[1] his attention had been strained and his eyes dazzled, and he had sat down with an aesthetic headache. He had looked, moreover, not only at all the pictures, but at all the copies that were going forward around them, in the hands of 20 those innumerable young women in irreproachable toilets who devote themselves, in France, to the propagation of masterpieces; and, if the truth must be told, he had often admired the copy much more than the original. His physiognomy would have sufficiently indicated that he was a shrewd and capable fellow, and in truth he had often sat up all night over a bristling 25 bundle of accounts, and heard the cock crow without a yawn. But Raphael and Titian and Rubens were a new kind of arithmetic, and they inspired our friend, for the first time in his life, with a vague self-mistrust.

Henry James: The American (1877)

1. Describe your impressions of the central character as he emerges in each extract.
2. Making use of illustration and quotation, show in the case of each passage how the use of point of view:

   (a) colours the way character is presented to us;
   (b) affects the writer's diction, tone and sentence structure. (Do not forget to examine both punctuation and the way in which ideas in sentences are connected.)

In the next two sections we will examine in greater depth the resources of the first and third person.

---

[1] Baedeker: the 'little red guide-book' previously mentioned – a famous handbook for travellers. Asterisks indicate pictures etc. which are specially commended.

THE CREDENTIALS OF 'I'

The most common mistake readers make when confronted by a piece of writing in the first person is to assume immediately that the author and the 'I' who addresses the reader are one and the same. While some writing may convince us by its purpose and tone that the 'I' is simply an extension of the author's everyday self – 'sincerity', however, is a notoriously slippery literary concept – we should always beware of coming too quickly to this conclusion. A narrator can be used, for instance, simply as the fairly impersonal vehicle for telling a story – the proverbial 'fly on the wall'. Or again a narrator may be a 'persona' – a mask through which the author speaks – and he or she is therefore to be assessed in much the same way as any fictional creation. In fact, when we come to examine irony, we will see that a familiar ironic manoeuvre involves the impersonation of a first-person narrator who is quietly allowed to destroy himself out of his own mouth, while remaining oblivious to the effect he is producing on the reader. The 'I' we meet in a narration or description may be reliable or unreliable – or a mixture of both. (Read, for example, Katherine Mansfield's story 'Je Ne Parle Pas Français' (1920) or Ford Madox Ford's *The Good Soldier* (1915) to see how a narrator may remain tellingly blind to the full significance of what he has to tell us.)

It may be helpful at this point to consider the way, in everyday experience, we form an impression of somebody we are meeting for the first time. We observe the individual's appearance, of course – features, dress and gestures. (Some people make great claims concerning what we can learn from studying 'body language'.) We also listen to the speaker's voice, and consciously or unconsciously it will raise a number of questions in our mind. What does this voice tell us about our interlocutor's social background and level of education? Does the tone assume a position of superiority or a degree of intimacy? Is this person reticent or eager to impress? Does the voice suggest a certain type with whom we are already familiar? Are we fairly certain that our first impressions are accurate, or would we be wise to suspend judgement? And so on. The questions are virtually endless.

Getting to know a fictional first-person narrator is a roughly analogous process, though, of course, the introduction is effected purely through a series of words on the page. We need to remember, too, that in a literary context, there is always an important third party present – the author. We must never entirely forget that it is the author who is manipulating the strings behind the puppet narrator; and while the puppet is made to move in a life-like way, the writer-creator must also convey to the reader what opinion is to be formed on this figure who dances before our very eyes. In other words, not only the subject matter, but also the tone – the 'voicing' of the first person narrator – must establish a set of credentials, so that we can recognize what sort of person we are dealing with and the kind of judgements the author implicitly has made on him or her. Perhaps if we listen carefully enough to the voice of the narrator, we will detect the

author's own voice whispering in the background 'This fellow is
transparently an obtuse fool, isn't he?' or 'Don't leap to any simple
judgements on her character – there's more to her than is immediately
apparent'. The way in which the 'signals' are transmitted by an author
may be a subtle process, but the successful use of the first person narrative
point of view requires this ability to establish what *seems* to be an external
framework of values against which we place and judge the 'I' who
addresses us.

In order to approach this quite complex matter in a more concrete way,
we would like you to consider the questions which follow this next pairing
of extracts, both of which are concerned in different ways to define the
nature of what we might term a 'master-servant relationship.'

Sometimes of a morning, as I've sat in bed sucking down the early cup of tea
and watched Jeeves flitting about the room and putting out the raiment for
the day, I've wondered what the deuce I should do if the fellow ever took it
into his head to leave me. It's not so bad when I'm in New York, but in
London the anxiety is frightful. There used to be all sorts of attempts on the 5
part of low blighters to sneak him away from me. Young Reggie Foljambe
to my certain knowledge offered him double what I was giving him, and
Alistair Bingham-Reeves, who's got a man who had been known to press his
trousers sideways, used to look at him, when he came to see me, with a kind
of glittering, hungry eye which disturbed me deucedly. Bally pirates! 10

The thing, you see, is that Jeeves is so dashed competent. You can spot it
even in the way he shoves studs into a shirt.

I rely on him absolutely in every crisis, and he never lets me down. And
what's more, he can always be counted on to extend himself on behalf of any
pal of mine who happens to be to all appearances knee-deep in the bouillon. 15
Take the rather rummy case, for instance, of dear old Bicky and his uncle,
the hard-boiled egg.

It happened after I had been in America for a few months. I got back to
the flat latish one night, and when Jeeves brought me the final drink he said:

'Mr Bickersteth called to see you this evening, sir, while you were out.' 20

'Oh?' I said.

'Twice, sir. He appeared a trifle agitated.'

'What, pipped?'

'He gave that impression, sir.'

I sipped the whisky. I was sorry if Bicky was in trouble, but, as a matter of 25
fact, I was rather glad to have something I could discuss freely with Jeeves
just then, because things had been a bit strained between us for some time,
and it had been rather difficult to hit on anything to talk about that wasn't
apt to take a personal turn. You see, I had decided – rightly or wrongly – to
grow a moustache, and this had cut Jeeves to the quick. He couldn't stick the 30
thing at any price, and I had been living ever since in an atmosphere of bally
disapproval till I was getting jolly fed up with it. What I mean is, while
there's no doubt that in certain matters of dress Jeeves's judgement is
absolutely sound and should be followed, it seemed to me that it was getting
a bit too thick if he was going to edit my face as well as my costume. No one 35
can call me an unreasonable chappie, and many's the time I've given in like a

lamb when Jeeves has voted against one of my pet suits or ties; but when it comes to a valet's staking out a claim on your upper lip you've simply got to have a bit of the good old bulldog pluck and defy the blighter.

> P. G. Wodehouse: 'Jeeves and the Hard-Boiled Egg' taken from
> *Carry on Jeeves!* (1925)

When I saw Finn waiting for me at the corner of the street I knew at once that something had gone wrong. Finn usually waits for me in bed, or leaning up against the side of the door with his eyes closed. Moreover, I had been delayed by the strike. I hate the journey back to England anyway; and until I have been able to bury my head so deep in dear London that I can forget that   5
I have ever been away I am inconsolable. So you may imagine how unhappy it makes me to have to cool my heels at Newhaven, waiting for the trains to run again, and with the smells of France still fresh in my nostrils. On this occasion too the bottles of cognac which I always smuggle had been taken from me by the Customs, so that when closing time came I was utterly   10
abandoned to the torments of a morbid self scrutiny. The invigorating objectivity of true contemplation is something which a man of my temperament cannot achieve in unfamiliar towns in England, even when he has not also to be worrying about trains. Trains are bad for the nerves at the best of times. What did people have nightmares about before there were   15
trains? So all this being considered, it was an odd thing that Finn should be waiting for me in the road.

As soon as I saw Finn I stopped and put the cases down. They were full of French books and very heavy. I shouted 'Hey!' and Finn came slowly on. He never makes haste. I find it hard to explain to people about Finn. He isn't   20
exactly my servant. He seems more often like my manager. Sometimes I support him, and sometimes he supports me; it depends. It's somehow clear that we aren't equals. His name is Peter O'Finney, but you needn't mind about that, as he is always called Finn, and he is a sort of remote cousin of mine, or so he used to claim, and I never troubled to verify this. But people   25
do get the impression that he is my servant, and I often have this impression too, though it would be hard to say exactly what features of the situation suggest it. Sometimes I think that it is just that Finn is a humble and self-effacing person and so automatically takes second place. When we are short of beds it is always Finn who sleeps on the floor, and this seems thoroughly   30
natural. It is true that I am always giving Finn orders, but this is because Finn seems not to have many ideas of his own about how to employ his time. Some of my friends think that Finn is cracked, but this is not so; he knows very well what he is about.

> Iris Murdoch: *Under the Net* (1954)

1. The first passage is full of a certain kind of slang – for instance, 'Bally pirates!' (line 10). Locate similar examples of this type of language and suggest what it tells us about (a) the narrator, Bertie Wooster, and (b) the social background and period in which he is set.
2. Which of the following comments more accurately reflects what you feel is Wodehouse's implicit attitude towards Bertie Wooster?

(a) 'A lovable fool at whom we smile – harsher judgements would be out of place.'

(b) 'A helples social parasite who belongs to a class Wodehouse despises.'

By what means does Wodehouse convey his view of Bertie?

3. The narrator of the second passage, Jake Donaghue, uses language such as 'utterly abandoned to the torments of a morbid self scrutiny' lines 10–11), but there are descents to a more colloquial level (for example, 'cool my heels', line 7). What impression do you form of this narrator – his outlook and his cast of mind – from the language he uses?

4. You probably found it fairly easy to establish what Wodehouse thinks about Bertie. Is it as clear what Iris Murdoch intends the reader to make of Jake Donaghue's credentials?

5. Both narrators spend some time trying to define the nature of their relationship with their 'servant'. In so doing, what does each narrator reveal about *himself*? Is one narrator, for example, more self-aware than the other? More assertive? More unconsciously self-revealing?

We would not like to leave you with the impression that point of view is only important and influential in fiction writing. In virtually every kind of composition, from our earlier example of a cookery recipe (see page 2) to the writing of history, authors will, consciously or unconsciously, adopt a certain stance to the reader. This will certainly be influenced by the kind of readership they are aiming at and the kind of relationship they wish to achieve: most writers have some kind of audience in mind, even if it is only a vague picture of an ideally sympathetic reader. Sometimes the attitude to the reader will be virtually determined by the nature of the subject itself or by convention: for example, in writing up a report on a scientific experiment, a particular kind of format is almost preordained and a certain objectivity obligatory.

To underline the importance of point of view in connection with non-fictional writing, we would like you to read the following two examples. Both use the first person and both were written in the eighteenth century. One is taken from a private letter, the other from an article written for a periodical. Assess the way in which the nature of the audience has in each case influenced the writer's treatment of the subject and the kind of language used.

The Funeral of George II

Arlington Street, Nov. 13, 1760.

Do you know, I had the curiosity to go to the burying t'other night; I had never seen a royal funeral; nay, I walked as a rag of quality, which I found would be, and so it was, the easiest way of seeing it. It is absolutely a noble sight. The Prince's Chamber, hung with purple, and a quantity of silver   5 lamps, the coffin under a canopy of purple velvet, and six vast chandeliers of silver on high stands, had a very good effect. The Ambassador from Tripoli and his son were carried to see that chamber. The procession through a line of foot-guards, every seventh man bearing a torch, the horse-guards lining the outside, their officers with drawn sabres and crape sashes on horseback,   10 the drums muffled, the fifes, bells tolling, and minute guns, all this was very solemn. But the charm was the entrance of the Abbey, where we were received by the Dean and Chapter in rich robes, the choir and almsmen all bearing torches; the whole Abbey so illuminated, that one saw it to greater advantage than by day; the tombs, long aisles, and fretted roof, all   15 appearing distinctly, and with the happiest chiaroscuro.[1] There wanted nothing but incense, and little chapels here and there, with priests saying mass for the repose of the defunct – yet one could not complain of its not being catholic enough. I had been in dread of being coupled with some boy of ten years old – but the heralds were not very accurate, and I walked with   20 George Grenville, taller and older enough to keep me in countenance. When we came to the chapel of Henry the Seventh, all solemnity and decorum ceased – no order was observed, people set or stood where they could or would, the yeomen of the guard were crying out for help, oppressed by the immense weight of the coffin, the Bishop read sadly, and blundered in the   25 prayers, the fine chapter, *Man that is born of a woman*, was chanted, not read, and the anthem, besides being unmeasurably tedious, would have served as well for a nuptial. The real serious part was the figure of the Duke of Cumberland, heightened by a thousand melancholy circumstances. He had a dark brown adonis,[2] and a cloak of black cloth, with a train of five   30 yards. Attending the funeral of a father, however little reason he had so to love him, could not be pleasant. His leg extremely bad, yet forced to stand upon it near two hours, his face bloated and distorted with his late paralytic stroke, which has affected, too, one of his eyes, and placed over the mouth of the vault, into which, in all probability, he must himself so soon descend –   35 think how unpleasant a situation! He bore it all with a firm and unaffected countenance. This grave scene was fully contrasted by the burlesque Duke of Newcastle. He fell into a fit of crying the moment he came into the chapel, and flung himself back in a stall, the Archbishop hovering over him with a smelling-bottle – but in two minutes his curiosity got the better of his   40 hypocrisy, and he ran about the chapel with his glass to spy who was or was not there, spying with one hand, and mopping his eyes with t'other. Then returned the fear of catching cold, and the Duke of Cumberland, who was sinking with heat, felt himself weighed down, and turning round, found it was the Duke of Newcastle standing upon his train to avoid the chill of the   45 marble. It was very theatric to look down into the vault, where the coffin lay, attended by mourners with lights. Clavering, the Groom of the Bedchamber, refused to sit up with the body, and was dismissed by the King's order.

Horace Walpole: *Letter to George Montagu*

---

[1] *chiaroscuro*: made up of light and dark shadings, as in a picture.

[2] *adonis*: a kind of wig.

When I am in a serious Humour, I very often walk by my self in *Westminster* Abby; where the Gloominess of the Place, and the Use to which it is applied, with the Solemnity of the Building, and the Condition of the People who lye in it, are apt to fill the Mind with a kind of Melancholy, or rather Thoughtfulness, that is not disagreeable. I Yesterday pass'd a whole 　5 afternoon in the Churchyard, the Cloysters, and the Church, amusing my self with the Tombstones and Inscriptions that I met with in those several Regions of the Dead. Most of them recorded nothing else of the buried Person, but that he was born upon one Day and died upon another: The whole History of his Life being comprehended in those two Circumstances, 　10 that are common to all Mankind. I could not but look upon these Registers of Existence, whether of Brass or Marble, as a kind of Satyr upon the departed Persons; who had left no other Memorial of them, but that they were born and that they died. They put me in mind of several Persons mentioned in the Battels of Heroic Poems, who have sounding Names given 　15 them, for no other Reason but that they may be killed, and are celebrated for nothing but being knocked on the Head . . .

Upon going into the Church, I entertained my self with the digging of a Grave; and saw in every Shovel-full of it that was thrown up, the Fragment of a Bone or Skull intermixt with a kind of fresh mouldering Earth that some 　20 time or other had a place in the Composition of an human Body. Upon this, I began to consider with my self what innumerable Multitudes of People lay confused together under the Pavement of that ancient Cathedral; how Men and Women, Friends and Enemies, Priests and Soldiers, Monks and Prebendaries, were crumbled amongst one another, and blended together in 　25 the same common Mass; how Beauty, Strength, and Youth, with Old-age, Weakness, and Deformity, lay undistinguished in the same promiscuous Heap of Matter.

After having thus surveyed this great Magazine of Mortality, as it were, in the Lump, I examined it more particularly by the Accounts which I found on 　30 several of the Monuments which are raised in every Quarter of that ancient Fabrick. Some of them were covered with such extravagant Epitaphs that, if it were possible for the dead Person to be acquainted with them, he would blush at the praises which his Friends have bestowed upon him. There are others so excessively modest, that they deliver the Character of the Peron 　35 departed in *Greek* or *Hebrew*, and by that means are not understood once in a Twelve-month. In the Poetical Quarter, I found there were Poets who had no Monuments, and Monuments which had no Poets. I observed indeed that the present War had filled the Church with many of these uninhabited Monuments, which had been erected to the Memory of Persons whose 　40 Bodies were perhaps buried in the Plains of *Blenheim*, or in the Bosom of the Ocean . . .

I have left the Repository of our *English* Kings for the Contemplation of another Day, when I shall find my Mind disposed for so serious an Amusement. I know that Entertainments of this nature are apt to raise dark 　45 and dismal Thoughts in timorous Minds, and gloomy Imaginations; but for my own part, though I am always serious, I do not know what it is to be melancholy; and can therefore take a View of Nature in her deep and solemn Scenes, with the same pleasure as in her most gay and delightful ones. By this means I can improve my self with those Objects, which others consider with 　50

Terror. When I look upon the Tombs of the Great, every Emotion of Envy dies in me; when I read the Epitaphs of the Beautiful, every inordinate Desire goes out; when I meet with the Grief of Parents upon a Tomb-stone, my Heart melts with Compassion; when I see the Tomb of the Parents themselves, I consider the Vanity of grieving for those whom we must   55
quickly follow: When I see Kings lying by those who deposed them, when I consider rival Wits placed Side by Side, or the holy Men that divided the World with their Contests and Disputes, I reflect with Sorrow and Astonishment on the little Competitions, Factions, and Debates of Mankind. When I read the several Dates of the Tombs, of some that died   60
Yesterday, and some 600 Years ago, I consider that great Day when we shall all of us be Contemporaries, and make our Appearance together.

Addison: The Spectator, No. 26 (1711)

When you have discussed the way(s) in which each author's perception of his reader affects the language he adopts, give your opinion on this comment: 'Walpole is sincerely persenting *himself*, whereas Addison is posturing to create a picture of himself which he imagines will impress the reader.'

WHERE IS THE AUTHOR?

You will already have gathered that the idea of the *distance* at which the reader is placed from the narrative is central to a consideration of point of view. Are we, to use the analogy of film, looking at a character, setting or event in full close-up through a single fixed lens, or perhaps more detachedly through a selection of different shots of varying focal length and from different angles? Another crucial question which has great relevance to the use of a third person point of view concerns the extent to which the author himself is 'present' in what he writes – or *apparently* 'absent'.

We have already defined what is involved in an omniscient point of view, and observed that an author may decide, in various ways, to surrender areas of the potential god's-eye vision (see page 118). We need now to make another crucial distinction: omniscient narrators may appear in an *intrusive* form – that is, they may in their capacity as Author not only narrate but also freely comment on their characters or settings, analyze actions or motives by directly addressing the reader, or even introduce widely their own views on the human condition. On the other hand a narrator can, of course, remain *unintrusive* or *impersonal*. (Incidentally, an extreme example of this apparent unintrusiveness is to be found in the stream of consciousness technique in which a direct internal monologue registers the flux of experience, both memory and immediate sensation and impression, as it flows through the mind of a central character. If you wish to remind yourself of how this point of view may be used, you should turn back to pages 89 and 95 for examples by one of its greatest pioneers, James Joyce.)

If you are sharp-eyed, you perhaps noticed what may seem an odd piece of capitalization earlier in the last paragraph: why should one usage of 'author' merit a capital 'A', while on another occasion the word begins, as you would expect, with a small 'a'? In fact, we intend 'author' to indicate the person whose name appears on the cover of a given book and who sits down to consider such technical matters as the use of point of view. By 'the Author' we signify the authorial voice, projected in the resulting narrative. This is no mere piece of theoretical hair-splitting. Just as it is vital to distinguish a writer from the persona adopted in the first person, so we should not necessarily assume that the Author who addresses us in a work signed by Fielding or Dickens is in all respects that person. The role of the Author *may* be an extension of the everyday character of the author, but clearly he or she is, in one sense, 'invented' to fulfil certain narrative functions, and can therefore aspire to an urbanity or sureness in breadth of vision which is seldom to be enjoyed in daily life.

We should now be in a position to consider some examples of the Author's role. You will find that the following three passages have been arranged to show a pattern of an increasingly intrusive authorial presence. In the first extract, for instance, though Jane Austen is clearly guiding our responses, she does this primarily through the presentation of one dominant, and a number of related, points of view. (Note: you should not assume from this that she habitually adopts this self-effacing approach.) The second passage by Samuel Butler blends the points of view of two characters who are at cross-purposes with the frequent intrusion of his authorial voice. The third passage is marked by George Eliot's sage-like manner as she brings one of her creations to the centre of the stage and comments on him at some length. We have provided questions at the end of each extract which we hope will lead you into important areas of discussion.

The scene is set in Bath where Anne Elliot is slowly re-establishing her intimacy with Captain Wentworth after having been persuaded some years earlier that marriage to him would be unwise. While Anne is paying a visit to the Musgroves — her sister, Mary, has married into this family — Anne's elder sister, Elizabeth, and her father arrive unexpectedly.

The door was thrown open for Sir Walter and Miss Elliot, whose entrance seemed to give a general chill. Anne felt an instant oppression, and, wherever she looked, saw symptoms of the same. The comfort, the freedom, the gaiety of the room was over, hushed into cold composure, determined silence, or insipid talk, to meet the heartless elegance of her father and sister.   5
How mortifying to feel that it was so!

Her jealous eye was satisfied in one particular. Captain Wentworth was acknowledged again by each, by Elizabeth more graciously than before. She even addressed him once, and looked at him more than once. Elizabeth was, in fact, revolving a great measure. The sequel explained it. After the waste of   10
a few minutes in saying the proper nothings, she began to give the invitation which was to comprise all the remaining dues of the Musgroves. 'To-

morrow evening, to meet a few friends, no formal party.' It was all said very gracefully, and the cards with which she had provided herself, the 'Miss Elliot at home,' were laid on the table, with a courteous, comprehensive 15 smile to all; and one smile and one card more decidedly for Captain Wentworth. The truth was, that Elizabeth had been long enough in Bath, to understand the importance of a man of such an air and appearance as his. The past was nothing. The present was that Captain Wentworth would move about well in her drawing-room. The card was pointedly given, and Sir 20 Walter and Elizabeth arose and disappeared.

The interruption had been short, though severe; and ease and animation returned to most of those they left, as the door shut them out, but not to Anne. She could think only of the invitation she had with such astonishment witnessed; and of the manner in which it had been received, a manner of 25 doubtful meaning, of surprise rather than gratification, of polite acknowledgment rather than acceptance. She knew him; she saw disdain in his eye, and could not venture to believe that he had determined to accept such an offering, as atonement for all the insolence of the past. Her spirits sank. He held the card in his hand after they were gone, as if deeply considering it. 30

'Only think of Elizabeth's including every body!' whispered Mary very audibly. 'I do not wonder Captain Wentworth is delighted! You see he cannot put the card out of his hand.'

Anne caught his eye, saw his cheeks glow, and his mouth form itself into a momentary expression of contempt, and turned away, that she might 35 neither see nor hear more to vex her.

The party separated.

Jane Austen: *Persuasion* (1818)

1. Anne Elliot's point of view dominates here. It is frequently presented by means of a 'narrated interior monologue' – that is, though the third person and past tense are used, the reader is to understand that the immediate thoughts and feelings of the character concerned are being recorded.

   (a) Comment on the use of narrated interior monologue to register Anne Elliot's impressions.
   (b) Show how Jane Austen uses Anne Elliot's point of view to create the mood of the occasion;
   (c) and to suggest reactions and judgements in connection with other characters present.

2. Do you think we are intended to regard Anne Elliot as a sympathetic and reliable observer? Give reasons for your view.

3. Locate at least two parts of the passage in which other points of view are introduced and comment on what you think the reader is intended to feel about the characters concerned.

4. Did you find it straightforward to separate the authorial point of view from that of Anne Elliot? Are there any *explicit* or *implicit* intrusions of authorial judgement?

It has been discovered that Ellen, a servant in the Pontifex household, is pregnant. Christiana Pontifex, whose husband is a clergyman, is wondering — somewhat fancifully in view of the boy's lack of years — whether her own son, Ernest, could be the father of the child. In fact, the extent of Ernest's 'guilt' is to have taken pity on Ellen's plight and, before the servant was dismissed, to have given her his watch.

Then came the question — horrid thought! — as to who was the partner of Ellen's guilt? Was it, could it be, her own son, her darling Ernest? Ernest was getting a big boy now. She could excuse any woman for taking a fancy to him; as for himself, why she was sure he was behind no young man of his age in appreciation of the charms of a nice-looking young woman. So long as he   5
was innocent she did not mind this, but oh, if he were guilty!

She could not bear to think of it, and yet it would be mere cowardice not to look such a matter in the face — her hope was in the Lord, and she was ready to bear cheerfully and make the best of any suffering He might think fit to lay upon her. That the baby must be either a boy or a girl — this much,   10
at any rate, was clear. No less clear was it that the child, if a boy, would resemble Theobald, and if a girl, herself. Resemblance, whether of body or mind, generally leaped over a generation. The guilt of the parents must not be shared by the innocent offspring of shame oh! no — and such a child as this would be . . . She was off in one of her reveries at once.   15

The child was in the act of being consecrated Archbishop of Canterbury when Theobald came in from a visit in the parish and was told of the shocking discovery . . .

'Come here, my poor, pale-faced, heavy-eyed boy', Christiana said to Ernest in her kindest manner; 'come and sit down by me, and we will have a   20
little quiet confidential talk together, will we not?'

The boy went mechanically to the sofa. Whenever his mother wanted what she called a confidential talk with him she always selected the sofa as the most suitable ground on which to open her campaign. All mothers do this; the sofa is to them what the dining-room is to fathers. In the present   25
case the sofa was particularly well adapted for a strategic purpose, being an old-fashioned one with a high back, mattress, bolsters and cushions. Once safely penned into one of its deep corners, it was like a dentist's chair, not too easy to get out of again. Here she could get at him better to pull him about, if this seemed desirable, or if she thought fit to cry she could bury her head in   30
the sofa cushion and abandon herself to an agony of grief which seldom failed of its effect. None of her favourite manoeuvres were so easily adopted in her usual seat, the armchair on the right-hand side of the fireplace, and so well did her son know from his mother's tone that this was going to be a sofa conversation that he took his place like a lamb as soon as she began to speak   35
and before she could reach the sofa herself.

'My dearest boy,' began his mother, taking hold of his hand and placing it within her own, 'promise me never to be afraid either of your dear papa or of me; promise me this, my dear, as you love me, promise it to me,' and she kissed him again and again and stroked his hair. But with her other hand she   40
still kept hold of his; she had got him and she meant to keep him.

The lad hung down his head and promised. What else could he do?

'You know there is no one, dear, dear Ernest, who loves you so much as

your papa and I do; no one who watches so carefully over your interests or
who is so anxious to enter into all your little joys and troubles as we are; but,   45
my dearest boy, it grieves me sometimes to think that you have not that
perfect love for and confidence in us which you ought to have. You know,
my darling, that it would be as much our pleasure as our duty to watch over
the development of your moral and spiritual nature, but alas! you will not let
us see your moral and spiritual nature. At times we are almost inclined to   50
doubt whether you have a moral and spiritual nature at all. Of your inner
life, my dear, we know nothing beyond such scraps as we can gleam in spite
of you, from little things which escape you almost before you know that you
have said them.'
   The boy winced at this. It made him feel hot and uncomfortable all over.   55
He knew well how careful he ought to be, and yet, do what he could, from
time to time his forgetfulness of the part betrayed him into unreserve. His
mother saw that he winced, and enjoyed the scratch which she had given
him. Had she felt less confident of victory she had better have forgone the
pleasure of touching as it were the eyes at the end of the snail's horns in order   60
to enjoy seeing the snail draw them in again – but she knew that when she
had got him well down into the sofa, and held his hand, she had the enemy
almost absolutely at her mercy, and could do pretty much what she
liked . . .
   Ernest could never stand being spoken to in this way by his mother: for he   65
still believed that she loved him, and that he was fond of her and had a friend
in her – up to a certain point. But his mother was beginning to come to the
end of her tether; she had played the domestic confidence trick upon him
times without number already. Over and over again had she wheedled from
him all she wanted to know, and afterwards got him into the most horrible   70
scrape by telling the whole to Theobald . . .
   'I see, my dearest,' continued his mother, 'either that I am mistaken, and
that there is nothing on your mind, or that you will not unburden yourself to
me: but oh, Ernest, tell me at least this much; is there nothing that you repent
of, nothing which makes you unhappy in connection with that miserable girl   75
Ellen?'
   Ernest's heart failed him. 'I am a dead boy now,' he said to himself. He
had not the faintest conception what his mother was driving at, and thought
she suspected about the watch; but he held his ground.
   I do not believe he was much more of a coward than his neighbours, only   80
he did not know that all sensible people are cowards when they are off their
beat, or when they think they are going to be roughly handled . . .

Samuel Butler: The Way of All Flesh (1903)

Many different narrative techniques are at work in this passage: there is
dialogue in direct speech combined with the description of setting and the
movement of characters etc.; we are given information about past
experiences which have a bearing on the present interview; metaphor
(there is one important extended metaphor) and simile guide our
response; the author combines narrated interior monologue with an
external, judgemental view of his characters; an element of ironic humour
is produced both as a result of the contradictions in Christiana's response,

of which she is unaware, and the essential misunderstanding between mother and son; and in the tone of the passage there are several marked contrasts – most noticeably between the kind of language Butler puts into Christiana's mouth and the authorial voice he adopts.

Bearing these points in mind, write an analysis of the narrative techniques Butler uses in the passage. You may find it useful to centre your answer around the questions of the ways in which Butler (a) enlists the reader's sympathies on Ernest's behalf, and (b) exposes Christiana to criticism.

Lydgate, a doctor who hopes to contribute to the advance of medical research, has bought a practice in Middlemarch.

He was at a starting-point which makes many a man's career a fine subject for betting, if there were any gentlemen given to that amusement who could appreciate the complicated probabilities of an arduous purpose, with all the possible thwartings and furtherings of circumstance, all the niceties of inward balance, by which a man swims and makes his point or else is carried   5
headlong. The risk would remain, even with close knowledge of Lydgate's character; for character too is a process and an unfolding. The man was still in the making, as much as the Middlemarch doctor and immortal discoverer, and there were both virtues and faults capable of shrinking or expanding. The faults will not, I hope, be a reason for the withdrawal of   10
your interest in him. Among our valued friends is there not some one or other who is a little too self-confident and disdainful; whose distinguished mind is a little spotted with commonness; who is a little pinched here and protuberant there with native prejudices; or whose better energies are liable to lapse down the wrong channel under the influence of transient   15
solicitations? All these things might be alleged against Lydgate, his conceit was of the arrogant sort, never simpering, never impertinent, but massive in its claims and benevolently contemptuous. He would do a great deal for noodles, being sorry for them, and feeling quite sure that they could have no power over him: he had thought of joining the Saint Simonians[1] when he   20
was in Paris, in order to turn them against some of their own doctrines. All his faults were marked by kindred traits, and were those of a man who had a fine baritone, whose clothes hung well upon him, and who even in his ordinary gestures had an air of inbred distinction. Where then lay the spots of commonness? says a young lady enamoured of that careless grace. How   25
could there be any commonness in a man so well-bred, so ambitious of social distinction, so generous and unusual in his views of social duty? As easily as there may be stupidity in a man of genius if you take him unawares on the wrong subject, or as many a man who has the best will to advance the social millennium might be ill-inspired in imagining its lighter pleasures; unable to   30
go beyond Offenbach's music, or the brilliant punning in the last burlesque. Lydgate's spots of commonness lay in the complexion of his prejudices, which, in spite of noble intentions and sympathy, were half of them such as are found in ordinary men of the world: that distinction of mind which

---

[1] *Saint Simonians*: group which based its ideals of world peace, broadly socialist organization of society and reverence for women on the teachings of the Comte de Saint-Simon (1760–1825).

belonged to his intellectual ardour, did not penetrate his feeling and 35
judgement about furniture, or women, or the desirability of its being known
(without his telling) that he was better born than other country surgeons. He
did not mean to think of furniture at present; but whenever he did so, it was
to be feared that neither biology nor schemes of reform would lift him above
the vulgarity of feeling that there would be an incompatibility in his 40
furniture not being of the best.

As to women, he had once already been drawn headlong by impetuous
folly, which he meant to be final, since marriage at some distant period
would of course not be impetuous.

George Eliot: *Middlemarch* (1871–2)

1. This is clearly an introductory view of Lydgate. In your own words,
   what kind of man is he presented as being? Does this introduction to
   him suggest any foreshadowing possibilities of what is likely to
   happen to him?
2. (a) What stance does the Author adopt towards this character –
       and the reader?
   (b) How do the particular qualities of George Eliot's authorial
       voice compare with those of Samuel Butler in the previous
       extract?
3. How would you reply to the reader who observed: 'I do wish the
   Author would stop treading water and get on with the story'?

THE SELF-CONSCIOUS NARRATOR

George Eliot prepared the way for making a preliminary judgement on
Lydgate which will possess just the carefully calculated emphasis she feels
is appropriate at this stage. One of the keys to an understanding of her
approach is to perceive how strongly the Author manifests an *awareness*
of the reader. Indeed, the tone assumes the presence of different kinds of
reader when at one point the Author pre-empts the response of 'a young
lady enamoured of that careless grace'. Earlier the reader had been
directly addressed – 'the faults will not, I hope, be a reason for the
withdrawal of your interest in him' – and his own experience had been
directly appealed to. (How flattering to be taken almost as an equal in an
unfolding relationship with such a wise and judicious narrator!) Lydgate
is clearly being weighed in the Author's meticulously balanced scales.
George Eliot's authorial attitude, though occasionally playful, suggests
that, because serious matters are being considered, the Author will not be
afraid to call on a direct line of access to the reader.

There is often fundamental disagreement among writers and critics on
the desirability of this kind of authorial intrusiveness. One narrative
tradition runs right from Cervantes, who had a great influence on the
early development of the English novel, and includes eighteenth century
novelists such as Fielding and later Victorian novelists such as Dickens
and Thackeray as well as George Eliot. In this tradition, the Author is

always a potent personal presence. Thackeray described the novel as 'a sort of confidential talk'. As the puppet-master, the Author is entitled to address the reader and to comment on his or her own creations. On the other hand, novelists such as Joyce favour a more impersonal approach, regarding addresses to the 'dear reader' as a clumsy fracturing of narrative realism.

What we mean by the 'self-conscious narrator' is an extreme extension of the intrusive authorial element in narration, whereby Authors draw the reader's attention to the fact that we are reading a fiction of which they are the controlling intelligence. The Author makes the reader a kind of accomplice. He or she may do this, as Sterne often does to comic effect in *Tristram Shandy* (1760–67), by taking us into his or her confidence about the problems of writing; the reader may be teased about the likely outcome of events; or possibly forced to stand back from the narrative during a lengthy digression. There are all kinds of interesting games that can be played between Authors and readers, as the Authors break their fictional cover to remind us that the 'reality' of a narrative is on one level no more than a cleverly sustained illusion. The effects of such a procedure are complex: paradoxically the self-conscious narrator, while *apparently* shattering an impression of realism, may finally bewitch the reader into total acceptance of a fictional spell. It is not so much *what* is done as *the way in which* it is done that matters in a case of fictional sleight of hand. Consider the success, for example, of the following use of the self-conscious narrator. The passage is taken from Kurt Vonnegut's *Breakfast of Champions* (1973).

Wayne Hoobler smiled now, not because he was happy but because, with so little to do, he thought he might as well show off his teeth. They were excellent teeth. The Adult Correctional Institution at Shepherdstown was proud of its dentistry program.

It was such a famous dental program, in fact, that it had been written up in   5
medical journals and in the *Reader's Digest*, which was the dying planet's most popular magazine. The theory behind the program was that many ex-convicts could not or would not get jobs because of their appearances, and good looks began with good teeth.

The program was so famous, in fact, that police even in neighboring   10
states, when they picked up a poor man with expensively maintained teeth, fillings and bridgework and all that, were likely to ask him, 'All right, boy – how many years you spend in Shepherdstown?'

Wayne Hoobler heard some of the orders which a waitress called to the bartender in the cocktail lounge. Wayne heard her call, 'Gilbey's and   15
quinine, with a twist.' He had no idea what that was – or a Manhattan or a brandy Alexander or a sloe gin fizz. 'Give me a Johnny Walker Rob Roy,' she called, 'and a Southern Comfort on the rocks, and a Bloody Mary with Wolfschmidt's.'

Wayne's only experiences with alcohol had had to do with drinking   20
cleaning fluids and eating shoe polish and so on. He had no fondness for alcohol.

'Give me a Black and White and water,' he heard the waitress say, and Wayne should have pricked up his ears at that. That particular drink wasn't for any ordinary person. That drink was for the person who had created all   25
Wayne's misery to date, who could kill him or make him a millionaire or send him back to prison or do whatever he damn pleased with Wayne. That drink was for me.

I had come to the Arts Festival incognito. I was there to watch a confrontation between two human beings I had created: Dwayne Hoover   30
and Kilgore Trout. I was not eager to be recognized. The waitress lit the hurricane lamp on my table. I pinched out the flame with my fingers. I had bought a pair of sunglasses at a Holiday Inn outside of Ashtabula, Ohio, where I spent the night before. I wore them in the darkness now. They looked like this: 35

The lenses were silvered, were mirrors to anyone looking my way. Anyone wanting to know what my eyes were like was confronted with his or her own twin reflections. Where other people in the cocktail lounge had eyes, I had two holes into another universe. I had *leaks*.[1] . . .

'This is a very bad book you're writing,' I said to myself behind my *leaks*.   40
'I know,' I said.

'You're afraid you'll kill yourself the way your mother did,' I said.
'I know,' I said.

There in the cocktail lounge, peering out through my leaks at a world of my own invention, I mouthed this word: *schizophrenia*.   45

The sound and appearance of the word had fascinated me for many years. It sounded and looked to me like a human being sneezing in a blizzard of soapflakes.

I did not and do not know for certain that I have that disease. This much I knew and know: I was making myself hideously uncomfortable by not   50
narrowing my attention to details of life which were immediately important, and by refusing to believe what my neighbors believed.

I am better now.

Word of honor: I am better now.

I was really sick for a while, though.   55

1. Locate and comment on specific examples of when the self-conscious narrator is most notable.

---

[1] *leaks*: earlier the narrator has written: 'he called mirrors *leaks*. It amused him to pretend that mirrors were holes between two universes'.

2. Why the clumsy drawing of the sunglasses? Should a writer not rely on words alone?
3. Give your final view of the success of the writing here. You should take into account Vonnegut's treatment of the idea of illusion and reality and the manner in which he presents the Author as the *inventor* of a fiction. Say also what you make of the tone here: is it 'flippancy teetering on the edge of breakdown'?

THE CHOICE OF AN UNUSUAL POINT OF VIEW

So far we have assumed that point of view generally involves the selection of a fairly recognizable human perspective. Sometimes, however, experiments with an unexpected angle of vision may yield interesting results. Those essays that we were forced to write on 'The Life of an Old Penny' or 'Written from Inside a Ping-Pong Ball' may have been little more than almost punitive tests of ingenuity and invention, but when Swift, for instance, in Book I of *Gulliver's Travels* (1726) makes us look through the eyes of a giant at a world of human midgets – and then in Book II exactly reverses the process – the point of view leads to some novel, even alarming, conclusions. The choice of an unexpected or even fantastic point of view may enable the writer to cleanse the doors of perception so that we examine some aspect of human experience with fresh eyes. Consider whether this is successfully done in the following extract taken from the conclusion of T. F. Powys's story 'The Bucket and the Rope' (from *God's Eyes a'Twinkle*, 1947)

'Yes, there was Mr Dendy!' exclaimed the bucket, 'a true and joyful countryman, doing his proper tasks. What could harm him? What could prevent him from living out his life contentedly and going down, as a good man should, gently into the grave? Surely never was a poor man created who meant so well.'   5

'Look at him now,' said the rope quietly; 'at first when he kicked you over I wondered if I should be strong enough to hold him. He struggled horribly, and I fancy that when he first felt me tighten round his throat he would have changed his mind. He tried to catch me to lessen the dreadful feeling of suffocation.'   10

'You must have hurt him very much,' observed the bucket, 'for his face became quite black, and his eyes bulged out of his head. I wonder you did not let him fall for in his death agony he kicked his legs and swung round, but you held him fast. Why did he do it?'

'I believe the reason was,' replied the rope, 'that Mr Dendy did not like to   15 see others happy.'

'That is not easy to believe,' remarked the bucket, 'when one considers how happy he was himself.'

'His wife made him so,' said the rope, 'and feeling her success with him she naturally wished to make another happy too.'   20

'What could be more proper?' said the bucket.

'It was this summer,' continued the rope, 'and the master, having saved a few guineas, bought for himself a new Sunday suit. "You look so well in it,"

his wife told him, "that you should go to church more often, for people will
know how well you are getting on when they see you in your new clothes."   25
Now, it was the time when Mr Dendy began to go to church of an evening
that I noticed passing this shed the same young man who had given Betty a
kiss in the by-street when Mr Dendy was drinking a glass in the little tavern.
He still looked unhappy.'

'A chance for Betty to turn his sorrow into joy!' laughed the bucket.   30

'She wished to do so, and they met in this very shed, on a Sunday evening,
when Mr Dendy was supposed to be gone to church.'

'But had he gone?' asked the bucket.

'No,' replied the rope. 'He had only put on his best clothes and walked
out, as if to go. Instead of going to church, he came to this shed, took me up,   35
and bound me round a large bundle of straw. The bundle he placed against
the wall of the shed, where there was a little chink, and, creeping under the
straw to hide himself, he waited.'

'For the pleasure of witnessing the kindness of his wife, I suppose,' said
the bucket.   40

'One would have thought so,' replied the rope, 'but the look upon
Mr Dendy's face when he saw what was going on did not warrant such a
supposition.'

'Perhaps he thought,' reasoned the bucket, 'that Betty should have
remained at home and warmed the rabbit pie for his supper; for the sermon   45
preached by Mr Hayball always made him extremely hungry, and Betty was
not to be expected to know that he was not at church. I have seen the pigs fed
so often, and I know how hungry animals are, and, as food keeps a man alive
and prevents him from becoming a dead carcass, it is natural that a man
should wish the woman that he keeps to prepare food for him, even though   50
she may prefer to be loving and kind to another man.'

'You should have heard Mr Dendy,' said the rope; 'he gnashed his teeth
and moaned horribly, and when his wife's friend seemed to be altogether
forgetting his sorrow, being come, as the lyric poet says, "Where comfort
is —" Mr Dendy crept out of the bundle and hid in the lane, snarling like a   55
bitten dog.'

'His hunger, I suppose, had gone beyond the proper bounds,' suggested
the bucket.

'It is difficult,' said the rope, after a few minutes' silence, as the body
swung to and fro, 'for us to decide what could have troubled this good man.   60
No one had robbed him. No one had beaten or hurt him, and never once
since they had been married had Betty refused his embraces.'

1. What has, in fact, happened to make Mr. Dendy take his own life?
2. What effect does T. F. Powys produce by using this particular
   point of view?

A SHORT NOTE ON POINT OF VIEW AND THE NOVEL TRADITION

The three writers who, in the eighteenth century, have a claim to being
'parents' of the English novel, all exhibit markedly different methods of
narration. Defoe, in novels such as *Robinson Crusoe* (1719) and *Moll*

Flanders (1722), submerges himself in the first person narrator who purports to be telling his or her story, and we are given a racy memoir. Richardson, in very long novels such as *Pamela* (1740–41) and *Clarissa Harlowe* (1747–8), adopts the epistolary form – his novels are composed entirely of letters written by the participants in events. Fielding in *The History of the Adventures of Joseph Andrews* (1742) and *Tom Jones* (1749) uses the third person and periodically intervenes with good-humoured urbanity as the Author to guide the reader through the world he has created. (For an example of the tone Fielding adopts, turn ahead to page 160). By the time Sterne's *Tristram Shandy* appears (1760–67), the whole business of narrative technique in the novel can already be subjected to high-spirited parody: Sterne's self-conscious narrator constantly reveals to us the way in which the complexity of actual experience proliferates beyond the capacity of any form of narrative to contain it.

To jump to more recent times – and what a jump this is, over the heads of the great Victorian masters of the novel – novelists such as Henry James and Conrad place a concern with point of view right at the centre of their novels. James's *The Ambassadors* (1903) and Conrad's *The Secret Agent* (1907), to take just two notable examples, are built on the awareness that reality is generally perceived in a distorted form as a result of our preconceptions and prejudices – and where we happen to be standing at the time! (Remember our opening examples, page 112, which showed that the scorer himself thought he had brought off a spectacularly difficult goal, but his effort seemed a mere formality from the press-box.) This sense of the relativity of any character's point of view is incorporated into the very narrative structure of the two novels we mentioned. The way in which the story is unfolded *is* the story.

Some novelists in our century, such as Joyce, have experimented with the stream of consciousness method (see page 127). Others, for instance, Faulkner in *The Sound and the Fury* (1929), have combined in the same novel the immediacy of a number of first person accounts, in relation to central events, with the objectivity and comprehensiveness which only an omniscient narrator can fully provide. The pressure behind this kind of narrative structure is the perception which Lawrence Durrell gives to one of his characters, the novelist Pursewarden, in *Balthazar* (1958):

> We live . . . lives based upon selected fictions. Our view of reality is conditioned by our position in space and time . . . Thus every interpretation of reality is based upon a unique position. Two paces east or west and the whole picture is changed.

Of course, we can do no more here than touch the surface of a vast and complex subject. If you wish to continue this area of study, we suggest you begin by consulting Percy Lubbock's *The Craft of Fiction* (1921) and Wayne C. Booth's *The Rhetoric of Fiction* (1961). Even more usefully, you should read closely some of the novels in the following list, all of which repay careful study in terms of their narrative structure. Perhaps, if you are working in a group with other students, each member could read one of these novels and prepare a short paper on its use of point of view.

Defoe: *Robinson Crusoe* (1719); Fielding: *Tom Jones* (1749); Sterne: *Tristram Shandy* (1760–67); Smollett: *Humphrey Clinker* (1771); Emily Brontë: *Wuthering Heights* (1847); Dickens: *Bleak House* (1852–3), *Great Expectations* (1860–61); Collins: *The Moonstone* (1868); Henry James: *The Turn of the Screw* (1898), *The Ambassadors* (1903); Conrad: *Nostromo* (1904), *The Secret Agent* (1907); Joyce: *A Portrait of the Artist as a Young Man* (1914–15); Ford Madox Ford: *The Good Soldier* (1915); F. Scott Fitzgerald: *The Great Gatsby* (1925); Virginia Woolf: *Mrs Dalloway* (1925); Faulkner: *The Sound and the Fury* (1929); Flann O'Brien: *At Swim – Two – Birds* (1939); Beckett: *Malone Dies* (1958); Golding: *The Inheritors* (1955), *Rites of Passage* (1980).

6

Irony

You may remember the passage by Jonathan Swift from his essay 'A Modest Proposal', quoted in our Introduction on page 64. We suggest that you reread it as an excellent example of a writer skilfully using irony – the topic which we are now to consider. Indeed, some critics consider Swift to be the master-ironist, and an appreciation of this passage can show us a great deal about this most tricky of subjects. This is how Swift's narrator continues his proposal:

I have reckoned upon a medium, that a child just born will weigh 12 pounds, and in a solar year, if tolerably nursed, increaseth to 28 pounds.

I grant this food will be somewhat dear, and therefore very proper for landlords, who, as they have already devoured most of the parents seem to have the best title to the children. 5

Infant's flesh will be in season throughout the year, but more plentiful in March, and a little before and after; for we are told by a grave author, an eminent French physician, that fish being a prolific diet, there are more children born in Roman Catholic countries about nine months after Lent, than at any other season; therefore reckoning a year after Lent, the markets 10 will be more glutted than usual, because the number of Popish infants, is at least three to one in this kingdom, and therefore it will have one other collateral advantage, by lessening the number of Papists among us.

I have already computed the charge of nursing a beggar's child (in which list I reckon all cottagers, labourers, and four-fifths of the farmers) to be 15 about two shillings per annum, rags included; and I believe no gentleman would repine to give ten shillings for the carcass of a good fat child, which, as I have said will make four good dishes of excellent nutritive meat, when he hath only some particular friend, or his own family to dine with him. Thus the squire will learn to be a good landlord, and grow popular among his 20 tenants, the mother will have eight shillings neat profit, and be fit for work till she produces another child.

Those who are more thrifty (as I must confess the times require) may flay the carcass; the skin of which, artificially dressed, will make admirable gloves for ladies, and summer boots for fine gentlemen. 25

Swift's aim in the passage was to draw attention to the conditions of dire poverty and hunger that prevailed in his native Ireland. He did this by shocking his readers with the suggestion that the best method of alleviating the poverty and hunger was for the Irish to breed children for sale as food for the rich. Clearly, Swift was not putting this forward as a

serious solution. Or is it so clear? Consider the following comments that
were made about this extract.

(i) The writer of this passage must have been a heartless savage himself,
even to consider such a solution to poverty. How would he like it if it
were his children who were going to be eaten?

(ii) How can the writer assert these views in such a clinical style which
assumes that all reasonable readers will approve of treating Irish   5
children as if they were cattle or pigs? Surely his tone should register
disapproval. What he is saying so coldly is as bad as Hitler's treatment
of the Jews. If he can't see this, he must be mad!

Now, if Swift were putting forward such a solution in all seriousness,
then these two comments would be justified. To suggest cannibalism as
the answer to the eighteenth century Irish economic situation, and to
suggest it in such an urbane tone, *is* heartless and *is* savage and we *would*
be justified in doubting Swift's sanity. But he is not suggesting any such
course of action; rather he is attempting to show, by means of satire, the
heartlessness and the savagery (and, perhaps, even the madness) of the
rulers of the Irish people who could permit the state of affairs in which the
natives were forced to sell their children, not as food but as servants of the
rich in order to avoid starvation. It is as if, from behind this smokescreen,
Swift is saying to the English rulers and landlords of Ireland: 'you have
already battened on the lives of my fellow countrymen; why not go the
whole hog, then, and literally start eating our children?' This view is fairly
clearly suggested when, virtually breaking his ironic cover for a moment,
Swift writes that Irish children will be very 'proper' food for landlords
'who, as they have already devoured most of the parents seem to have the
best title to the children'. The landlords have 'devoured' the parents
metaphorically by their harsh treatment of tenants and their high rents;
what Swift's satire does is to take that metaphor of careless greed –
'devoured' – and transform it into a most potent 'literal' suggestion for
the ruling class's future policy – as a 'mere' extension of their present
behaviour. The element of exaggeration is a powerful satirical device.
Bearing in mind the second mistaken response quoted earlier, you should
see that the apparently reasonable tone of the proposal – as if this were the
carefully considered plan of a public-spirited economist to which all must
give their unqualified assent – aids Swift's ironic attack. The tone he
adopts serves to arouse the reader's anger against an outlook – one which
Swift himself found totally objectionable – which is so purely 'rational' as
to regard people as mere commodities to be sold in the market-place.

What our two critics have failed to see is the element of camouflage or
disguise in what Swift was saying. He appeared on the surface to be saying
one thing, (breed Irish children for food), but in reality, he was saying
another (the exploitation of the Irish is to be condemned). This element of
camouflage, this distinction between appearance and reality, is fundamental to irony. Irony always operates on two levels and it is the

secondary, or disguised meaning, that is the important one. But the nature of the disguise will alter from example to example. Perhaps if you remember that the term 'irony' has its origins in a Greek word meaning a 'dissembler' – a person who conceals intentions or opinions under a feigned guise – then you will not be tempted to make the same error of judgement as those who made the comments on Swift's 'modest proposal'.

Of course, the irony will be lost on the readers if, like our two students, they fail to penetrate the disguise. So it should be part of the purpose of ironists to signal their ironic intentions with some clarity. They must, of course, be careful not to make the irony too obvious, or much of its impact will be dissipated. On the other hand, irony will fail if the author is in some ways like the man going to a fancy-dress party disguised, complete with parrot and wooden leg, as Long John Silver, and whose disguise is so convincing that none of his fellow-guests can recognize the man behind it, seeing only Long John. Ironists have to calculate carefully both the means by which their disguise is penetrated and the timing of this process of *éclaircissement*, or enlightenment. Much of the pleasure in going to a fancy-dress party is to be recognized finally as yourself. The pleasure for readers is analogous, for in reading irony, *part* of the satisfaction comes from detecting the irony through the camouflage and feeling that they are now 'in the know', almost as part of an exclusive club. The appreciation of irony is very challenging and some critics have even suggested that it is the most challenging aspect of practical criticism. In his book, *Glossary of Literary Terms*, which we have already recommended to you, M. H. Abrams has said that 'following the intricate manoeuvres of a great ironist . . . is an ultimate test of a student's skill in reading.'

To give you some initial practice in following these 'intricate manoeuvres', we have printed four short passages which all depend to some extent on the writer's use of irony for their effectiveness. Read each of the passages carefully to see if you can appreciate the distinction between what the writer appears to be saying and what he or she really means.

(a) [Captain Blifil] was one day engaged with Mr Allworthy in a discourse on charity: in which the captain, with great learning, proved to Mr Allworthy, that the word charity in Scripture nowhere means benefi-cence or generosity. . . . 'Those,' he said, 'came nearer to the Scripture meaning, who understood by it candour, or the forming of a benevolent   5 opinion of our brethren, and passing a favourable judgement on their actions; a virtue much higher, and more extensive in its nature, than a pitiful distribution of alms, which, though we would never so much prejudice, or even ruin our families, could never reach many; whereas charity, in the other and truer sense, might be extended to all   10 mankind.' . . . Mr Allworthy answered, 'He could not dispute with the Captain in the Greek language, and therefore could say nothing as to the true sense of the word which is translated charity; but that he had

always thought it was interpreted to consist in action, and that giving
alms constituted at least one branch of that virtue.'   15

Henry Fielding: *The History of Tom Jones* (1749)

(b) Of the three popes, John the Twenty-third was the first victim: he fled
and was brought back a prisoner: the most scandalous charges were
suppressed; the vicar of Christ was only accused of piracy, murder,
rape, sodomy and incest.

Edward Gibbon: *Decline and Fall of the Roman Empire* (1788)

(c) It was true that the appointment (to a headmistressship) was not much
to offer. The school owed its independent existence to masculine pride
rather than to educational necessity. Thirty years earlier the County
Council decided that a daily train journey to Kingsport, suitable
enough to Grammar School boys, was unsafe for girls. Girls were   5
delicate. Life imperilled them. So four grim tall apartment houses were
bought cheap on Kiplington North Cliff, . . . and there for a quarter of
a century the High School mouldered gently into unregretted
inefficiency.

Winifred Holtby: *South Riding* (1936)

(d) Tom Sponson, at fifty-three, was thoroughly successful man. He had
worked up a first-class business, married a charming wife, and built
himself a good house in the London suburbs that was neither so
modern as to be pretentious nor so conventional as to be dull. He had
good taste. His son, Bob, nineteen, was doing well at Oxford; his   5
daughter, April, aged sixteen, who was at a good school, had no wish to
use make-up, to wear low frocks, or to flirt. She still regarded herself as
too young for these trifling amusements. Yet she was gay, affectionate,
and thoroughly enjoyed life. All the same, for some time Tom had been
aware that he was working very hard for very little. His wife, Louie,   10
gave him a peck in the morning when he left for the office and, if she
were not at a party, a peck in the evening when he came home. And it
was obvious that her life was completely filled with the children, with
their clothes, with keeping her figure slim, with keeping the house clean
and smart, with her charities, her bridge, her tennis, her friends, and her   15
parties.

Joyce Cary: 'The Breakout' (from *Spring Song and Other
Stories*, 1960)

In your thinking about these passages, you will probably have
commented on:

(i) the way that Fielding criticises Captain Blifil's hypocrisy;
(ii) the way that Gibbon suggests that this pope was guilty
     more serious charges than those mentioned;
(iii) the County Councillors being shown as short-sightedly sexist and,
      perhaps, even as dull and crassly insensitive to the educational
      needs of girls;

(iv) the way the intentionally threadbare adjectives – 'thoroughly successful', 'charming', 'good' – make us question Tom Sponson's real fulfilment, and prepare us for the second half of the paragraph which begins to reveal his emotional isolation.

These points should have alerted you to an important element in irony – that more often than not, ironists make a judgement upon their subject(s) and invite their readers to share in this judgement. We are asked to make a moral judgement on Captain Blifil's views, and presumably Henry Fielding is keen for us to condemn the Captain as he himself clearly does. The use of irony is a major weapon in the satirist's armory and consequently is often found in writers who are interested in commenting on human nature.

A second element that your discussion of the ironic effects of these four passages may well have raised is that all the authors are using the humour that stems from a contradiction or an incongruity as part of their technique. For example, we are invited to smile at the beliefs of Winifred Holtby's councillors, but in smiling at them we are at the same time making a judgement on their behaviour and attitudes. We might say that, whereas comedy on its own makes us laugh, irony goes a stage further than comedy and makes us relate our laughter to judgement.

After this preliminary discussion of irony, we can now move on to an examination of some of the different ways writers use irony.

(i) *Using a speaker to put forward views which the reader can see as objectionable or foolish in some way*
This is a classic ironic manoeuvre and one with which you already have some familiarity, for it is the one that Swift uses in the extract from 'A Modest Proposal'. You will remember that Swift's disguise or persona as a rational, thoughtful speaker is intended to alert the reader to the appalling conditions in Ireland. Many ironists have used this technique, which emphasizes for the perceptive reader the ironist's real point of view. At the same time, the reader is entertained.

In this next passage, very different in tone from Swift's, the writer again hides behind a mask ('I') to put forward views which the reader is expected at least to question. What do you think is the target of his ironic manoeuvring?

Two people are discussing Shakespeare's Macbeth *having mistaken it for a detective story. They are trying to discover who really killed Duncan.*

'I've found out,' I said triumphantly, 'the name of the murderer!' 'You mean it wasn't Macduff?' she said. 'Macduff is as innocent of those murders,' I said, 'as Macbeth and the Macbeth woman.' I opened the copy of the play, which I had with me, and turned to Act II, Scene 2. 'Here,' I said, 'you will see where Lady Macbeth says, "I laid their daggers ready. He could not miss   5 'em. Had he not resembled my father as he slept, I had done it." Do you see?' 'No,' said the American woman, bluntly, 'I don't.' 'But it's simple!' I

exclaimed. 'I wonder I didn't see it years ago. The reason Duncan resembled
Lady Macbeth's father as he slept is that *it actually was her father!*' 'Good
God!' breathed my companion softly. 'Lady Macbeth's father killed the   10
King,' I said, 'and, hearing someone coming, thrust the body under the bed
and crawled into the bed himself.' 'But,' said the lady, 'you can't have a
murderer who only appears in the story once. You can't have that.' 'I know
that,' I said, and I turned to Act II, Scene 4. 'It says here, "Enter Ross with   15
an old Man." Now, that old man is never identified and it is my contention
he was old Mr Macbeth, whose ambition it was to make his daughter Queen.
There you have your motive.' 'But even then,' cried the American lady, 'He's
still a minor character!' 'Not,' I said, gleefully, ' when you realize that he was   20
also *one of the weird sisters in disguise!*' 'You mean one of the three witches?'
'Precisely,' I said.

James Thurber: 'The Macbeth Murder Mystery' (from *Vintage
Thurber*, 1963)

Clearly, to be able both to appreciate the passage and to answer our
question, you will need two things: a familiarity with *Macbeth* and some
knowledge of the conventions of the detective story. Otherwise much of
Thurber's irony will be lost and his disguise will remain impenetrable.

As a further exercise – and incidentally one which indicates the
difficulty in deciding whether a passage is or is not ironic – we ask you to
read the following passage, written at a time when great landowners were
changing the face of their estates by 'landscape gardening'. We have
added two pairs of statements after the extract and you might like to see
which of the statements you find yourself in most agreement with.

'My dear sir,' said Mr Milestone, 'accord me your permission to wave the
wand of enchantment over your grounds. The rocks shall be blown up, the
trees shall be cut down, the wilderness and all its goats shall vanish like mist.
Pagodas and Chinese bridges, gravel walks and shrubberies, bowling-
greens, canals, and clumps of larch shall rise upon its ruins. One age, sir, has   5
brought to light the treasures of ancient learning; a second has penetrated
into the depths of metaphysics; a third has brought to perfection the science
of astronomy; but it was reserved for the exclusive genius of the present
times, to invent the noble art of picturesque gardening, which has given, as it
were, a new tint to the complexion of nature, and a new outline to the   10
physiognomy of the universe.'

Thomas Love Peacock: *Headlong Hall* (1816)

(i) (a) The author approves of Mr Milestone's views on landscape
           gardening.
     (b) The author disapproves of Mr Milestone's views on landscape
           gardening.
(ii) (a) The author is pleased by Mr Milestone.
     (b) The author is displeased by Mr Milestone.

If you found it difficult to decide what attitude Peacock has towards Mr Milestone and his views – and it isn't easy – then you might find our comments on page 149 helpful.

(ii) *Using a speaker who is innocently naive*
This is a popular ironic technique which is a variant on the manoeuvre we have just been examining. In this case, the author impersonates a speaker who, because of naive simplicity or stupidity, is confidently unaware of the reality of what he or she is saying. Thus it is left to the readers, either on their own or with the aid of another character, to infer this reality. Chaucer in his 'Prologue to the Canterbury Tales' is the classic example of this, where the 'simple' narrator unwittingly reveals a character's greed or hypocrisy while, at the same time, ironically assuring us that this hypocrite is a 'good fellow' who holds 'good opinions'. Swift is a master of this technique and uses it in Book II of *Gulliver's Travels* (1726) to satirize, among other things, England's political, religious and judicial institutions. Gulliver holds a number of conversations with the King of Brobdingnag. The King, as a result of Gulliver's descriptions of conditions in England and his own subsequent questioning, comes to the conclusion that 'the bulk of your natives [are] the most pernicious race of little odious vermin that nature ever suffered to crawl upon the surface of the earth.'

Read the following passage in which Gulliver is giving some apparently bland descriptions of the English parliament. Decide what it is in Gulliver's observations that is likely to prompt the king into making the judgement we quoted above.

I then spoke at large upon the constitution of an English parliament, partly made up of an illustrious body called the House of Peers, persons of the noblest blood, and of the most ancient and ample patrimonies. I described that extraordinary care always taken of their education in arts and arms, to qualify them for being counsellors born to the king and kingdom, to have a   5
share in the legislature, to be members of the highest court of judicature from whence there could be no appeal; and to be champions always ready for the defence of their prince and country by their valour, conduct and fidelity. That these were the ornament and bulwark of the kingdom, worthy followers of their most renowned ancestors, whose honour had been the   10
reward of their virtue, from which their posterity were never once known to degenerate . . . That the other part of the parliament consisted of an assembly called the House of Commons, who were all principal gentlemen, freely picked and culled out by the people themselves, for their great abilities, and love of their country, to represent the wisdom of the whole   15
nation.

(iii) *Irony of self-betrayal*
In this next passage, Lorna Merrifield, a seventeen-year old girl who has been befriended by a doctor and his wife, is describing a visit to the home of the doctor's mother.

One day . . . they took me in the car to the country, to see Jim's mother. The baby was put in a carry-cot at the back of the car. He began to cry, and without a word of a lie, Jim said to him over his shoulder, 'Oh shut your gob, you little bastard.' I did not know what to do, and Mavis [the doctor's wife] was smoking a cigarette. Dad would not dream of saying such a thing to   5
Trevor or I.

When we arrived at Jim's mother's place, Jim said, 'It's a fourteenth-century cottage, Lorna.' I could well believe it. It was very cracked and old, and it made one wonder how Jim could let his old mother live in this tumbledown cottage, as he was so good to everyone else. So Mavis knocked   10
at the door, and the old lady came. There was not much anyone could do to the inside. Mavis said, 'Isn't it charming, Lorna?' If that was a joke, it was going too far. I said to the old Mrs Darby, 'Are you going to be rehoused?' but she did not understand this, and I explained how you have to apply to the Council, and keep at them. But it was funny that the Council had not   15
done something already, when they go round condemning. Then old Mrs Darby said, 'My dear, I shall be rehoused in the Grave.' I did not know where to look.

> Muriel Spark: 'You Should Have Seen the Mess' (from *The Go-Away Bird and Other Stories*, 1958)

(i) What impression do you form of Lorna from this extract?
(ii) Is Lorna aware of the impression she makes on people? How do you know?
(iii) What do you think is the effect of the following lines?
    (a) 'I did not know what to do, and Mavis was smoking a cigarette.' (lines 4–5)
    (b) 'I could well believe it.' (line 8)
    (c) 'If that was a joke, it was going too far.' (lines 12–13)
    (d) 'But it was funny that the Council had not done something already, when they go round condemning.' (lines 15–16)
(iv) Earlier in the story Lorna prides herself on the fact that at school she 'was always good at English'. What do you think Muriel Spark intends the *reader* to think about Lorna's prose style?

You probably came to the conclusion that Lorna was blissfully unaware that, while describing 'in her own words' her visit to the fourteenth-century cottage, she has unwittingly revealed her true self: her misjudgements, her prejudices and her social *faux-pas*. Rather than condemn her for her errors, Muriel Spark, we feel sure, wants us to smile at Lorna: her irony is gentle, not biting as Swift's can be. But it is irony nonetheless and the passage does illustrate the very frequently used ironic device of having a character inadvertently betray himself or herself. In this case the author impersonates a character, speaking in her voice. Usually, the speakers so used are self-confident and unaware that they have revealed their true self, thus giving the perceptive reader an opportunity to penetrate the 'appearance' and appreciate the 'reality'.

So far in this discussion we have used the word 'speak', but of course a character does not only reveal himself through speech and so an author can achieve a similar betrayal through impersonating a character's thoughts (which can be either directly or indirectly reported) or writings. For instance, in this next extract, Mr Collins, a clergyman, proposes marriage to Elizabeth Bennett by letter.

What does the letter reveal about Mr Collins's character and interests?

My reasons for marrying are, first, that I think it a right thing for every clergyman in easy circumstances (like myself) to set the example of matrimony in his parish. Secondly, that I am convinced it will add very greatly to my happiness; and thirdly – which perhaps I ought to have mentioned earlier, that it is the particular advice and recommendation of the   5
very noble lady whom I have the honour of calling patroness.

. . . Allow me, by the way, to observe, my fair cousin, that I do not reckon the notice and kindness of Lady Catherine de Bourgh as among the least of the advantages in my power to offer. You will find her manners beyond anything I can describe; and your wit and vivacity I think must be acceptable   10
to her, especially when tempered with the silence and respect which her rank will inevitably excite. Thus much for my general intention in favour of matrimony; it remains to be told why my views were directed to Longbourn instead of my own neighbourhood, where I assure you there are many amiable young women. But the fact is, that being, as I am, to inherit this   15
estate after the death of your honoured father, (who, however, may live many years longer,) I could not satisfy myself without resolving to chose a wife from among his daughters, that the loss to them might be as little as possible, when the melancholy event takes place – which, however, as I have already said, may not be for several years. This has been my motive, my fair   20
cousin, and I flatter myself it will not sink me in your esteem. And now nothing remains for me but to assure you in the most animated language of the violence of my affection. To fortune I am perfectly indifferent, and shall make no demand of that nature on your father, since I am well aware that it could not be complied with; and that one thousand pounds in the 4 per cents,   25
which will not be yours till after your mother's decease, is all that you may ever be entitled to. On that head, therefore, I shall be uniformly silent; and you may assure yourself that no ungenerous reproach shall ever pass my lips when we are married.

Jane Austen: *Pride and Prejudice* (1813)

Before we conclude this section, it would be as well to sound two cautionary notes:

(i) that this ironic betrayal can sometimes work to the advantage of a character, for occasionally it will reveal the character to be better than he or she thinks, and perhaps the reader will smile at this unawareness. Huck Finn in Mark Twain's novel is a good example of this, for Huck's self-disparagement is often not at all justified;

(ii) however villainous, hypocritical or stupid a character might be, the fact that he or she is presented to us 'from the inside' means that the author has had to engage in some imaginative sympathy with

the speaker's point of view – and so, consequently, has the reader, 'there but for the grace of God go I.'
who may then be forced into a position of critical self-awareness –
'there but for the grace of God go I.'

Or do you think that some of the examples of irony you have come across so far simply encourage the reader to adopt a condescending and superior judgemental attitude?

IRONY DETECTION
We have already said that the ironist can be a slippery customer to deal with. Detecting irony is sometimes like our response to that kind of cryptic conversationalist who is given to making asides, the level of seriousness of which leaves us guessing. Is the comment made in all innocence? Or is there an edge of criticism suggested?

We have pointed to the *context* as being one crucial determining factor in our detection of irony. If you were to walk into a church and see a golden plaque which, commemorating many years of service by some Sunday School Superintendent, said 'She hath done all she could', you would read it as an unquestioned tribute. However, exactly the same words in a different context – in the mouth of a detractor, if our superintendent happened to be a character in a novel – could be aimed with withering irony.

The most reputable critics can disagree in their response to irony – or even in their judgement as to whether it is present in a passage. In the examples we have used so far from Swift (see pages 140 and 146), there would probably be little disagreement about the general use to which irony is put. However, in connection with Book IV of Swift's *Gulliver's Travels*, critics have presented diametrically opposed reactions. These are largely dependent on the way they judge Gulliver's credentials as a narrator at this point and the extent to which strongly critical irony is directed at Swift's persona.

We have already warned that irony can cut two or more ways, for while it may carry criticism, it can at the same time go hand in hand with a considerable strength of authorial self-identification. When, for example, you read the passage by Peacock (see page 145), you may have found it difficult to pin down a definite 'for' or 'against' judgement on Mr Milestone. Pompous, conceited and garrulous he may be; but he is not without the wit and amusing inventiveness of the lovable fool – though the reader, of course, will laugh at Mr Milestone for reasons which the character himself could not appreciate! A sense of *joie d'esprit* comes through this characterization, suggesting that while Peacock has seen through Mr Milestone – and wishes his reader to do the same – he nevertheless is half in love with this character, into whom he breathes the breath of life.

We have made frequent reference to Swift in this chapter. Defoe is another eighteenth century writer whose alleged irony has provoked strong critical disagreement. Some readers of Defoe feel that he submerges himself so fully in his first person narratives, and identifies so completely with the persona he creates, that ironies which may emerge for the sophisticated reader were simply not intended. Others feel that Defoe is a much more self-aware literary artist capable of concocting the most delicious ironies.

As an exercise in the detection of irony, we would like you to read carefully the two following passages by Defoe. Decide where the *possible* irony occurs in each, and then state whether you feel it is intended. Incidentally, do you think you are more or less likely to be led into detecting ironies in these passages by their isolation from the wider context of the novels?

Robinson Crusoe has been shipwrecked on a deserted island.

I had now been thirteen days on shore, and had been eleven times on board the ship; in which time I had brought away all that one pair of hands could well be suppos'd capable to bring, tho' I believe verily, had the calm weather held, I should have brought away the whole ship piece by piece. But preparing the 12th time to go on board, I found the wind begin to rise;　5 however, at low water I went on board, and tho' I thought I had rumag'd the cabbin so effectually, as that nothing more could be found, yet I discover'd a locker with drawers in it, in one of which I found two or three razors, and one pair of large sizzers, with some ten or a dozen of good knives and forks; in another I found about thirty six pounds' value in money, some European　10 coin, some Brasil, some pieces of eight, some gold, some silver.

I smil'd to my self at the sight of this money. "O drug!" said I aloud, "what are thou good for? Thou art not worth to me, no, not the taking off of the ground; one of those knives is worth all this heap; I have no manner of use for thee, e'en remain where thou art, and go to the bottom as a creature　15 whose life is not worth saving." However, upon second thoughts, I took it away, and wrapping all this in a piece of canvas, I began to think of making another raft, but while I was preparing this, I found the sky overcast, and the wind began to rise, and in a quarter of an hour it blew a fresh gale from the shore; it presently occur'd to me that it was in vain to pretend to make a raft　20 with the wind off shore, and that it was my business to be gone before the tide of flood began, otherwise I might not be able to reach the shore at all. Accordingly I let my self down into the water, and swam across the channel which lay between the ship and the sands, and even that with difficulty enough, partly with the weight of the things I had about me, and partly the　25 roughness of the water, for the wind rose very hastily, and before it was quite high water it blew a storm.

But I was gotten home to my little tent, where I lay with all my wealth about me very secure. It blew very hard all that night, and in the morning when I look'd out, behold, no more ship was to be seen; I was a little　30 surpriz'd, but recover'd my self with this satisfactory reflection, viz. that I had lost no time, nor abated no diligence to get every thing out of her that could be useful to me, and that indeed there was little left in her that I was able to bring away if I had had more time.

Robinson Crusoe (1719)

Moll Flanders finds herself living in straitened circumstances in London.

I went out now by daylight, and wandered about I knew not whither, and in search of I knew not what, when the devil put a snare in my way of a dreadful nature indeed, and such a one as I have never had before or since. Going through Aldersgate Street, there was a pretty little child had been at a dancing-school, and was agoing home all alone; and my prompter, like a   5
true devil, set me upon this innocent creature. I talked to it, and it prattled to me again, and I took it by the hand and led it along till I came to a paved alley that goes into Bartholomew Close, and I led it in there. The child said, that was not its way home. I said, 'Yes, my dear, it is; I'll show you the way home'. The child had a little necklace on of gold beads, and I had my eye   10
upon that, and in the dark of the alley I stooped, pretending to mend the child's clog that was loose, and took off her necklace, and the child never felt it, and so led the child on again. Here, I say, the devil put me upon killing the child in the dark alley, that it might not cry, but the very thought frightened me so that I was ready to drop down; but I turned the child about and bade it   15
go back again, for that was not its way home; the child said, so she would; and I went through into Bartholomew Close, and then turned round to another passage that goes into Long Lane, so away into Charterhouse Yard and out into St John's Street; then crossing into Smithfield, went down Chick Lane, and into Field Lane, to Holborn Bridge, when, mixing with the   20
crowd of people usually passing there, it was not possible to have been found out; and thus I made my second sally into the world.

The thoughts of this booty put out all the thoughts of the first, and the reflections I had made wore quickly off; poverty hardened my heart, and my own necessities made me regardless of anything. The last affair left no great   25
concern upon me, for as I did the poor child no harm, I only thought I had given the parents a just reproof for their negligence, in leaving the poor lamb to come home by itself, and it would teach them to take more care another time.

This string of beads was worth about £12 or £14. I suppose it might have   30
been formerly the mother's, for it was too big for the child's wear, but that, perhaps, the vanity of the mother to have her child look fine at the dancing-school, had made her let the child wear it; and no doubt the child had a maid sent to take care of it, but she, like a careless jade, was taken up perhaps with some fellow that had met her, and so the poor baby wandered till it fell into   35
my hands.

However, I did the child no harm; I did not so much as fright it, for I had a great many tender thoughts about me yet, and did nothing but what, as I may say, mere necessity drove me to.

Moll Flanders (1722)

THE IRONIC STANCE

In all the examples of ironic manoeuvres that we have so far looked at, the author, in some way or other, has been impersonating a character. What we shall now consider is the irony in which the author does not use a persona, but either makes ironic comments which set the tone for the passage or writes the whole work in a detached ironic mode. The element of detachment or seeming impersonality is characteristic of this type of irony. In this case, the ironists seem to withdraw and to write in a modest, unassuming way. They will often seem matter-of-fact and are prone to understate, with the result that a reader can experience some difficulty in deciding whether the writer is being ironic or not. Readers must always be on the alert for any signals from the author to help them decide. These may include not only the context itself but also such stylistic devices as innuendo, exaggeration, ambiguity and contrast and contradiction.

To give you an idea of the various ways in which this kind of irony operates, we have printed three very different passages, the first of which is also quoted in A. E. Dyson's very useful book on irony, *The Crazy Fabric*. They are followed by some notes which, we hope, will show you how the ironic effect is achieved.

Gibbon is writing of the Jews
This inflexible perseverance which appeared so odious or so ridiculous to the ancient world, assumes a more awful character, since Providence has deigned to reveal to us the mysterious history of the chosen people. But the devout and even scrupulous attachment to the Mosaic religion, so conspicuous among the Jews who lived under the second temple, becomes   5
still more surprizing if it is compared with the stubborn incredulity of their forefathers. When the law was given in thunder from Mount Sinai; when the tides of the ocean and the course of the planets were suspended for the convenience of the Israelites; and when temporal rewards and punishments were the immediate consequences of their piety or disobedience; they   10
perpetually relapsed into rebellion against the visible majesty of their Divine King, placed the idols of the nations in the sanctuary of Jehovah, and imitated every fantastic ceremony that was practised in the tents of the Arabs, or in the cities of Phoenicia. As the protection of Heaven was deservedly withdrawn from the ungrateful race, their faith acquired a   15
proportionable degree of vigour and purity. The contemporaries of Moses and Joshua had beheld with careless indifference the most amazing miracles. Under the pressure of every calamity, the belief of those miracles has preserved the Jews of a later period from the universal contagion of idolatry; and, in contradiction to every known principle of the human mind, that   20
singular people seems to have yielded a stronger and more ready assent to the traditions of their remote ancestors than to the evidence of their own senses.

Edward Gibbon: *Decline and Fall of the Roman Empire* (1788)

Mankind, says a Chinese manuscript, which my friend M. was obliging enough to read and explain to me, for the first seventy thousand ages ate their meat raw, clawing or biting it from the living animal, just as they do in Abyssinia to this day. This period is not obscurely hinted at by their great Confucius in the second chapter of his Mundane Mutations, where he   5
designates a kind of golden age by the term Cho-fang, literally the Cook's holiday. The manuscript goes on to say, that the art of roasting, or rather broiling (which I take to be the elder brother) was accidentally discovered in

the manner following. The swine-herd, Ho-ti, having gone out into the woods one morning, as his manner was, to collect mast for his hogs, left his 10 cottage in the care of his eldest son Bo-bo, a great lubberly boy, who being fond of playing with fire, as younkers of his age commonly are, let some sparks escape into a bundle of straw, which kindling quickly, spread the conflagration over every part of their poor mansion till it was reduced to ashes. Together with the cottage (a sorry antediluvian make-shift of a 15 building, you may think it), what was of much more importance, a fine litter of new-farrowed pigs, no less than nine in number, perished.

Charles Lamb: 'A Dissertation upon Roast Pig' (from *Essays of Elia*, 1823)

Now it is the autumn again; the people are all coming back. The recess of summer is over, when holidays are taken, newspapers shrink, history itself seems momentarily to falter and stop. But the papers are thickening and filling again; things seem to be happening; back from Corfu and Sete, Positano and Leningrad, the people are parking their cars and campers in 5 their drives, and opening their diaries, and calling up other people on the telephone. The deckchairs on the beach have been put away, and a weak sun shines on the promenade; there is fresh fighting in Vietnam, while McGovern campaigns ineffectually against Nixon. In the chemists' shops in town, they have removed the sunglasses and the insect-bite lotions, for the 10 summer visitors have left, and have stocked up on sleeping tablets and Librium, the staples of the year-round trade; there is direct rule in Ulster, and a gun-battle has taken place in the Falls Road. The new autumn colours are in the boutiques; there is now on the market a fresh inter-uterine device, reckoned to be ninety-nine per cent safe. Everywhere there are new 15 developments, new indignities; the intelligent people survey the autumn world, and liberal and radical hackles rise, and fresh faces are about, and the sun shines fitfully, and the telephones ring.

Malcolm Bradbury: *The History Man* (1975)

1. Gibbon: Major events like the crossing of the Red Sea understated, described in a deflating and condescending manner as if they were everyday occurrences – 'the convenience of the Israelites', 'deigned to reveal'; use of phrases like 'still more surprizing', 'visible majesty', 'amazing miracles', which seem *at face value* to acknowledge God's power, actually lead to suspicions that the Biblical stories may not be true; Gibbon pretends not to notice the Jews' illogicality or ingratitude, though his account makes it clear to the reader. Doubts about God suggested – why choose such a foolish ('singular') people who, it is suggested, are irrational ('in contradiction to every known principle of the human mind')? Apparent defence of the subject is, in fact, an ironic undermining of it. With friends like Gibbon, who needs enemies!
2. Lamb: Mock-serious and mock-scholarly treatment of mundane subject; comically excessive and portentous language ('dissertation', 'not obscurely hinted at', 'conflagration', 'antediluvian') mixed with the colloquial ('great lubberly boy', 'bundle of straw', 'make-shift'); citing of

spurious authorities ('a Chinese manuscript', 'the second chapter of his Mundane Mutations'); ludicrous detail ('ate their meat raw, clawing or biting it from the living animal'); author seeming to take pains to get his facts right ('Cho-fang, literally the Cook's holiday', 'the art of roasting, or rather broiling (which I take to be the elder brother)'.

3. Bradbury: Irony of juxtaposition: the trivial ('a weak sun shines on the promenade', 'the Chemists . . . have stocked up on sleeping tablets and Librium') placed, as a contrast, next to the serious ('there is fresh fighting in Vietnam', 'there is direct rule in Ulster') reducing everything, seemingly, to the same level. Rhythm and movement of sentences is weighty and dignified, ironically contrasting with the level of importance of subject-matter. Suggestion that events are manufactured to a pre-ordained pattern ('Now it is autumn again . . . the papers are thickening and filling again', 'everywhere there are new developments, new in-dignities'), carrying with it a hint that perhaps 'liberal and radical' consciences operate on the same automatic circuit.

DRAMATIC IRONY: IRONY OF SITUATION

So far in this chapter we have been discussing verbal irony – ironic manoeuvres in which an author can impersonate a character's words and thoughts or take an ironic stance towards what is being described. But there is another type of irony to which our reaction will be to acknowledge not, as in the case of verbal irony, that the writer is being ironical, but that the situation being described is in itself ironical. For example, we would probably be tempted to exclaim 'Isn't that ironic?' if a trenchant campaigner against pornography were to be found watching and enjoying a particularly lurid sex-film, or if a chief constable were to be stopped for speeding by one of his own officers. In both of these examples, it is the situation itself that is ironic and writers will often exploit the potentialities offered: in our examples, perhaps to expose hypocrisy in the one and perhaps to emphasize equality before the law in the other.

We can say that a situation is potentially ironic when a character is unaware of the incongruity inherent in it and the reader or audience is allowed by the writer to perceive this incongruity while 'the victim' is not allowed to. In addition, the 'victim' of an ironic situation somehow has to 'deserve' his or her 'fate' because the writer usually has a moral purpose in devising such a situation, as in our two examples of the pornographer and the policeman. Thus it is ironic that the sexually lax Mollie Seagrim in Fielding's *Tom Jones* should be swearing to Jones that 'I can never love any other man as long as I live' while hiding another lover in her room – and is confidently unaware that he is soon to be discovered. It is ironic that the hideous old woman sitting at the foot of the guillotine in Dickens's *A Tale of Two Cities* should complain at the absence of the most influential of their number, ignorant of the fact that she has already, and deservedly, been murdered. In many ironic situations, the irony is that those involved often speak with more truth than they realize, or speak truths that no one expects from their lips.

Another related form of dramatic irony often used to great effect is that in which a character embarks on a course of action that in fact will lead to the least expected end. The irony is made that much sharper if the reader, or even another character, is aware of facts which the character does not know. The theatre furnishes us with many examples of this. King Duncan in *Macbeth* visits Macbeth's castle expecting to be treated as an honoured guest, whereas the audience knows that it is his host's intention to murder him. Lear expects harmony and peace from his division of his kingdom between his daughters, but he only precipitates disaster. This situational irony is, of course, not solely confined to the theatre: it is also to be found in prose literature. For instance, the reader is aware of the machinations of the beautiful yet small-minded Rosamund Vincy to marry Dr Lydgate in George Eliot's *Middlemarch*, while at the same time knowing of Lydgate's determination to remain a bachelor so as to further his medical research. The irony is compounded by the fact that Lydgate often seeks Rosamund's company, thinking he is merely visiting her and her family out of politeness, but the result is that he becomes trapped in a loveless marriage. As a further illustration of this type of irony, we suggest you consider the following passage.

Angela Moping is convinced that Mr Loveday, who has been committed to a lunatic asylum after he knocked a young woman from her bicycle and then strangled her, is now perfectly sane. She campaigns strongly for Mr Loveday's release.

From that day onwards for many weeks Angela had a new purpose in life. She moved about the ordinary routine of her home with an abstracted air and an unfamiliar, reserved courtesy which greatly disconcerted Lady Moping.

'I believe the child's in love. I only pray that it isn't that uncouth   5
Egbertson boy.'

She read a great deal in the library, she cross-examined any guests who had pretensions to legal or medical knowledge, she showed extreme goodwill to old Sir Roderick Lane-Foscote, their Member. The names 'alienist', 'barrister' or 'government official' now had for her the glamour   10
that formerly surrounded film actors and professional wrestlers. She was a woman with a cause, and before the end of the hunting season she had triumphed. Mr Loveday achieved his liberty.

The doctor at the asylum showed reluctance but no real opposition. Sir Roderick wrote to the Home Office. The necessary papers were signed, and   15
at last the day came when Mr Loveday took leave of the home where he had spent such long and useful years.

His departure was marked by some ceremony. Angela and Sir Roderick Lane-Foscote sat with the doctors on the stage of the gymnasium. Below them were assembled everyone in the institution who was thought to be   20
stable enough to endure the excitement.

Lord Moping, with a few suitable expressions of regret, presented Mr Loveday on behalf of the wealthier lunatics with a gold cigarette case; those who supposed themselves to be emperors showered him with decorations and titles of honour. The warders gave him a silver watch and   25 many of the non-paying inmates were in tears on the day of the presentation.

The doctor made the main speech of the afternoon. 'Remember,' he remarked, 'that you leave behind you nothing but our warmest good wishes. You are bound to us by ties that none will forget. Time will only deepen our sense of debt to you. If at any time in the future you should grow tired of   30 your life in the world, there will always be a welcome for you here. Your post will be open.'

A dozen or so variously afflicted lunatics hopped and skipped after him down the drive until the iron gates opened and Mr Loveday stepped into his freedom. His small trunk had already gone to the station; he elected to walk.   35 He had been reticent about his plans, but he was well provided with money, and the general impression was that he would go to London and enjoy himself a little before visiting his step-sister in Plymouth.

It was to the surprise of all that he returned within two hours of his liberation. He was smiling whimsically, a gentle, self-regarding smile of   40 reminiscence.

'I have come back,' he informed the doctor. 'I think that now I shall be here for good.'

'But, Loveday, what a short holiday. I'm afraid that you have hardly enjoyed yourself at all.'   45

'Oh yes, sir, thank you, sir, I've enjoyed myself *very much*. I'd been promising myself one little treat, all these years. It was short, sir, but *most* enjoyable. Now I shall be able to settle down again to my work here without any regrets.'

Half a mile up the road from the asylum gates, they later discovered an   50 abandoned bicycle. It was a lady's machine of some antiquity. Quite near it in the ditch lay the strangled body of a young woman, who, riding home to her tea, had chanced to overtake Mr Loveday, as he strode along, musing on his opportunities.

Evelyn Waugh: 'Mr Loveday's Little Outing' (1936)

(i) Comment on the effect of the final sentence.
(ii) What elements in the passage ironically foreshadow the final outcome? When you read the passage through a second time, do any further ironies emerge?
(iii) What judgement does Waugh suggest concerning Angela Moping's conduct?
(iv) Give your opinion on this reaction to the ending of the story: 'If this is irony, it's of a very sick nature. How can an author be so callous as to attempt to extract humour from such subjects as mental illness and senseless murder?'

There are, perhaps, some further types of irony of situation that we should consider before we leave the question; they are part of what we might call a 'general' irony of situation – for some writers consider that the whole of human life is ironic, in that human beings are unaware of, or prefer not to think about, the incongruities that are inherent in our situation. For instance, we like to think that we have more control over our own fates than perhaps we really have, especially since our individual genetic, social and psychological make-up may restrict us much more than we care to admit. Some writers see the whole of human life as incongruous and ironic when compared to the one certain fact in our lives, our death, and they consider that our struggles against this fact are inherently comic and absurd. Some see us struggling against an inescapable course of cause and effect, without our always perceiving the links. In other words, for some writers, people have either become a plaything for the gods or a source of amusement as they watch their struggles in life from on high. Only God (or the gods) can perceive the ultimate reality, whereas people are always unaware of the whole of their situation.

This general irony is, of course, a very large subject. Because it is embodied in the whole fabric of a novel – its plot, characterization, settings and thematic structure – it is one which we do not have space to develop here. However, we should add that for some writers, irony may be a method of *withholding* their judgement: they do not seek to expose the discrepancy between appearance and reality in order to enforce a definite moral viewpoint; rather they hope to unfold both the complexity and the relativity of all human perceptions, in the face of which any absolute judgement is felt to be impossible.

A NOTE ON SARCASM

One of the commonest mistakes students make is to confuse irony with sarcasm, and from the way these terms are sometimes used, it would appear that to many they are interchangeable – 'he's being sarcastic' being every bit as serviceable as 'he's being ironic'. Though some people consider that sarcasm is only a crude form of irony, we would argue that there is a difference between the two. An element common to all sarcasm is the desire to hurt or wound. In the passage that follows, the sarcastic schoolmaster, Mr Wellings 'ruled entirely by the lash of his tongue' and the image of the whip or lash does illustrate clearly this particular aspect of sarcasm, an aspect that is not present in all irony.

You will also have seen from the work that you have been doing that irony is capable of great subtlety and that readers must always be at their sharpest to perceive and gauge its effects. There is no such problem with sarcasm. Since there is never any doubt as to its intended effect (for the meaning is clearly revealed), no one is likely to be left puzzled by or unaware of it. In the passage we have chosen to illustrate sarcasm, no one in the class, especially the unfortunate Corbett, will be left wondering what Mr Wellings's true opinion and intention is. Wellings is the mathematics master in Ian Hay's *The Lighter Side of School Life* (1914). He addresses a newcomer to his class.

'Let me see,' Wellings would drawl, 'I am afraid I can't recall your name for the moment. Have you a visiting card about you?'

Here the initiated would chuckle with anticipatory relish, and the offender, a little taken aback, would either glare defiantly or efface himself behind his book.   5

'I am addressing you, sir – you in the back bench, with the intelligent countenance and the black-edged finger-nails,' Wellings would continue in silky tones. 'I asked you a question just now. Have you a visiting card about you?'

A thousand brilliant repartees would flash through the brain of the   10
obstreperous one. But somehow, in Wellings' mild and apologetic presence, they all seemed either irrelevant or fatuous. He usually ended by growling, 'No.'

'Then what is your name – or possibly title? Forgive me for not knowing.'

'Corbett.' It is extraordinary how ridiculous one's surname always sounds 15
when one is compelled to announce it in public.

'Thank you. Will you kindly stand up, Mr Corbett, in order that we may study you in greater detail? I must apologise for not having heard of you before. Indeed, it is surprising that one of your remarkable appearance should hitherto have escaped my notice in my walks abroad. The world   20
knows nothing of its greatest men: how true that is. However, this is no time for moralizing. What I wanted to bring to your distinguished notice is this – that you must not behave like a yahoo in my mathematical set. During the past ten minutes you have kicked one of your neighbours and cuffed another; you have partaken of a good deal of unwholesome and (as it came   25
out of your pocket) probably unclean refreshment; and you have indulged in several childish and obscene gestures. These daredevil exploits took place while I was writing on the blackboard; but I think it only fair to mention to you that I have eyes in the back of my head – a fact upon which any member of this set could have enlightened you. But possibly they do not presume to   30
address a person of your eminence. I have no idea, of course, with what class of society you are accustomed to mingle; but here – *here* – that sort of thing is simply not done, really! I am so sorry! But the hour will soon be over, and then you can have a nice game of shove-halfpenny, or whatever your favourite sport is, in the gutter. But at present I must ask you to curb your   35
natural instincts. That is all thank you very much. You may sit down now.'

Perhaps you would like to write a companion piece of sarcasm to this in which an older Corbett gets his revenge on Mr Wellings!

7

Tone

It is perhaps helpful when discussing the tone of a particular piece of writing to think of it, not as something written, but as something spoken. This is not to minimize the often marked difference between spoken and written language; but if you imagine writers as speaking aloud to you, it is usually easier to gauge their tone and attitude towards you, the reader. To pursue this a little further, most of us find it fairly easy to differentiate between people's tones of voice when they are addressing us, because we usually accurately receive and interpret the signals that speakers transmit. 'There's no milk in the fridge' could be the remark of someone extremely angry at this lack, or the remark of someone who is resigned to what may be an habitual state of affairs, or simply a plain statement of fact. 'Sit down' could be spoken pleadingly, commandingly, politely, gently (in fact, you could quite easily add an almost endless list yourself) and most of us are able to recognize the particular tone being used by the speaker – and we react accordingly.

A speaker can guide our response in a variety of ways: the speed at which he or she speaks; the emphasis placed on certain words; the volume of the speech; the gestures and facial expressions that accompany the words. It is our social training and experience that enable us to give the intended response. If we do misinterpret the speaker's tone, we may possibly find ourselves in an awkward situation, for instance, laughing at something meant to be taken seriously.

Tone, then, is the speaker's attitude towards and relationship with the audience. Similarly with the written word. All writers assume an attitude towards their audience and subject matter and readers must learn to recognize the signals that transmit the author's intention. Whereas in speech we have to recognize and respond to such things as pitch and stress, in written English we must be on the lookout for different signals – and it is a sensitivity to and awareness of these signals that should be the aim of every critical reader. The signals that we should try to respond to are, in fact, all the areas we have so far covered in this book: for diction, imagery, grammatical structure, rhythm and point-of-view all play a part in determining the overall tone. In trying to establish the tone of a particular passage, you will probably find yourself considering these elements, but it has to be said that this is not always an easy task, for even experienced readers of literature may find it difficult at times to pin down an author's tone precisely. You will have seen some of this difficulty already in the section on irony, where it was clear that experienced as well as inexperienced readers can easily fail to detect the ironic intentions of a writer. Yet being ironical is only one of innumerable tones that a writer can use.

Irony, is a rather special case, because writers who are ironical in tone are being deliberately deceptive. When reading non-ironic writers, you are not expected to penetrate a disguise, but rather should try to respond to the tone used, to try to find exact words to describe it and to be aware of any shifts in tone that may take place within the passage. It can be helpful in pinning down a writer's tone if you imagine him or her reading the passage aloud, as if performing it for you. You will remember that in our opening chapter we suggested oral reading as a very good way into a passage, because in preparing such a reading, you have to think closely about the tone of voice you will adopt.

Two very brief words of warning before we look at some examples: (i) tone is not something that exists on its own, as a separable entity in a passage: it is the product of a writer's diction, imagery, syntax, rhythm and point of view; (ii) there are innumerable possible tones a writer may adopt and the few illustrations we give are by no means exhaustive.

At the end of our first two examples, we have suggested some ways in which the tone might be described. See if you agree with us.

Henry Fielding is bidding farewell to his readers at the end of his very long novel, Tom Jones (1749).

> We are now, reader arrived at the last stage of our long journey. As we have, therefore, travelled together through so many pages, let us behave to one another like fellow-travellers in a stage-coach, who have passed several days in the company of each other; and who, not withstanding any bickerings or little animosities which may have occurred on the road, generally make all   5
> up at last, and mount, for the last time, into their vehicle with cheerfulness and good humour; since after this one stage, it may possibly happen to us, as it commonly happens to them, never to meet more . . . And now, my friend, I take this opportunity (as I shall have no other) of heartily wishing thee well. If I have been an entertaining companion to thee, I promise thee it is   10
> what I have desired.

> (Book XVIII, chap. 1)

(Warm, open, generous, frank, good-hearted, relaxed, expansive)

The following is one of the most famous of all political speeches:

> Fourscore and seven years ago our fathers brought forth upon this continent a new nation, conceived in liberty, and dedicated to the proposition that all men are created equal. Now we are engaged in a great Civil War, testing whether that nation or any nation so conceived and dedicated can long endure. We are met on a great battlefield of war.   5
> We have come to dedicate a portion of that field as a final resting place of those who gave their lives that the nation might live. It is altogether fitting

that we should do this. But in a larger sense we cannot dedicate, we cannot consecrate, we cannot hallow this ground. The brave men, living and dead, who struggled here, have consecrated it far above our power to add or   10
detract. The world will little note, nor long remember what we say here, but it can never forget what they did here. It is for us, the living, rather to be dedicated here to the unfinished work they have thus so far so nobly advanced. It is rather for us to be here dedicated to the great task remaining before us, that from these honoured dead we take increased devotion to that   15
cause for which they gave the last full measure of devotion; that we here highly resolve that the dead shall not have died in vain, that the nation shall, under God, have a new birth of freedom, and that the government of the people, by the people, and for the people, shall not perish from the earth.

Abraham Lincoln: 'The Gettysburg Address' (1863)

(dignified, solemn, stately, measured, formal, rhetorical, emotional)

Now try your hand at assessing the tone of the following two extracts. We would add one word of advice. We described the previous two extracts in terms which should already be a part of your critical vocabulary. However, to give any full and significant analysis of tone – or, indeed, to discuss any aspect of a writer's style – it is vital to *quote* from the passage in question. This will add a concrete and illustrative quality to the descriptive labels you use. We hope you will adopt this approach.

The bouncer lay sprawled on [the] floor unconscious, with a knife in his hand. I leaned down and pulled the knife loose and threw it down a back stairway. The bouncer breathed stertorously and his hand was limp.
I stepped over him and opened a door marked "Office" in flaked black paint. There was a small scarred desk close to a partly boarded-up window.   5
The torso of a man was bolt upright in the chair. The chair had a high back which just reached to the nape of the man's neck. His head was folded back over the high back of the chair so that his nose pointed at the boarded-up window. Just folded, like a handkerchief or a hinge.

Raymond Chandler: *Farewell, My Lovely* (1940)

My dear wife Carrie and I have just been a week in our new house, 'The Laurels', Brickfield Terrace, Holloway – a nice, six-roomed residence, not counting basement, with a front breakfast-parlour. We have a little front garden, and there is a flight of ten steps up to the front door, which, by-the-by, we keep locked with the chain up. Cummings, Gowing, and our other   15
intimate friends always come to the little side entrance, which saves the servant the trouble of going up to the front door, thereby taking her from her work. We have a nice little back garden which runs down to the railway. We were rather afraid of the noise of the trains at first, but the landlord said we should not notice them after a bit, and took £2 off the rent. He was   20
certainly right; and beyond the cracking of the garden wall at the bottom, we have suffered no inconvenience.
After my work in the City, I like to be at home. What's the good of a

home, if you are never in it? 'Home, Sweet Home', that's my motto. I am
always in of an evening. Our old friend Gowing may drop in without   25
ceremony; so may Cummings, who lives opposite. My dear wife Caroline
and I are pleased to see them, if they like to drop in on us . . . In the evening,
Cummings unexpectedly dropped in to show me a meerschaum pipe he had
won in a raffle in the City, and told me to handle it carefully, as it would spoil
the colouring if the hand was moist. He said he wouldn't stay, as he didn't   30
care much for the smell of the paint, and fell over the scraper as he went out.
Must get the scraper removed, or else I shall get into a *scrape*. I don't often
make jokes.

George and Weedon Grossmith: *The Diary of a Nobody* (1892)

We have already suggested that tone is the signalling of the writer's
attitude to his or her subject matter – and to the reader. Readers
sometimes go astray when, instead of establishing and responding to the
actual tone of a piece of prose, they assume that the writer's attitude must
be the one which they themselves would adopt to the same material. In
fact, it is helpful to adopt the starting-point that no subject is, for
instance, intrinsically comic or tragic, light-hearted or serious. It is all a
matter of the author's treatment. If an author is addressing the topic, say,
of death or of a lover's infidelity, the reader may anticipate a certain
attitude on the author's part, but should never take this for granted. For
instance, this next passage concerns the pain of violent toothache, which
forces the sufferer to take a carelessly administered dose of a potentially
fatal drug. Yet the writer's treatment of this material, his tone, allows us
to laugh at the whole incident. We would like you to define how the
author creates the characteristic tone of this passage.

*Mr Povey has asked the two girls, Constance and Sophia, if there is any
laudanum in their house to relieve his toothache. Laudanum, a tincture of
opium, is a dangerous drug which was nevertheless widely used, until fairly
recent times, as a pain-killer.*

With youthful cries and alarms they succeeded in pouring four mortal dark
drops (one more than Constance intended) into a cup containing a little
water. And as they handed the cup to Mr Povey their faces were the faces of
affrighted comical conspirators. They felt so old and they looked so young.
Mr Povey imbibed eagerly of the potion, put the cup on the mantelpiece,   5
and then tilted his head to the right so as to submerge the affected tooth. In
this posture he remained awaiting the sweet influence of the remedy. The
girls, out of a nice modesty, turned away, for Mr Povey must not swallow
the medicine, and they preferred to leave him unhampered in the solution of
a delicate problem. When next they examined him, he was leaning back in   10
the rocking-chair with his mouth open and his eyes shut.
'Has it done you any good, Mr Povey?'
'I think I'll lie down on the sofa for a minute,' was Mr Povey's strange
reply; and forthwith he sprang up and flung himself on to the horsehair sofa
between the fireplace and the window, where he lay stripped of all his   15
dignity, a mere beaten animal in a grey suit with peculiar coat-tails, and a

very creased waistcoat, and a lapel that was planted with pins, and a paper
collar and close-fitting paper cuffs.

Constance ran after him with the antimacassar, which she spread softly
on his shoulders; and Sophia put another one over his thin little legs, all   20
drawn up.

They then gazed at their handiwork, with secret self-accusations and the
most dreadful misgivings.

'He surely never swallowed it!' Constance whispered.

'He's asleep, anyhow,' said Sophia, more loudly.   25

Mr Povey was certainly asleep, and his mouth was very wide open – like a
shop door. The only question was whether his sleep was not an eternal sleep;
the only question was whether he was not out of his pain for ever.

Then he snored – horribly; his snore seemed a portent of disaster.

Sophia approached him as though he were a bomb, and stared, growing   30
bolder, into his mouth.

'Oh, Con,' she summoned her sister, 'do come and look! It's too droll!'

In an instant all their four eyes were exploring the singular landscape of
Mr Povey's mouth. In a corner, to the right of that interior, was one sizeable
fragment of a tooth, that was attached to Mr Povey by the slenderest tie, so   35
that each respiration of Mr Povey, when his body slightly heaved and the
gale moaned in the cavern, this tooth moved separately, showing that its
long connection with Mr Povey was drawing to a close.

Arnold Bennett: The Old Wives' Tale (1908)

If you feel you would like some extra practice in assessing the tone of a
passage, we suggest that you look back at some of the extracts we have
already used in the book. Particularly useful ones to consider are the
following:

Mark Twain on page 41   Dr Johnson on Page 103
Churchill on page 106   H. L. Mencken on page 8
Evelyn Waugh on page 155   George Orwell on page 55
D. H. Lawrence on page 23   Joseph Conrad on page 33

Naturally, it would be a mistake to think that a writer never changes the
tone during the course of a work. Shifts into understatement or
overstatement, for instance, may be very significant.

Into which category does the following example fall, and what is the
effect achieved?

. . . the First Division (of the second Battalion of the Welsh Regiment) had
been in constant hard fighting since the previous August; in eight months
the battalion had lost its full fighting strength five times over. The last
occasion was at Richebourg on May 9th, one of the worst disasters hitherto.
The Division's epitaph in the official communiqué read: 'Meeting with   5
considerable opposition in the direction of the Rue de Bois, our attacks were
not pressed.'

Robert Graves: Goodbye to All That (1929)

The reader also needs to be alive to the kind of effect that can be produced by a sudden descent into anti-climax. Consider the following two examples:

A. Slowly and majestically, the ponderous horses lumbered into a walk. The spears, which had been pointing in the air, bowed to a horizontal line and pointed at each other. King Pellinore and Sir Grummore could be seen to be thumping their horses' sides with their heels for all they were worth, and in a few minutes the splendid animals had shambled   5 into an earth-shaking imitation of a trot.

T. H. White: The Sword in the Stone (1938)

B. Today Aunt Alexandra and her missionary circle were fighting the good fight all over the house. From the kitchen, I heard Mrs Grace Merriweather giving a report in the living-room on the squalid lives of the Mrunas, it sounded like to me. They put the women out in huts when their time came, whatever that was; they had no sense of family – I knew   5 that'd distress Aunty – they subjected their children to terrible ordeals when they were thirteen; they were crawling with yaws and earworms, they chewed and spat out the bark of a tree into a communal pot and then got drunk on it.
Immediately thereafter the ladies adjourned for refreshments.   10

Harper Lee: To Kill a Mocking Bird (1960)

Changes in tone from, for example, an elevated to a colloquial or vulgar level of diction, and the deflating effect this produces, will often be clearly marked by an author. Other changes can be more subtle – the blending, for instance, of different levels of seriousness – and readers often underestimate the extent to which a writer's tone can simultaneously incorporate a range of possible responses. Readers must be for ever on the alert to identify these tonal changes and contrasts and to gauge the effect that the author intended by them. To illustrate this, we suggest you read this passage from George Eliot's *Daniel Deronda* (1876) in which the changes in tone are very important in establishing our attitude to the situation and the characters involved. In what tone does George Eliot write about each of the characters and in what tones do they converse with each other?

Mr Bult has come to pay court to the rich heiress, Catherine Arrowpoint and is a little disconcerted to find Klesmer, a foreigner and a musician, already in the room.

Meanwhile enters the expectant peer, Mr Bult, an esteemed party man who, rather neutral in private life, had strong opinions concerning the districts of the Niger, was much at home also in the Brazils, spoke with decision of affairs in the South Seas, was studious of his parliamentary and itinerant speeches, and had the general solidity and suffusive pinkness of a healthy   5 Briton on the central table-land of life. Catherine, aware of a tacit understanding that he was an undeniable husband for an heiress, had nothing to say against him but that he was thoroughly tiresome to her. Mr Bult was amiably confident, and had no idea that his insensibility to counterpoint[1] could ever be reckoned against him. Klesmer he hardly regarded in the light of a serious human being who ought to have a vote; and he did not mind Miss Arrowpoint's addiction to music any more than her probable expenses in antique lace. He was consequently a little amazed at an after-dinner out-burst of Klesmer's on the lack of idealism in English politics, which left all mutuality between distant races to be determined simply by the need of a market; the crusades, to his mind, had at least this excuse, that they had a banner of sentiment round which generous feelings could rally: of course, the scoundrels rallied too, but what then? – they rally in equal force round your advertisement van of 'Buy cheap, sell dear'. On this theme Klesmer's eloquence, gesticulatory and other, went on for a little while like stray fireworks accidentally ignited, and then sank into immovable silence. Mr Bult was not surprised that Klesmer's opinions should be flighty, but was astonished at his command of English idiom and his ability to put a point in a way that would have told at a constituents' dinner – to be accounted for probably by his being a Pole, or a Czech, or something of that fermenting sort, in a state of political refugeeism which had obliged him to make a profession of his music; and that evening in the drawing-room he for the first time went up to Klesmer at the piano, Miss Arrowpoint being near, and said –

'I had no idea before that you were a political man.'

Klesmer's only answer was to fold his arms, put out his nether lip, and stare at Mr Bult.

'You must have been used to public speaking. You speak uncommonly well, though I don't agree with you. From what you said about sentiment, I fancy you are a Panslavist.'[2]

'No; my name is Elijah. I am the Wandering Jew,[3]' said Klesmer, flashing a smile at Miss Arrowpoint, and suddenly making a mysterious wind-like rush backwards and forwards on the piano. Mr Bult felt this buffoonery rather offensive and Polish, but – Miss Arrowpoint being there – did not like to move away.

'Herr Klesmer has cosmopolitan ideas,' said Miss Arrowpoint, trying to make the best of the situation. 'He looks forward to a fusion of races.'

'With all my heart,' said Mr Bult, willing to be gracious. 'I was sure he had too much talent to be a mere musician.'

'Ah sir, you are under some mistake there,' said Klesmer, firing up. 'No man has too much talent to be a musician. Most men have too little. A creative artist is no more a mere musician than a great statesman is a mere politician. We are not ingenious puppets, sir, who live in a box and look out on the world only when it is gaping for amusement. We help to rule the nations and make the age as much as any other public men. We count ourselves on level benches with legislators. And a man who speaks

---

[1] *counterpoint*: the technique involving the simultaneous sounding of two or more parts or melodies.

[2] *Panslavist*: someone who believed in the union of all the Slavic peoples.

[3] *the Wandering Jew*: according to a legend, the Wandering Jew was condemned to wander the world until Christ's second coming as a punishment for insulting Christ as he carried his cross to Calvary and urging him to go faster.

effectively through music is compelled to something more difficult than
parliamentary eloquence.'
　With the last word Klesmer wheeled from the piano and walked away.
　Miss Arrowpoint coloured, and Mr Bult observed with his usual　55
phlegmatic solidity, 'Your pianist does not think small beer of himself.'

As tone is the indicator of the writer's attitude, it is inevitably the main
element to which a reader is liable to take exception. This may be the
result of a kind of temperamental clash between author and reader, or
perhaps the product of a shift in taste from one period to our own; for we
know that the views on, say, war or the place of women in society which
were a commonplace to one generation are often heretical to the next.
While we do well not to assume the inherently superior wisdom of our
own age (or ourselves), it is undoubtedly true that some prose, widely
acceptable in its own period, possesses a tone which produces uneasiness
in many modern readers. The final extract in this chapter is a case in point.
To be fair, there were contemporaries of Dickens who found his death-
bed scenes involving children far too maudlin; yet most of his Victorian
readers – and apparently the author himself – seemed to lap them up. The
tone of this kind of writing now seems open to the charge of
sentimentality – which we might define as the extraction of an excessive
emotion from a given cause and the open invitation to the reader to
wallow indulgently in the bath of steamy feelings so produced.
　Do you find the following extract open to this charge?
　What is the effect of the tone on the reader? (One reader has
commented that it was impossible to read it without breaking out into
laughter; but is this not a heartlessly cynical response?)

She was dead. No sleep so beautiful and calm, so free from trace of pain, so
fair to look upon. She seemed a creature fresh from the hand of God, and
waiting for the breath of life; not one who had lived and suffered death.
　Her couch was dressed with here and there some winter berries and green
leaves, gathered in a spot she had been used to favour. 'When I die, put near　5
me something that has loved the light, and had the sky above it always.'
Those were her words.
　She was dead. Dear, gentle, patient, noble Nell was dead. Her little bird –
a poor slight thing the pressure of a finger would have crushed – was stirring
nimbly in its cage; and the strong heart of its child mistress was mute and　10
motionless for ever.
　Where were the traces of her early cares, her sufferings, and fatigues? All
gone. Sorrow was dead indeed in her, but peace and perfect happiness were
born; imaged in her tranquil beauty and profound repose.
　And still her former self lay there, unaltered in this change. Yes. The old　15
fireside had smiled upon that same sweet face; it had passed like a dream,
through haunts of misery and care; at the door of the poor schoolmaster on
the summer evening, before the furnace fire upon the cold wet night, at the
still bedside of the dying boy, there had been the same mild lovely look. So
shall we know the angels in their majesty, after death.　20

　　　　　Charles Dickens: *The Old Curiosity Shop* (1841)

8

Some practice in answering examination questions

We trust that working through the previous chapters will have improved your responsiveness to prose. We now move to the specific business of the demands of prose criticism in an examination. In one sense, if you have carefully followed the material we have studied throughout the book, this chapter may well be superfluous; and yet students do sometimes make errors under the pressure of an examination, and we feel that any extra practice or assistance we can provide towards the achievement of a better grade should not be denied you. This is the essential function of this chapter, which we have attempted to make as practical and specific as possible.

The following passage was set for the 1980 Joint Matriculation Board's 'A' level examination. We suggest that you attempt to answer the questions yourself under examination conditions, taking no more than an hour over this, before you read our comments on the questions. These we have divided into three parts:

(i) what an examiner would be looking for when marking;
(ii) selections from answers written in examination, together with our comments;
(iii) quotations from the 1980 examiners' report on this question.

As a matter of general approach we would recommend two important, if obvious, procedures. First, you should spend at least ten minutes carefully reading any passage set in an examination. You should read the passage several times before picking up your pen – unless as an aid to your initial response you find it useful to jot down notes or to ring and underline key parts of the passage. So often in reading candidates' answers, examiners can see changes of mind on important issues as an answer develops, which is a sure sign that the candidates have committed themselves to paper before giving the question sufficient thought. Second, you should read through *all* the questions set before starting to answer the first one. This will enable you to avoid possible areas of overlapping which might cause you to include a lot of material in an earlier answer which should, in fact, be at the centre of a later one.

Now try this question.

Read the following passage, which is the opening of an early twentieth-century novel, and answer the questions which follow.

He felt very old.

Older than the old face at the table before him, than the office furniture, which had been there before he was born, than his father's portrait over the desk; older even than the tulip-tree bowing its graceful head to his window. Very old.   5

They said the tulip-tree blossomed no more than once in a hundred years. It was an ancient tree, biding its time as ancient things may. But Lancaster felt older even than that.

It had been a trying day. Helwise had made it trying, to begin with. She had come down to breakfast in a black print flickering with white spots, and   10
a whirlpool frame of mind, grievance after grievance spinning musically to the surface, only to be submerged again in the twinkling of an eye. In the intervals of digesting a troublesome correspondence, he found himself flinging life-belts of common sense after long-sunk bits of wreckage, gaining nothing but an impulse of helpless annoyance and growing dislike for the   15
flickering spots. Helwise was his aunt and housekeeper, and though she could add nearly a score of years to his thirty-seven, the weight of time lay infinitely lighter upon her shoulders than on his; perhaps because she twitched them so gracefully from under every descending yoke. Her delicate face and softly-greying hair gave the impression of a serene mind and a   20
fading constitution, and if you were not, vulgarly speaking, up to snuff, you ran and did things for Helwise that Helwise ought to have been doing for you, and she always let you. But the serenity was sheer illusion and the constitution was tough. Closer inspection found her racing through life with the objectless hurry of a cinema express. She shimmered along a permanent   25
way of mazy speech, and when you lived close to her you were always breathless and hurried, and the air was never quiet. She had the aimless velocity of a trundled hoop, and accomplished about as much.

Various printed notices drifted across the table on the rippling and bubbling of worries. She had a passionate habit of joining societies in all   30
capacities, from President or Secretary to General Bottle-Washer, of getting herself appointed on innumerable county committees. As Lancaster's aunt she was considered 'the right person', and as Lancaster's aunt she took it for granted that his fingers should straighten the tangle of her ensuing bewilderment, and make her trundling path smooth.   35

He glanced through the circulars quickly, folding them neatly and adding them to his own collection. He was very business-like in his movements. The sheep and the goats of his correspondence were separated right and left; each envelope had its pencilled name and date; while the more important took cover in an elastic band and an inner pocket. His brown hands were   40
methodical and deft; his weighing eyes implied a steady brain; his glance at the clock showed a sense of routine always alert. He was speed without hurry; while she, like the picture-train, rushed wildly and got nowhere.

A business-man born and made, you would have said of Lancelot Lancaster, not of stocks and shares or rustling parchments, but an acute,   45
sound man of the land, a lean, light, open-air man often in the saddle, with no aim beyond a clear-sighted judgment of terms and tenants, nor any desire

more whimsical than a steady prosperity. It was only when you looked at his mouth, with its hint of patience and repression, of longing held in leash and idealism shrouded like a sin, that you wondered if he was not, after all, only   50 very well-trained.

(a) Show how the writer brings out the feeling of growing old experienced by Lancaster.
(b) How effectively does the writer employ imagery to describe Helwise's personality in lines 9–35?
(c) Describe the impression which you have formed of Lancaster in the last two paragraphs and show how the writer's use of language conveys that impression.
(d) Discuss the effectiveness of the passage as the opening of a novel.

(a) *(i) What the examiner is looking for*
The examiner will have three areas in which to award marks:

1. the abruptness and isolation of the opening sentence, which immediately draws attention to Lancaster's feeling old. The general structure of the second paragraph is also significant with its rather weary, repeated pattern of 'older than . . .' and 'older even than . . .' which, together with the emphatic repetition of the key word, prepares for the culminating isolation of 'Very old' at the end of the paragraph;

2. (probably the most important area in terms of marks available.) The way in which the writer shows that Lancaster compares himself with what is old and generally static – 'the old face', 'the office furniture which had been there before he was born', 'his father's portrait', 'the tulip tree' which is described as 'ancient'. You would be expected to comment on the fact that the writer has chosen to introduce these objects in a pattern which shows increasing 'ancientness' and concludes with the absurdly exaggerated feeling that Lancaster has of being older than something which 'blossomed no more than once in a hundred years';

3. the contrast with Helwise who, despite being nearly 'a score of years' older than Lancaster, does not seem to feel or show her age – 'the weight of time [lying] infinitely lighter upon her shoulders than on his'. This contrast is heightened as Helwise is constantly linked with diction suggesting giddy movement – 'flickering', 'a whirlpool', 'spinning', 'twinkling' etc.

(a) *(ii) Some examination answers*
You should try to be very precise in your answers. Examiners will not reward vagueness such as 'the author effectively conveys Lancaster's feelings of growing old by going through a number of relatively old objects' or 'the author also mentions that Helwise "could add nearly a score of years to his thirty-seven."' Both of these comments show sloppiness of thought.

Other candidates tried to disguise their inability to answer the question merely by paraphrasing the author's words, thus ignoring the examiner's request to 'show *how*'. No marks would be given for an answer that tells us 'Lancaster is compared to the office furniture which has been situated there before his birth and he feels older than an ancient portrait of his father . . . and older than a graceful tulip-tree outside his window'. Neither does the examiner want you to speculate on matters that go beyond what the passage tells us – 'the furniture in his office is quite conceivably that which he grew up with, so perhaps he has memories of that same furniture as a child' is a comment that would gain no marks.

However, candidates who established a symbolic link between the tulip-tree which 'blossomed no more than once in a hundred years' and the author's final judgement that Lancaster's sense of premature age results from a kind of self-repression ('longing held in leash') would probably find that their ingenuity was rewarded.

Here is an example of quite a good answer, though it fails to achieve maximum marks partially because it makes no mention of the arresting opening line: 'Lancaster's ageing process is mental rather than physical; he is described as feeling older than the objects which surround him: the portrait of his father, the office furniture and the tulip-tree outside, which seem to ascend in age until the comic climax of the tree flowering only once every hundred years is reached. The writer also emphasizes this effect through the numerous repetitions of "old" and "older" and the slow, deliberate speed of the first two paragraphs. [This needs clarification, see (a) (i).] The introduction of Helwise comes as a great contrast to Lancaster and as she is shown to be vivacious, despite being twenty years older than her nephew, this adds to the feeling he has of growing old.'

(a) *(iii) Examiners' report*
'It was generally felt that this question was well-answered, though more attention should have been paid to the *methods* used . . . Thus, simply listing the objects mentioned in the opening eight lines was not a complete answer; exaggeration, comparison, emphasis were there to be seen, as well as the sentence structure. Innocently, the 'old face' became that of Helwise . . . .; unforgivably, Lancaster's thirty-seven years were made to represent senescence if not senility.'

(b) *(i) What the examiner is looking for*
An examiner would expect you to do two things in your answer: firstly, to point out the imagery that the writer is using (and this is the simpler of your tasks) and secondly, to show the effectiveness of this imagery in describing Helwise's personality. Do not make the mistake of assuming your task is over when you have demonstrated what imagery the author is using, for far too frequently candidates ignore the terms in which a question is set, either because it seems too difficult or because they have not read it carefully enough. Rest assured that if you do not answer the question in the precise terms in which it is couched, or if you twist it so

that the question becomes the one you yourself would like to have been set, then no marks will be coming your way!

There are three main images in Lines 9–35 and they are all extended ones:

1. the comparison of Helwise to a whirlpool: 'a whirlpool frame of mind'; 'grievance after grievance spinning musically to the surface, only to be submerged in the twinkling of an eye'; Lancaster's flinging 'life-belts of commonsense after long sunk bits of wreckage'; 'the rippling and bubbling of worries';

2. the comparison of Helwise to a cinema express train: 'racing through life with the objectless hurry of a cinema express train'; 'she shimmered along a permanent way [i.e. a railway track] of mazy speech';

3. the comparison of Helwise to a hoop: 'the aimless velocity of a trundled hoop'; 'her trundling path'.

To demonstrate the effectiveness of these images, you should point out that they all describe things which suggest speed, vigour and somewhat undisciplined energy; that they all indicate a circularity of movement, returning forever to the same place after their energetic course. (Remember that the train is no ordinary train, but one that endlessly repeats its journey on film.) These images suggest a gadfly personality of extravagantly superficial activity which is, in fact, aimless or – as the third image we referred to implies – even puerile.

(b) *(ii) Some examination answers*

It is obviously important when answering this question that you are clear in your own mind what imagery is (if you are unsure, reread the relevant chapter in this book, particularly pages 56), for if you wrote about Helwise's appearance and dress, as many candidates did, then you penalize yourself for irrelevance. Such comments as ' "a black print flickering with white spots" gives us an image of her appearance' or 'the impression given of Helwise's face gives the image of a pleasant, gentle lady' show no appreciation of the nature of imagery and can get no reward from the examiner. Had the writer of the first comment written something along these lines – 'The image of the "flickering" of the spots on Helwise's patterned dress suggests that she is giddily always in motion and adds to our sense of her mercurial character' – he or she would have shown a definite understanding of what was meant by an image and his or her conclusion would also be clearly relevant to the question.

Candidates who understood what imagery was, yet did little more than point out the images connected with Helwise, fared only marginally better than candidates ignorant of the term. You are expected to show some critical insight and appreciation of the reasons for the writer's choice of imagery; you should not remain content with image-spotting followed by remarks such as 'these images all convey the feeling that is needed for a description of Helwise' or 'the imagery used is very effective in conveying Helwise's personality'. Nor is there any reward for long chunks of the passage quoted without any comment. Many answers demonstrated a reluctance to comment in *enough detail* on the effectiveness of the imagery. In this category we would place remarks such as 'Helwise seemed to be always in a hurry; this is conveyed by the following lines – "closer inspection . . . objectless hurry of a cinema express"' or 'the reader can obviously see that this lady is very scatterbrained. The use of the phrase "whirlpool frame of mind" puts this across effectively'. While showing some small degree of critical insight, these comments are not developed sufficiently. Much more successful was the following answer: 'The imagery used is extensive and expressive and Helwise's character is well-described. Such words as "whirlpool" mind and grievances "spinning musically to the surface" show us her light-headed, confused state of mind. This extended image [which the candidate quotes] continues to reveal to us a woman of shallow though expressive intelligence, likeable, but not without the capacity to cause annoyance over an extensive period . . . Likening Helwise to a "trundling hoop" shows her lack of direction ("aimless velocity") and lack of real accomplishment – it reminds us of a childish activity. Her course through life, dictated by her "whirlpool mind", is baseless and without ambition or success. Similarly, likening her to a "cinema express" and "the objectless hurry" thus pictured, enhances this image of a vital woman, given to exploding suddenly upon the scene, but always wasting great energies upon nothing as she steams rapidly to nowhere. Her contrast and qualities antipathetic to Lancaster are obvious.'

Perhaps an examiner would say that this candidate has not commented fully on the links between the images, but is still worthy of a high mark. Incidentally, though it hardly detracts from the good quality of the answer, did you notice that on one occasion the candidate uses the word 'image' in the misleadingly non-literary sense we referred to in the opening paragraph of this section?

(b) *(iii) Examiners' report*
' "How effectively", the question began, but most writers were content to append a few images to their celebration of Helwise's personality . . . having first caught your image, you then *explain it*. You ask yourself what, for example, a whirlpool *is* and *does*. Only then are you in a position to comment on its effectiveness . . . Little or no credit could be given for the mere writing out of images and saying that they were "effective".'

As a footnote here we would draw your attention to something that should be obvious enough: the wording of the question – 'How effectively . . . ?' – leaves it open to the candidate to express adverse criticism. This is not to recommend wholesale demolition; but you should never simply assume that the passage presented for your appreciation is flawless, nor hesitate to express, with the appropriate intellectual grace, your own opinion, if the question gives you scope for this. For instance, do you think that the image contained in lines 33–35 ('she took it for granted . . . make her trundling path smooth') is entirely successful? Is the writer of the passage not guilty here of a clumsy mixed metaphor as she runs together the ideas of disentangling (a ball of wool or string?) with the revival of the 'hoop image' from the previous paragraph? The examiner would reward some accurately supported opinion on this point, a view underlined by a later comment from the examiners' report which, in connection with question (d), where again there is scope for the expression of personal opinion, states with a touch of acerbity: 'It may be that here again the appeal to the candidate for a personal opinion was too staggering, for most candidates sought refuge in unabashed, unselective praise . . . Is it asking too much to hope that next year the new candidates will have the confidence to trust and support a critical judgement?'

(c) *(i) What the examiner is looking for*
The question has two distinct parts: the first asks for your impressions of Lancaster and the second asks you to show how the writer has conveyed this impression through her use of language. As the question also states, you must take all your evidence from the last two paragraphs; consequently, the examiner will ignore anything you write about other parts of the passage, so your efforts in this direction will have been wasted.

You would be expected to make points like these about Lancaster: that he is efficient and well-organized (for example, the way in which he methodically deals with his correspondence), and that he works in a similarly diligent and sensible way on the estate, dealing with its problems and hoping to make a comfortable living from it; but that beneath this respectable exterior and this efficient estate management, there lies a desire to break away and to embark on some exciting new venture or more self-fulfilling role in life.

In answer to the second part of the question, the examiner would hope to read such critical insights as:

1. the author's use of direct statement (she *tells* us that Lancaster 'was very business-like in his movements', that 'his brown hands were methodical and deft');

2. the diction is generally plain and connected with the world of offices, management and estates ('pencilled', 'elastic-band', 'stocks and shares', 'terms and tenants' etc.) – it is a kind of language in marked contrast to the metaphorical flights that Helwise's directionless energy has inspired in the author, and it tends to suggest in Lancaster a 'compartmentalized' view of priorities which mechanically allocates each item to its proper place ('sheep and goats' – a wryly appropriate blending of a biblical/agricultural image – and 'right and left');

3. the movement of the sentences which describe his actions is balanced and sedate ('His brown hands'/'his weighing eyes'/'his glance at the clock');

4. the way in which the author enlists our support ('you would have said . . .') for a view of Lancaster that she subsequently undermines.

(c) *(ii) Some examination answers*

It would be a mistake to assume, as many candidates did, that they could gain high marks by concentrating mainly on the first part of the question dealing with Lancaster's character, neglecting that part which requires them to comment on 'the writer's use of language'. It was relatively easy to score some marks with answers such as: 'from the penultimate paragraph one gains the impression of a careful and pedantic man, steady and business-like in his action' or 'the impression formed in the last two paragraphs is that of a middle-aged, methodical, tidy, hardworking man'. Candidates who supported their judgements with textual evidence were rewarded more highly than those who merely gave their impressions. Rarer were candidates who were perceptive enough to realize that Lancaster was a man of the land and who made such comments as 'the very brownness of his hands adds to his strength, emphasizing his outdoor life; he is often "in the saddle" and his "business" (to do with the estate) is based on a stolid wish to be steadily prosperous'. Most answers did give some recognition to the fact that the impression of Lancaster originally given by the author was 'thrown into doubt' by her comments in the final three and a half lines.

Almost without exception, candidates found it difficult to comment on the writer's use of language. One way out of the difficulty was to pretend that the question had never been asked. A second, and more popular, escape was to pay lip-service to the question – 'the writer's use of language is very effective in conveying Lancaster's character' or 'therefore, as one can see [one can't without the candidate telling one!] the use of these descriptive words help to convey his character' – and to trust that the examiner will assume either the candidate is as wise and perceptive as the examiner and therefore there is no need to bother with details that they each know the other knows! or that, but for the pressure of time, the candidate would have produced the definitive answer and hopes that the examiner will nonetheless give a reward. He will – no marks!

Only a handful of candidates tried to answer the question – 'the writer uses short, evenly-balanced syntax, giving a picture of a methodical, well-prepared man' (this comment was supported by a couple of references and illustrations). Even comments like this were thin and only sporadically scattered through scripts. Some candidates thought that a reiteration of Lancaster's character with a few remarks praising the accurate or well-chosen language would suffice. Not so! The candidate who gave a good answer to this part of the question would have received a high reward. Remember, as a cardinal rule, always answer *all* parts of a question *thoroughly*.

(c) *(iii) Examiners' report*

'Perhaps this question would have alerted the candidates more successfully if it had been divided into parts (i) and (ii), for the great majority paid little or no attention to the use of language. There were some curious impressions of Lancaster: he became a cowboy, a much-travelled tourist [those brown hands] and a nephew consumed with barely concealed malevolence towards his aunt . . . Few indeed were the writers who stopped to examine sentence structure, balance and rhythm of phrases, length and choice of descriptive vocabulary, etc. Many were those who made unexplained "lifts" of words and phrases from the text, put them in inverted commas and trusted that these might be accepted as bona fide scrutiny of language use.'

(d) *(i) What the examiner is looking for*
An examiner could justifiably expect to meet some of the following points:

1. there is a very striking and arresting opening sentence;

2. we are introduced to two unusual and contrasting characters who are closely linked in a situation and scene that could lead to friction;

3. one of the characters has reached a crisis in his life – 'feeling old';

4. there is clearly scope for further development in his character, as we are told that his mouth gives the impression of 'longing held in leash and idealism shrouded in sin'.

All of these points could be expected to attract the readers' attention at the beginning of a novel and to encourage them, at the very least, to continue reading further into the work.

(d) *(ii) Some examination answers*
An important, yet commonsensical point first. Though this is the final question of the four, it is just as important as any of the preceding three, yet many candidates produced skimpy answers if at all, presumably because they had run out of time. Thus, an answer along the lines of 'this could be very effective as the opening of a novel since the direct statement of the first line would make a powerful impression on the reader, and the following paragraphs lead him into the novel' could not be expected to gain high marks. Neither could the approach of some candidates who thought that long quotations from the text or a paraphrase of its contents, followed by some speculative remarks as to future developments, would be a sufficient answer.
As in any examination answer, if you are going to quote, make sure that your quotations are (1) quite short, (2) relevant and (3) support the critical point you are making. No credit will be given for quotations merely lifted from the passage without any visible means of support. We suggested earlier that most advice on 'examination technique' is a matter of mere commonsense. Yet it does seem necessary to stress the point that when a marks total for each question is included on the examination

paper and the examiner can award six marks, candidates should realize that they are expected to produce an answer of some depth made up of several distinct points.

However, most candidates did make something out of this question and comments along the lines of 'it is effective because it suggests an air of mystery about the character of a superficially ordinary man' or 'the contrast between his character and the colourful one of Helwise sets up a range of interesting possibilities' were at least straining in the right direction. Not so was this catch-all answer: 'most novels open with some form of description either of people or the scene in which they are set so this passage is not far from the norm'. So what? Finally, part of an answer that shows some of the insight an examiner would reward quite generously:

'I believe this passage would form an interesting opening . . . the extract ends with an unresolved situation. We know the respective positions of Lancaster and Helwise, but the final sentence of the extract leaves the possibility of confrontation, with the first sign of Lancaster breaking through the shroud of oppression. The very beginning of the passage is also striking and its very weariness catches the reader's attention. It is only reasonable to assume that the reader will wish to read on to discover exactly why Lancaster, at thirty-seven years of age, is in such a pitiable state of mind . . . Helwise, who is so different, must also affect the reader's imagination. She has already been portrayed as generally amusing in a strange sort of way [*too vague*] and I believe the reader will wish to learn more of her, particularly as it seems likely that Lancaster is about to rebel against her dependency on him.'

(d) *(iii) Examiners' report*

'The usual response was to summarize the contents of the excerpt and add a few speculations about the quarrels between Helwise and Lancaster. What was needed was a comment on the way the author had written these opening paragraphs, the emphasis she had given to certain aspects of personality, and the effect of these upon a reader starting the book.'

The examiners ended their report on a characteristic note – something of this kind is included virtually every year:

'. . . The examining panel achieved complete unanimity in deploring, resignedly, the depressing standards of all too many candidates. Pride over precision, care over choice and use of words, consistency over spelling forms (right or wrong), knowledge and use of basic structural and punctuation rules – these seem to have become declining qualities in this examination. Yet the examination panel, which represents teachers of a wide range of ages and backgrounds, recognize that such qualities are an essential basis for a merited pass in English at this level. It will be the policy of the panel to continue to reward well-presented and accurate writing, and to penalize careless and casually written scripts . . .'

You should be able to sympathize with the Lancaster-like note of weariness in these remarks if you remember that examiners have to read a large number of scripts in a relatively short space of time. It is not always an agreeable process. Candidates will get examiners on their side by making life relatively easy for them – by clear, logical presentation of ideas in neat, correct and succinct English. While this is an examination in literature, once bad English or illegibility comes between what the candidate has to communicate and the examiner's ability to understand it, then the candidate is in danger of being heavily penalized.

We are grateful to the Joint Matriculation Board for permission to use this question and the Examiners' Report, though we should emphasize that the marking scheme is not the Board's but one we have devised ourselves.

For our second example of exercises set in prose analysis at 'A' level, we move to a type of exercise which poses a question couched in more general terms. For instance, you might be invited to read an extract of prose and then: 'Write a detailed critical appreciation of the passage, considering, in particular, the effect the author creates, the means he uses to that end, and your response to the passage as a whole.'

Here you have to decide for yourself both the general shape your answer will take, and the specific points it needs to include. On the positive side, this form of question may encourage an openness of response, on the negative side, candidates are given enough rope to hang themselves!

When tackling this kind of question, it may be useful for you to have in mind a number of questions of your own which you can put as an aid to start you thinking. You should remember the general 'three question approach' we introduced earlier (see page 6) or the questions we suggested as helpful to consider in relation to diction (see pages 24–25). However, there is no method, like a foolproof set of instructions or a simple check-list, which can be followed. As we have suggested before, the passage set for your appreciation should itself indicate to any sensitive reader what the important areas for consideration are. It would be a bad mistake to imagine that in answer to the general type of question we quoted above, the examiner is expecting to read two paragraphs on the passage's subject matter followed by paragraphs of equal length on its diction, imagery, sentence construction, use of narrative point of view and tone. Imagery, for example, might be of crucial importance in one extract and only a peripheral matter in another.

In the following question, taken from the Cambridge Board's 'A' level examination in English Literature (1981), you will see that there is a focus to the question – it concerns the state of mind of the central character – though the general approach is left very much to the candidate. We would like you again to write your own answer to the question, spending no more than one hour on it, and then turn to the material which follows. You will find two broad sections: (A.) comments on answers written by candidates; (B.) the marking scheme used by examiners.

Sensitive by nature to emanations from its prey and trembling with art in the morning air, the split tongue of the monster guided it forward. A graceful geometric pattern was left behind in the platinum dew. Death was in motion, death and destruction, death in the peaceful garden among all the pretty flowers. The bird, a fledgling wren, continued to chirp by the brick wall.   5

In mental pain, Randy gripped the bedroom windowsill and held his breath. There was nothing he could do; the snake would catch the bird and kill it before his eyes. He had told Aunt Rose again and again there was a nest of the things in the Algerian ivy, but she would not have it cleared out. It was lovely, she said. And now, because of the loveliness of the ivy, he had to   10 witness a grim murder.

'Let it fly away!' he whispered.

The bird did not fly away, but to Randy's immense relief something else did happen.

'Where you call yourself going, Mr Rattler?'   15

Josh's voice was soft, lazy, musical, and amused as the mattock lifted high and the muscles corded on his brown arms. Involuntarily Randy flinched. An explosive exhalation of breath came from Josh. With a loud whop, the mattock buried in the lawn.

'You done come in the wrong garden, son. Throw your head to the north,   20 throw your tail to the south. Before you die 'long about sundown, tell your brother and sister and all your relations stay away from my door.'

Thus perished one medium-sized rattlesnake in the prime of life.

For some reason, the death of the monster made a disturbing impression on Randy. The mercilessness with which Josh brought down the mattock   25 gave him a feeling of disquiet and anxiety. Why, in such a beautiful world, should life be thus destroyed? His view of the world that morning did not encompass with philosophical calm snakes or the murder of snakes. The swift hypodermic stab of poisonous fangs in a helpless little bird was intolerable, but the cruel whop of that mattock into the lawn was well-nigh   30 equally intolerable. Snakes, too, want to live, don't they?

Here, he believed, was a confounding dilemma for any man of good will. And there was no simple answer, in his view. The icy brain in that flat, horrible head presented a perturbing qualification of the benignity of Mother Nature. How can the pure at heart, who seek brotherhood and love   35 and all beautiful things, oppose the murdering snakes of this world? How else but by becoming a murdering snake oneself?

Something else disturbed him more. It could easily have happened, he knew, that Josh would not have noticed or would not have been in time. Pure chance had saved that little bird. Another might not be so lucky. He   40 had a vivid mental picture of fangs struck in a soft breast, the killing poison injected, then slow descent half alive down a slimy gullet. Benevolent Mother Nature was an unspeakable Harpy.

By the obvious extension of natural law, the frightful reality of human existence itself was nakedly exposed. Many kinds of snakes lay waiting, not   45 only for him, but also for those he loved. Wasn't this true, and if so, then how could a man of imagination not collapse into gibbering insanity, much less stand and face the world with a serene courage conscious in the midst of chaos and the dark?

(i) Give a brief account of the events being described in this passage.
(ii) Write a critical appraisal of the passage, paying attention to the presentation of Randy's state of mind and the questions that disturb him.

(A.) Question (i) asks for a *brief* answer: most candidates realized that they were being asked to provide a short summary before the real work of analysis began. Even so, a number of basic misreadings were apparent. For example:

(a) 'Randy reassured himself that it was not his fault if the bird was killed because he had told his Aunt Rose about the nest of snakes and she had refused to do anything about it.'
(Randy certainly has told his aunt about the nest of snakes, and because she has failed to remove the ivy 'he had to witness a grim murder'. The passage, however, provides no evidence of Randy shifting the blame for this to his aunt – nor does he reassure himself 'that it was not his fault'.)

(b) 'To save the little bird a slave hits the snake with a hammer.'
(The candidate does not know what a 'mattock' is and leaps to the conclusion that Josh is a slave, for which the passage provides no definite support. Most significantly, he or she fails to see that Josh simply kills the rattlesnake because it is in the garden – there is no evidence to support the view that he even sees the fledgling wren.)

Readings of this kind hardly provide a sound basis for the second part of the question. Analysis must rest on clear understanding.

One other point to bear in mind is that your summary should, by definition, consist largely of a reformulation of the central events described in the original in *your own words* – as far as is reasonably possible. Some candidates simply 'lifted' passages from the original and did not even have the honesty to put inverted commas around their wholesale quotations. The following, for instance, is clearly not acceptable as a summary:

Randy wonders how can the pure in heart, who seek brotherhood and love and all beautiful things, oppose the murdering snakes of this world. (See lines 35–36 of the original).

The following answer would certainly impress the examiner as being along the right lines, though it may be a little longer than is strictly necessary:

Randy watches apprehensively and helplessly from a bedroom window as a rattlesnake slithers across the lawn towards its prey, a small wren which remains pathetically oblivious to the danger. When Josh appears on the scene and quickly kills the snake, Randy feels immense relief, but this quickly fades as he begins to reflect that the snake, like the bird, had a right   5

to live. The merciless nature of the snake's death makes Randy consider the whole scheme of the natural world, including man's place in it. Must the virtuous commit violence in order to protect innocence? But then, in so doing, surely goodness turns to evil and the innocent end is corrupted? Is the guiding spirit behind nature, Randy reflects, simply one of 'kill or be killed'?   10
As Randy struggles to find an answer, he is also struck by the part that mere chance played in the survival, on this occasion, of the bird and the death of the snake. Finally, Randy is left wondering how anyone of imagination and sensitivity can keep madness at bay in the face of a hostile world in which man himself appears vulnerable to an arbitrary, cruel force which will   15
sooner or later destroy him.

We will consider the major, second question with reference to a rather weak answer followed by our comments. Reading a poor answer can, paradoxically, be very instructive: by showing in a glaring way what is missing, we can work towards deciding what would have to be present to form a good answer. You will see that one of the problems with this candidate's answer is its lack of shape: the candidate rambles from one point to the next. We feel, however, that you could order and develop some of the points we make in our comments – which, incidentally, run to considerably greater length than the answer itself! – to produce the basis of a very good answer. After you have read this material, perhaps you could put together something which approaches a 'model answer'. Bear in mind, however, that in literary studies there is no such thing as one single, ideal answer which is waiting in the abstract to be discovered; rather there are a number of different approaches, many of which might, each in its own terms, be brought to a pitch of excellence.

The author sets the scene pretty well, though it is a pity that he includes the details of the dew and the pretty flowers which make us think of a calm, pleasant morning scene. He could have made the garden more sinister and threatening and this would have prepared us better for the arrival of the snake.[1] Soon the atmosphere does become frightening,[2] however. The   5
reader is taken right inside Randy's mind and we look at everything that happens from his point of view.[3] The simple[4] language directly records his feelings, and the writing makes the reader feel as if he is actually present. The snake glides into the garden looking for its prey and for a moment Randy thinks the small bird is going to be killed. He wants the bird to fly away, but   10
it does not, and its life is only saved by the arrival of Josh on the scene.[5] The snake is described as a monster and represents all that is ugly and harsh in nature. It stands for Death,[6] and there is a strong sense of the horror[7] of death in the passage, but Randy should know that you have to kill to survive in nature – after all, even the bird eats worms, and I imagine that Randy   15
expects his mother to provide him with a three-course meal every night. Randy does not seem to realize at first that snakes have to hunt for their dinner. He seems mixed up in his feelings and probably is far too sentimental. Why should he make all this fuss over a small bird? Moreover, I think that the writer contradicts himself[8] several times in describing   20
Randy's feelings, and I would prefer him to come to some definite

conclusion.[9] The author is not sure about the nature of good and evil, and surely he is wrong to make Randy think of the snake as totally evil.[10] People have a biased view of snakes – they think of them as being repulsive and slimy, but I have a friend who keeps one as a pet – the snake crawls all over 25 him and never causes any harm. When I touched it once it felt warm and silky.[11] But to Randy and Josh snakes are the lowest of the low – something man has a right to kill.[12] But what right has man to interfere with the natural cycle?

The writer's style takes us right inside Randy's mind and he uses a lot of 30 vivid descriptive words.[13] As I have already said, it is a simple style, though the writer occasionally falls into the mistake of wrapping up what he wants to put over in long-winded phrases.[14] For example, I don't know what a 'Harpy' is, and I very much doubt whether Randy does either. There are a lot of words like this in the second half of the passage which a young boy is 35 hardly likely to have thought of and in the final paragraph it seems more like a man speaking than Randy.[15] Basically though the writing is very vivid, except for the boring bits I have mentioned, and the writer puts over a very good picture – it's almost as if you were actually there watching the snake moving across the lawn[16] – though I think I would have thrown a stone or 40 something to scare the bird away. Probably the writer had watched snakes very closely and he must have experienced something very similar in his own life – perhaps in his childhood. Perhaps he is, in fact, Randy himself.[17] There is certainly a lot of drama and the writer usually avoids boring the reader. Parts of this writing read almost like a scene from a play.[18] And the 45 writer combines his description with his hidden meanings and the important questions which force Randy for the first time to think about the whole meaning of life.[19] The writer leaves us with a very frightening picture in Randy's mind, as he is thinking of all the other snakes in the world – to him a terrifying idea – which may in the future attack him or other members of his 50 family. Probably later in the story somebody is going to suffer from a fatal snake bite.[20]

1. The author is aiming at precisely this sense of *incongruity* between the beautiful and peaceful setting and the intrusion of the menacing snake. (Note the irony that it is the 'loveliness of the ivy' which hides the nest of snakes.) This proximity of beauty and death prepares the reader for the 'confounding dilemma' which will later obsess Randy. The garden is a kind of Eden into which the snake enters – bringing with it a loss of innocence and unresolved complexities.

2. Too vague. At what point does the atmosphere become 'frightening'? Does the passage not begin with a frisson of horror as the snake is described closing inexorably on its prey? The candidate also needs to point to specific elements in the language which produce a sense of fear. He might have drawn our attention to the ominous repetition of the word 'death' in the third sentence of the extract or the direct description of Randy's 'mental pain' (line 6) and his gripping of the bedroom windowsill in apprehension.

3. Not true. While there are strong elements of a reported interior monologue (see page 129 for a definition of this term), the Author is

present, mediating Randy's thoughts in terms which frequently force the reader into a more detached appraisal of events – 'Benevolent Mother Nature was an unspeakable Harpy' (lines 42–43). The passage contains both the drama of immediate experience with the addition of an authorial tone which conveys its own attitude. Presumably it is the latter element that the candidate will later refer to as 'boring' – a woolly word which should probably be banned from all literary discussion! The failure to detect what the function of the Author's voice is in the passage leads the candidate into a number of confusions – of which we will say more later.

4. Is the diction and tone of the passage uniformly 'simple'? 'Snakes, too, want to live, don't they?' (line 31) is certainly direct enough and springs from Randy's immediate response. But there are many examples of a different kind of diction: '. . . . presented a perturbing qualification of the benignity of Mother Nature' (lines 34–35). Language of this type surely gives us the voice of the Author (see note 3), in a tone of something approaching whimsicality, filtering and implicitly commenting on Randy's impressions. For Randy, questions about the ultimate benevolence of nature may be novel and traumatic, but the Author's tone occasionally exhibits a faintly mocking irony which seeks to deflate the cosily sentimental view of 'Mother Nature' and draws attention to the fact that the Author, unlike the understandably naive Randy, lost his innocence a long time ago. The candidate's claim that the style of the passage is 'simple' will not stand up. Significantly, the candidate has not supported or illustrated this assertion by quotation, which is *indispensable* when discussing matters of style.

5. Notice at this point that the candidate retreats completely from analysis into mere narrative. The summary is not supporting any critical point, and question (i) gave all the opportunity needed simply to retell the story.

6. The matter is slightly more complex: in one of its aspects the snake certainly represents death; at the same time it is not entirely 'ugly', but rather is endowed with a kind of cold, streamlined beauty – 'trembling with art . . . A graceful geometric pattern was left behind' (lines 1–3). The candidate misses this kind of ambiguity (see also note 1) and seems to prefer imposing his or her own simplified view, which is chattily amplified in the next few lines.

7. Yes, but how is this sense of 'horror' produced? The candidate might have pointed to the powerful image in which Randy imagines what had seemed to be the inevitable death of the bird: 'swift hypodermic stab of poisonous fangs in a helpless little bird' (line 29) – connotations of an irresistibly clinical mode of mechanized death. Again, there is the mimetic (i.e. echoing, imitating the action described in its movement and syntax) description of 'then slow descent half alive down a slimy gullet' (line 42); or earlier, the striking, onomatopoeic rhythm of the snake's death-blow – 'cruel whop of that mattock' (line 30).

8. Randy's 'confusions' lie at the centre of the passage. Sometimes he

finds the only answer to a question is to ask another question. Often the argument is circular (lines 35–37). The candidate needs to show that he understands the exact nature of these questions – and appreciates that they are of some complexity. It is certainly not the author who is confused: he is portraying the contradictions that revolve in the boy's mind.

9. No simple conclusion is possible, only a sense of Randy's initiation into an age-old dilemma. It may be helpful at this point to quote from the examiners' marking scheme:

> The passage deals with the incompatibility between the goodness and beauty of the world and the cruelty, suffering and death that inhabit it. In other words, a consideration of the problem of evil . . . The dilemma is not answered, or resolved, though one can see an answer implied, for Randy, in the concluding sentences. 5

10. Randy does *not* think of snakes as being totally evil. This may be his first simplified view, but later, after the snake's death, he can feel a measure of sympathy for it and reflect that it had a right to life. The candidate must grasp this point to begin to understand the real issues the excerpt raises.

11. The candidate has already foisted a simplified view of snakes on Randy and lectured him for its inadequacies. Now the candidate introduces his own corrective – but this kind of personal reminiscence is largely irrelevant in a piece of critical writing. We want more light shed on the original passage. The weaker kind of candidate often introduces this kind of falsely personal note; it is also apparent elsewhere in the over-opinionated 'What right has man to interfere with the natural cycle' and the cocksure certainty that he knows better than Randy – e.g. he would have thrown a stone to scare the bird away! We have earlier encouraged candidates to express a personal opinion where there is scope for it, but here the opinions are largely puerile, and probably were introduced because the candidate finds it difficult to connect with the passage itself – though this may be unfairly cynical.

12. The attitudes of Randy and Josh need to be distinguished. Randy's response to snakes changes (see note 10). Josh's attitude is much more straightforward: he kills the rattlesnake with a kind of relish; he is not concerned with the wider situation – he knows nothing of the bird whose fate a moment before hung in the balance; he takes the uncomplicated view that rattlesnakes are dangerous and should be killed on sight if they stray into your garden, an outlook which is reflected in the simple jingle of his ethnic incantation ('Throw your head to the north . . .' – lines 20–22) and in the Author's short declarative summary which stands as a single paragraph and possesses a clinical tone: 'Thus perished one medium-sized rattlesnake in the prime of life' (line 23). Josh's attitude, therefore, provides a foil for Randy's more self-conscious, questioning state of mind.

13. Too vague. Where is the reference and quotation? Again the candidate is content with woolly generalization and avoids examining the mechanics of the language.

14. The candidate's own critical vocubulary is sometimes lacking. We have already commented on the loose use of the word 'boring' (see note 3), which later becomes the backhanded compliment to the author of avoiding 'boring the reader'. Lack of precision is particularly evident in the use of 'put over' ('convey' would be the more appropriate critical register) and 'long-winded' (does he mean tedious? over-pedantic? prolix?). Again, lack of quotation leaves the reader guessing as to the candidate's exact meaning. His next sentence may suggest he means words which are not in his own vocabulary.

15. Once more the absence of direct reference clouds the issue. There is again the failure to detect the function of the modulations of tone and the presence of the Author's voice in the passage (see notes 3 and 4).

16. While the creation of this sense of 'reality' is, of course, important, the candidate does not tackle the more demanding question of *how* the effect is produced through the language at work. Weaker candidates often fall back on this kind of uncritical praise – where the evidence is elsewhere suggestive of the fact that the candidate does not really like the passage very much. Is this 'all purpose comment' anything more than a piece of waffle?

17. More waffle and idle speculation. The comment that the Author may be 'Randy himself' brings into focus the candidate's refusal to see the extent to which the Author examines Randy's experience in a fairly detached tone (see note 4).

18. This is an interesting perception which needs to be shaped. There is a sense of Randy watching a drama: snake and bird are presented to us at first as 'monster' and 'prey', participants in a scene which has been played out many times before; Randy watches with helpless fascination from the gallery. Then at the climax there is an ironic reversal: the hunter becomes the hunted, the bringer of death is itself killed. At this point the drama turns into a kind of exemplum – a story designed to illustrate or embody a set of principles or ideas about life – and it brings disturbing knowledge to Randy.

19. What 'hidden meanings'? Again the candidate needs to go more fully into the questions – they are explicit enough – which disturb Randy (see notes 8 and 9). Moreover, there is something of an internal contradiction here. Earlier the candidate had complained 'Why all this fuss over a small bird?'; now the questions raised in Randy's mind are felt, in all too vague a way, to be 'important' and related to 'the whole meaning of life'. Is the candidate led into this error by a feeling that at the end of his 'analysis' he is obliged to pour over the passage the rich syrup of his unqualified esteem?

20. The candidate falls into a serious misreading by taking the final paragraph too literally. He has not realized that the snakes referred to

here now stand metaphorically for a pervasive sense of life's dangers and threats – the 'thousand natural shocks/That flesh is heir to', in Hamlet's words. The misunderstanding leads the candidate to offer the rather simple-minded prediction of the final sentence.

(B) *Examiners' marking scheme*

'The passage has a clear picture of a scene, followed by the reflections of Randy on what has taken place, the killing of the rattlesnake, the possible killing of the bird, and the cruelty of Nature. Candidates should be able, without much trouble, to give a coherent answer to (i), where what is required is not simply some re-description of the scene, but rather an   5
account that points up the significance of the events for Randy. This, of course, is not separate from (ii), where candidates are asked to consider how the state of mind, the quality of the disturbing impression, is conveyed, and indeed to show that they, the candidates, have understood what the questions are that disturb Randy.   10
The passage deals with the incompatibility between the goodness and beauty of the world and the cruelty, suffering and death that inhabit it. In other words, a consideration of the problem of evil, but encapsulated succinctly and in small compass. Candidates who attempt to grapple with issues raised by the passage, if they do so with some intelligence, should not   15
be penalized for irrelevance. The dilemma is not answered, or resolved, though one can see an answer implied, for Randy, in the concluding sentences.
Candidates should not have all that much trouble with this question, and we would want, I think, to reward those candidates who make something of   20
it, reaching beyond paraphrase and the associated bind, or repetition and retelling.
The question can be marked as a whole, or split up into two parts, as seems most suitable for the candidate whose work is before you.

You may be surprised to discover the very general terms in which this marking scheme is couched, unlike the more detailed and specific kind of marking scheme which operated in connection with the first type of question we examined. You should be encouraged, however, by the fact that the examiner who is marking by impression is open to a wide range of responses and will reward any answer which reveals a quality of mind sensitive to the use of language and capable of accounting for its discriminations. You may even feel that the tone of the examiners' scheme above suggests that we were too hard on the candidate whose work we analysed. Perhaps we seemed to dismiss it with the slightly bad-tempered air of over-rigorous and censorious judges turning on a whipping-boy. For your part, what kind of grade at 'A' level do you think the candidate deserves for this piece of work?

We conclude this chapter with another prose question from the Cambridge Board's 'A' level examination (1980), together with the relevant marking scheme.

Read the following passage carefully and answer the questions concerning it.

He was working on the edge of the common, beyond the small brook that ran in the dip at the bottom of the garden, carrying the garden path in continuation from the plank bridge on to the common. He had cut the rough turf and bracken, leaving the grey, dryish soil bare. But he was worried because he could not get the path straight, there was a pleat between his   5 brows. He had set up his sticks, and taken the sights between the big pine trees, but for some reason everything seemed wrong. He looked again, straining his keen blue eyes, that had a touch of the Viking in them, through the shadowy pine trees as through a doorway, at the green-grassed garden-path rising from the shadow of alders by the log bridge up to the sunlit   10 flowers. Tall white and purple columbines, and the butt-end of the old Hampshire cottage that crouched near the earth amid flowers, blossoming in the bit of shaggy wildness round about.

There was a sound of children's voices calling and talking: high, childish, girlish voices, slightly didactic and tinged with domineering: 'If you don't   15 come quick, nurse, I shall run out there to where there are snakes.' And nobody had the *sang-froid* to reply: 'Run then, little fool.' It was always, 'No, darling. Very well, darling. In a moment, darling. Darling, you *must* be patient.'

His heart was hard with disillusion: a continual gnawing and resistance.   20 But he worked on. What was there to do but submit!

The sunlight blazed down upon the earth, there was a vividness of flamy vegetation, of fierce seclusion amid the savage peace of the commons. Strange how the savage England lingers in patches: as here, amid these shaggy gorse commons, and marshy, snake infested places near the foot of   25 the south downs. The spirit of place lingering on primeval, as when the Saxons came, so long ago.

Ah, how he had loved it! The green garden path, the tufts of flowers, purple and white columbines, and great oriental red poppies with their black chaps and mulleins tall and yellow, this flamy garden which had been a   30 garden for a thousand years, scooped out in the little hollow among the snake-infested commons. He had made it flame with flowers, in a sun cup under its hedges and trees. So old, so old a place! And yet he had re-created it.

The timbered cottage with its sloping, cloak-like roof was old and   35 forgotten. It belonged to the old England of hamlets and yeomen. Lost all alone on the edge of the common, at the end of a wide, grassy, briar-entangled lane shaded with oak, it had never known the world of today. Not till Egbert came with his bride. And he had come to fill it with flowers.

The house was ancient and very uncomfortable. But he did not want to   40 alter it. Ah, marvellous to sit there in the wide, black, time-old chimney, at night when the wind roared overhead, and the wood which he had chopped himself sputtered on the hearth! Himself on one side the angle, and Winifred on the other.

Ah, how he had wanted her: Winifred! She was young and beautiful and   45 strong with life, like a flame in sunshine. She moved with a slow grace of energy like a blossoming, red-flowered bush in motion. She, too, seemed to

come out of the old England, ruddy, strong, with a certain crude, passionate
quiescence and a hawthorn robustness. And he, he was tall and slim and
agile, like an English archer with his long supple legs and fine movements.   50
Her hair was nut-brown and all in energic curls and tendrils. Her eyes were
nut-brown, too, like a robin's for brightness. And he was white-skinned with
fine, silky hair that had darkened from fair, and a slightly arched nose of an
old country family. They were a beautiful couple.

  (i) Give a brief account of the relation between man and nature being
       presented here.

 (ii) Say what your reaction to the passage is, making specific reference
       to the text.

Examiners' marking scheme

This is a passage that should allow the candidate a fair amount of lee-way. It
is a richly subjective piece (by Lawrence, of course), which provides
candidates with the kind of writing they are most sympathetic to. The build-
up of adjectival qualification, the evocation of the spirit of place (the
'primeval'), the use of natural imagery as objective correlative,[1] in other   5
words, the creation of a psychological landscape, all this should permit even
the weakest candidate to have something to say.

The first part of the question is aimed at all possible levels of performance.
Clearly, even the poorest can have some thoughts about this question, and
our problem will be to pick our way through the inevitable verbiage and   10
repetition that will afflict us. The second question is a critical question,
and candidates must be able to show the glimmerings of a literary response.

In marking of this kind, it is not possible to lay down hard external
criteria. Nonetheless, reference to the text does seem to be a basic
requirement for this kind of work, and where candidates show their abilities   15
with language they should be rewarded. Essentially, then, we are concerned
to recognize and reward any feeling for language, any sense of how writing
may create a world of imaginative life. In so far as candidates' reaction to the
passage may be very varied, some approving, others disliking it intensely, we
ourselves need not have prior positions as to whether or not Lawrence   20
succeeds here (or, if he succeeds, whether he ought to have succeeded). There
is more than a touch of *Blut und Erde*[2] in DHL, but at this date and at such a
cultural distance I doubt whether any candidate will notice the more
dubious resonances of the Lawrentian œuvre.

Because a senior examiner is here writing for the edification of his
fellow markers, a couple of footnotes are probably necessary:

1. *objective correlative*: a term introduced into literary criticism by
T. S. Eliot in his essay 'Hamlet and His Problems' (from *The Sacred
Wood*, 1920) and defined as 'the only way of expressing emotion in the
form of art . . . by finding . . . a set of objects, a situation, a chain of
events which shall be the formula of that *particular* emotion'. The term
refers to the precise means – a set of images or, in this extract, the
description of a scene – which are designed to evoke and express the state
of mind the writer wishes to convey to the reader.

2. *Blut und Erde*: from the German ('blood and earth'), a reference to Lawrence's celebration of the instinctive and intuitive life as against the purely intellectual. There is probably an allusion in this phrase to the 'spiritual fascism' of which Lawrence is sometimes accused.

The sources of the passages set for these questions are, in the order in which they appear, Constance Holme's *The Lonely Plough*, Calder Willingham's *To Eat a Peach* and D. H. Lawrence's *England, My England*.

9

Passages of prose for criticism

A. *Read the following excerpt from a novel and answer the questions which follow.*

A bus took him to the West End, where, among the crazy-coloured fountains of illumination, shattering the blue dusk with green and crimson fire, he found the café of his choice, a tea shop that had gone mad and turned Babylonian, a white palace with ten thousand lights. It towered above the older buildings like a citadel, which indeed it was, the outpost of a new age, 5
perhaps a new civilisation, perhaps a new barbarism; and behind the thin marble front were concrete and steel, just as behind the careless profusion of luxury were millions of pence, balanced to the last half-penny. Somewhere in the background, hidden away, behind the ten thousand lights and acres of white napery and bewildering, glittering rows of teapots, behind the 10
thousand waitresses and cashbox girls and black-coated floor managers and temperamental long-haired violinists, behind the mounds of shimmering bonbons and multi-coloured Viennese pastries, the cauldrons of stewed steak, the vanloads of harlequin ices, were a few men who went to work juggling with fractions of a farthing, who knew how many units of electricity 15
it took to finish a steak-and-kidney pudding and how many minutes and seconds a waitress (five-feet four in height and in average health) would need to carry a tray of given weight from the kitchen lift to the table in the far corner.

In short, there was a warm sensuous vulgar life flowering in the upper 20
storeys and cold science working in the basement. Such was the gigantic teashop into which Turgis marched, in search not of mere refreshment but of all the enchantment of unfamiliar luxury. Perhaps he knew in his heart that men have conquered half the known world, looted whole kingdoms, and never arrived at such luxury. 25

The place was built for him.

It was built for a great many other people too, and as usual they were all there. It steamed with humanity. The marble entrance-hall piled dizzily with bonbons and cakes, was as crowded and bustling as a railway station. The gloom and grime of the streets, the raw air, all November, were at once left 30
behind, forgotten: the atmosphere inside was golden, tropical, belonging to some high midsummer of confectionery. Disdaining the lifts, Turgis, once more excited by the sight, sound, and smell of it all, climbed the wide staircase until he reached his favourite floor, where an orchestra, led by a young Jewish violinist with wandering, lustrous eyes and a passion for 35
tremolo effects, acted as a magnet to a thousand girls. The door was swung open to him by a page: there burst, like a sugary bomb, the clatter of cups, the shrill chatter of white-and-vermillion girls, and, cleaving the golden-

scented air, the sensuous clamour of the strings; and, as he stood hesitating a
moment, half dazed, there came bowing, a sleek, grave man, older than he   40
was, and far more distinguished than he could ever hope to be, who
murmured deferentially: 'For one, sir? This way, please.' Shyly yet proudly
Turgis followed him.

   That was the snag really, though. The place was so crowded that you had
to take the seat they offered you; there was no picking and choosing your   45
company at the table. And, as usual, Turgis was not lucky. The vacant seat
which he was shown, and which he dare not refuse, was at a table already
occupied by three people, and not one of them remotely resembled a nice-
looking girl. There were two stout middle-aged women, voluble, perspiring,
and happy over cream buns, and a middle-aged man who, no doubt, had   50
been of no great size even before this expedition started, but was now very
small and huddled, and gave the impression that if the party stayed there
much longer he would shrink to nothing but spectacles, a nose, a collar, and
a pair of boots.

   (i) Consider the author's comment (lines 5–6): 'the outpost of a new
       age, perhaps a new civilisation, perhaps a new barbarism . . .'
       With reference to lines 1–25, discuss the ways by which the author
       has tried to make vivid his general impression of the tea shop and
       his views of it.
  (ii) Discuss the purpose and the effectiveness of the contrast between
       the last two paragraphs.
 (iii) Referring to the evidence of the whole passage, write briefly your
       impression of Turgis's personality and attitudes.
  (iv) 'The place was built for him' (line 26). Why do you think this
       comment is set on its own? Give reasons for your views.

                                    The Joint Matriculation Board (1979)

B. *Comment on the following passage. Consider such things as subject-
   matter, meaning, and the features of style which contribute to its full
   effect.*

Full moonlight drenched the city and searched it; there was not a niche left
to stand in. The effect was remorseless: London looked like the moon's
capital—shallow, cratered, extinct. It was late, but not yet midnight; now
the buses had stopped the polished roads and streets in this region sent for
minutes together a ghostly unbroken reflection up. The soaring new flats   5
and the crouching old shops and houses looked equally brittle under the
moon, which blazed in windows that looked its way. The futility of the
black-out became laughable: from the sky, presumably, you could see every
slate in the roofs, every whited kerb, every contour of the naked winter
flowerbeds in the park; and the lake, with its shining twists and tree-   10
darkened islands would be a landmark for miles, yes, miles, overhead.

   However, the sky, in whose glassiness floated no clouds, remained glassy-
silent. The Germans no longer came by the full moon. Something more
immaterial seemed to threaten, and to be keeping people at home. This day
between days was perhaps more than senses and nerves could bear. People   15

stayed indoors with a fervour that could be felt: the buildings strained with
battened-down human life, but not a beam, not a voice, not a note from a
radio escaped. Now and then under streets and buildings the earth rumbled:
the Underground sounded loudest at this time.

Outside the now gateless gates of the park, the road coming downhill   20
from the north-west turned south and became a street, down whose
perspective the traffic lights went through their unmeaning performance of
changing colour. From the promontory of pavement outside the gates you
saw at once up the road and down the street: from behind where you stood,
between the gateposts, appeared the lesser strangeness of grass and water   25
and trees. At this point, at this moment, three French soldiers, directed to a
hostel they could not find, stopped singing to listen derisively to the
waterbirds wakened up by the moon. Next, two wardens coming off duty
emerged from their post and crossed the road diagonally, each with an
elbow cupped inside a slung-on tin hat. The wardens turned their faces,   30
mauve in the moonlight, towards the Frenchmen with no expression at all.
The two sets of steps died in opposite directions, and, the birds subsiding,
nothing was heard or seen until, a little way down the street, a trickle of
people came out of the Underground, around the anti-panic brick wall.
These all disappeared quickly, in an abashed way, or as though dissolved in   35
the street by some white acid, but for a girl and a soldier who, by their way of
walking, seemed to have no destination but each other and to be not quite
certain even of that. Blotted into one shadow, he tall, she little, these two
proceeded towards the park. They looked in, but did not go in; they stood
there debating without speaking. Then, as though a command from the   40
street behind them had been received by their synchronized bodies, they
faced round to look back the way they had come.

Oxford Local Examinations Board (1981)

C. *Write a critical appreciation of the passage printed below. You may wish
to consider such matters as language, tone, movement.*

After this act of violence, the Captain proceeded to withdraw his men
towards their guard-house in the High Street. The mob were not so much
intimidated as incensed by what had been done. They pursued the soldiers
with execrations, accompanied by volleys of stones. As they pressed on
them, the rearmost soldiers turned, and again fired with fatal aim and   5
execution. It is not accurately known whether Porteous commanded this
second act of violence; but of course the odium of the whole transactions of
the fatal day attached to him, and to him alone. He arrived at the guard-
house, dismissed his soldiers, and went to make his report to the magistrates
concerning the unfortunate events of the day.   10

Apparently by this time Captain Porteous had begun to doubt the
propriety of his own conduct, and the reception he met with from the
magistrates was such as to make him still more anxious to gloss it over. He
denied that he had given orders to fire; he denied he had fired with his own
hand; he even produced the fusee which he carried as an officer for   15
examination; it was found still loaded. Of three cartridges which he was seen
to put in his pouch that morning, two were still there; a white handkerchief
was thrust into the muzzle of the piece, and returned unsoiled or blackened.

To the defence founded on these circumstances it was answered, that
Porteous had not used his own piece, but had been seen to take one from a 20
soldier. Among the many who had been killed and wounded by the unhappy
fire, there were several of better rank; for even the humanity of such soldiers
as fired over the heads of the mere rabble around the scaffold, proved in
some instances fatal to persons who were stationed in windows, or observed
the melancholy scene from a distance. The voice of public indignation was 25
loud and general; and, ere men's tempers had time to cool, the trial of
Captain Porteous took place before the High Court of Justiciary. After a
long and patient hearing, the jury had the difficult duty of balancing the
positive evidence of many persons, and those of respectability, who deposed
positively to the prisoner's commanding his soldiers to fire, and himself 30
firing his piece, of which some swore that they saw the smoke and flash, and
beheld a man drop at whom it was pointed, with the negative testimony of
others, who, though well stationed for seeing what had passed, neither heard
Porteous give orders to fire nor saw him fire himself; but, on the contrary,
averred that the first shot was fired by a soldier who stood close by him. A 35
great part of his defence was also founded on the turbulence of the mob,
which witnesses, according to their feelings, their predilections, and their
opportunities of observation, represented differently; some describing as a
formidable riot, what others represented as a trifling disturbance, such as
always used to take place on the like occasions, when the executioner of the 40
law, and the men commissioned to protect him in his task, were generally
exposed to some indignities. The verdict of the jury sufficiently shows how
the evidence preponderated in their minds. It declared that John Porteous
fired a gun among the people assembled at the execution; that he gave orders
to his soldiers to fire, by which many persons were killed and wounded; but, 45
at the same time, that the prisoner and his guard had been wounded and
beaten, by stones thrown at them by the multitude. Upon this verdict, the
Lords of Justiciary passed sentence of death against Captain John Porteous,
adjudging him, in the common form, to be hanged on a gibbet at the
common place of execution, on Wednesday, 8th September, 1736, and all his 50
movable property to be forfeited to the king's use, according to the Scottish
law in cases of wilful murder.

Cambridge Local Examinations Board (1980)

D. *Write a detailed critical appreciation of the following passage, considering, in particular, the effect the author creates, the means he uses to that
end, and your response to the passage as a whole.*

Mama's brother Mikhail died of typhus in Moscow. I took the letter from
the postman and brought it upstairs—the long latch-string ran through
loops under the banister. It was washday. The copper boiler steamed the
window. She was rinsing and wringing in a tub. When she read the news she
gave a cry and fainted. Her lips turned white. Her arm lay in the water, sleeve 5
and all. We two were alone in the house. I was terrified when she lay like that,
legs spread, her long hair undone, lids brown, mouth bloodless, death-like.
But then she got up and went to lie down. She wept all day. But in the
morning she cooked the oatmeal nevertheless. We were up early. 10
  My ancient times. Remoter than Egypt. No dawn, the foggy winters. In

darkness, the bulb was lit. The stove was cold. Papa shook the grates, and
raised an ashen dust. The grates grumbled and squealed. The puny shovel
clinked underneath. The Caporals gave Papa a bad cough. The chimneys in
their helmets sucked in the wind. Then the milkman came in his sleigh. The
snow was spoiled and rotten with manure and litter, dead rats, dogs. The   15
milkman in his sheepskin gave the bell a twist. It was brass, like the winding-
key of a clock. Helen pulled the latch and went down with a pitcher for the
milk. And then Ravitch, hung-over, came from his room, in his heavy
sweater, suspenders over the wool to keep it tighter to the body, the bowler
on his head, red in the face, his look guilty. He waited to be asked to sit.   20
   The morning light could not free itself from gloom and frost. Up and
down the street, the brick-recessed windows were dark, filled with darkness,
and schoolgirls by twos in their black skirts marched toward the convent.
And wagons, sledges, drays, the horses shuddering, the air drowned in
leaden green, the dung-stained ice, trails of ashes. Moses and his brothers   25
put on their caps and prayed together,
   '*Ma tovu ohaleha Yaakov. . . .*'
   'How goodly are thy tents, O Israel.'
Napoleon Street, rotten, toylike, crazy and filthy, riddled, flogged with
harsh weather—the boot-legger's boys reciting ancient prayers. To this   30
Moses' heart was attached with great power. Here was a wider range of
human feelings than he had ever again been able to find. The children of the
race, by a never-failing miracle, opened their eyes on one strange world after
another, age after age, and uttered the same prayer in each, eagerly loving
what they found. What was wrong with Napoleon Street? thought Herzog.   35
All he ever wanted was there. His mother did the wash, and mourned. His
father was desperate and frightened, but obstinately fighting. His brother
Shura with staring disingenuous eyes was plotting to master the world, to
become a millionaire. His brother Willie struggled with asthmatic fits.
Trying to breathe he gripped the table and rose on his toes like a cock about 40
to crow. His sister Helen had long white gloves which she washed in thick
suds. She wore them to her lessons at the conservatory, carrying a leather
music roll. Her diploma hung in a frame. *Mlle Hélène Herzog . . . avec
distinction.* His soft prim sister who played the piano.

The Welsh Joint Education Committee (1981)

E. *In the chapters preceding the extract printed below we read that Cecil
    Vyse has proposed to Lucy Honeychurch for the third time, having been
    attracted to her on holiday in Italy, not realising that part of her radiance
    comes from her love for another young man considered 'unsuitable' by
    her holiday companions. Mrs Honeychurch, Lucy's mother, is writing a
    letter to Cecil's mother. Freddy is Lucy's younger brother. The setting is
    Edwardian England.*
    Read the extract and then answer the questions that follow.

An Engagement

'Then the whole thing runs: "Dear Mrs Vyse,—Cecil has just asked my
permission about it, and I should be delighted if Lucy wishes it, and I have
told Lucy so. But Lucy seems very uncertain, and in these days young people

must decide for themselves. I know that Lucy likes your son, because she
tells me everything. But I do not know—"'   5
    'Look out!' cried Freddy.
    The curtains parted.
    Cecil's first movement was one of irritation. He couldn't bear the
Honeychurch habit of sitting in the dark to save the furniture. Instinctively
he gave the curtains a twitch, and sent them swinging down their poles.   10
Light entered. There was revealed a terrace, such as is owned by many villas,
with trees each side of it, and on it a little rustic seat, and two flower-beds.
But it was transfigured by the view beyond, for Windy Corner was built on
the range that overlooks the Sussex Weald. Lucy, who was in the little seat,
seemed on the edge of a green magic carpet which hovered in the air above   15
the tremulous world.
    Cecil entered.
    Appearing thus late in the story, Cecil must be at once described. He was
medieval. Like a Gothic statue. Tall and refined, with shoulders that seemed
braced square by an effort of the will, and a head that was tilted a little higher   20
than the usual level of vision, he resembled those fastidious saints who guard
the portals of a French cathedral. Well educated, well endowed, and not
deficient physically, he remained in the grip of a certain devil whom the
modern world knows as self-consciousness, and whom the medieval, with
dimmer vision, worshipped as asceticism. A Gothic statue implies celibacy,   25
just as a Greek statue implies fruition, and perhaps this was what Mr Beebe
meant. And Freddy, who ignored history and art, perhaps meant the same
when he failed to imagine Cecil wearing another fellow's cap.
    Mrs Honeychurch left her letter on the writing-table and moved towards
her young acquaintance.   30
    'Oh, Cecil!' she exclaimed—'oh, Cecil, do tell me!'
    'I promessi sposi,' said he.
    They stared at him anxiously.
    'She has accepted me,' he said, and the sound of the thing in English made
him flush and smile with pleasure, and look more human.   35
    'I am so glad,' said Mrs Honeychurch, while Freddy proffered a hand that
was yellow with chemicals. They wished that they also knew Italian, for our
phrases of approval and of amazement are so connected with little occasions
that we fear to use them on great ones. We are obliged to become vaguely
poetic, or to take refuge in Scriptural reminiscences.   40
    'Welcome as one of the family!' said Mrs Honeychurch, waving her hand
at the furniture. 'This is indeed a joyous day! I feel sure that you will make
dear Lucy happy.'
    'I hope so,' replied the young man, shifting his eyes to the ceiling.
    'We mothers—' simpered Mrs Honeychurch, and then realised that she   45
was affected, sentimental, bombastic—all the things she hated most. Why
could she not be as Freddy, who stood stiff in the middle of the room,
looking very cross and almost handsome?
    'I say, Lucy!' called Cecil, for conversation seemed to flag.

(i) What methods does the author use to reveal Cecil's character?
(ii) What do you find amusing in the passage? Discuss the ways in
     which the humorous effects are created.

(iii) Comment briefly on the effectiveness of the author's intrusion into the narrative as shown in each of the following within the passages:

    (a) 'Appearing thus late in the story, Cecil must be at once described.' (line 18).

    (b) 'for our phrases of approval and of amazement are so connected with little occasions that we fear to use them on 'great ones.' (lines 37–39).

(iv) Comment on the effect and significance of what is 'revealed' in lines 11–16.

The Joint Matriculation Board (1975)

F. *Read the following passage carefully and then answer the questions below it*:

It was beautiful then to see how Mr Jobbles swam down the long room and handed out his examination papers to the different candidates as he passed them. 'Twas a pity there should have been but five; the man did it so well, so quickly, with such a gusto! He should have been allowed to try his hand upon five hundred instead of five. His step was so rapid and his hand and   5 arm moved so dexterously, that no conceivable number would have been too many for him. But, even with five, he showed at once that the right man was in the right place. Mr Jobbles was created for the conducting of examinations.

And then the five candidates, who had hitherto been all ears, of a sudden   10 became all eyes, and devoted themselves to the papers before them.

It is a dreadful task that of answering examination papers – only to be exceeded in dreadfulness by the horrors of Mr Jobbles' viva voce[1] torments. A man has before him a string of questions, and he looks painfully down them, from question to question, searching for some allusion to that special   15 knowledge which he has within him. He too often finds that no such allusion is made. It appears that the Jobbles of the occasion has exactly known the blank spots of his mind and fitted them all. He has perhaps crammed himself with the winds and tides, and there is no more reference to those stormy subjects than if Luna[2] were extinct; but he has, unfortunately, been loose   20 about his botany, and question after question would appear to him to have been dictated by Sir Joseph Paxton[3] or the head-gardener at Kew. And then to his own blank face and puzzled look is opposed the fast scribbling of some botanic candidate, fast as though reams of folio could hardly contain all the knowledge which he is able to pour forth.   25

And so, with a mixture of fast-scribbling pens and blank faces, our five friends went to work. The examination lasted for four days, and it was arranged that on each of the four days each of the five candidates should be called up to undergo a certain quantum of Mr Jobbles' viva voce. This part

---

[1] viva voce: oral

[2] Luna: the moon

[3] Sir Joseph Paxton: distinguished architect and expert on gardening.

of his duty Mr Jobbles performed with a mildness of manner that was   30
beyond all praise. A mother training her first-born to say 'papa' could not
do so with a softer voice, or more affectionate demeanour.

(i) Explain *in your own words* the meaning of the following:
   (*a*) And then the five candidates, who had hitherto been all ears,
     of a sudden became all eyes . . . (lines 10–11).
   (*b*) . . . the fast scribbling of some botanic candidate, fast as
     though reams of folio could hardly contain all the knowledge
     he is able to pour forth. (lines 23–25).
(ii) Explain briefly what you understand by the term 'irony' and
   consider what evidence there is in the passage that the author is
   treating Mr Jobbles ironically.
(iii) Briefly describe the author's attitude to examinations and say how
   effectively you think he has conveyed it.

The Northern Ireland Board (1981)

The sources of the passages used for these questions set at 'A' level are
as follows: (A.) J. B. Priestley: *Angel Pavement* (1930); (B.) Elizabeth
Bowen: 'Mysterious Kôr' from the *Demon Lover* (1954); (C.) Sir Walter
Scott: *The Heart of Midlothian* (1818); (D.) Saul Bellow: *Herzog* (1964);
(E.) E. M. Forster: *A Room with a View* (1908); (F.) Anthony Trollope:
The Three Clerks (1858).

10

References to pairings of prose passages

We include the following thirty pairings of passages for your future study. Each pair concerns a related subject or theme, and the passages have generally been juxtaposed to present stimulating stylistic contrasts.

Most of the passages require no introduction, but where one is necessary, we have provided it.

1. *Portraits of the artist*
   Evelyn Waugh: *The Ordeal of Gilbert Pinfold* (1957), chap. 1 – 'It may happen in the next hundred years . . . as being almost as sinister as socialism'
   Joyce Cary: *The Horse's Mouth* (1944), chap. 2 – 'I could see my studio from where I stood . . . they were getting their own back'

2. *Religious observance*
   Aldous Huxley: *Antic Hay* (1923), chap. 1 – 'Gumbril, Theodore Gumbril Junior, B. A. Oxon., sat in his oaken stall . . . the organ presaged the coming *Te Deum*'
   Ronald Firbank: *Valmouth* (1919), chap. XI – 'Clad in a Persian-Renaissance gown . . . the eternal *she she she* of servants' voices'
   (At Hare-Hatch House it is the morning of the joint celebration of the marriage of Mrs Thoroughfare's son to a negress, who claims to be a Tahitian princess, and the christening of their baby.)

3. *Perspectives on the city*
   Saul Bellow: 'Looking for Mr Green' from *Mosby's Memoirs and Other Stories* (1969) – 'From here, his view was obstructed all the way to the South Branch . . . his neighbours didn't think they had to conceal him'
   (George Grebe is delivering 'relief cheques' – welfare payments – in the negro district of Chicago.)
   Henry Green: *Living* (1929), chap. 19 – 'What is a town then . . . Smell of the sea was at her, forcing itself on her'

4. *Escaping into fantasy?*
   James Thurber: 'The Secret Life of Walter Mitty' (1939) – 'We're going through! The Commander's voice was like thin ice breaking . . . he took them off again'
   John Updike: 'Wife-Wooing' from *Pigeon Feathers and Other Stories*

(1962) – 'Oh my love. Yes. Here we sit . . . the same trembling point, of beginning?'

5. *Only a child's imagination*

Saki (H. H. Munro): 'Sredni Vashtar' (1911) – 'Conradin was ten years old . . . the supply of nutmeg would have given out'

Angus Wilson: 'Raspberry Jam' from *The Wrong Set and Other Stories* (1949) – 'Upstairs, in the room which had been known as the nursery . . . and surrounded by unimaginative adults'

6. *Comic scrapes*

Kingsley Amis: *Lucky Jim* (1954), chap. 6 – 'Had he done all this himself . . . like the apprehension of something harmful or awful'

(Jim Dixon, who is spending the week-end with the Welches – he needs to impress Professor Welch in order to ensure that his lectureship at the university is made permanent – absents himself from an evening of amateur music-making in favour of a solitary drinking session at the local pub. He wakes the next morning to find that one of his unextinguished cigarettes has burnt the bedclothes, the bedside table and a rug.)

Tom Sharpe: *Porterhouse Blue* (1974), chap. 9 – 'Twenty minutes later he was still searching . . . not foreseen the dangers of icing'

(As a result of a strange chain of circumstances, Zipser, a student at Porterhouse College, Cambridge, has taken delivery of 'two gross of guaranteed electronically tested three-teat vending machine pack con- traceptives' intended for a public house. Zipser has already been 'gated' – confined to college – for a week, and he is now terrified of a discovery and a charge of being in 'felonious possession'.)

7. *Remembering mother*

John Osborne: *A Better Class of Person* (1981), chap. 7 – 'Mickey and I were eating Victoria plums . . . I couldn't wait to tell mine to Mickey'

William Golding: *Freefall* (1959), chap. 1 – 'Let me catch the picture . . . the warmth of a Christmas party'

8. *People with a mission*

Thomas Love Peacock: *Nightmare Abbey* (1818), chap. 2 – 'He – Scythrop – had some taste for romance reading . . . "golden candle- sticks with which I will illuminate the world." '

G. K. Chesterton: *The Man Who Was Thursday* (1908), chap. 4 – 'Gabriel Syme was not merely a detective . . . too quixotic to have cared for it otherwise'

9. *Work and play*

Alan Sillitoe: *Saturday Night and Sunday Morning* (1958), chap. 2 – 'the bright Monday-morning ring of the clocking-in machine . . . and talk to your mates now and again'

Dylan Thomas: 'Holiday Memory' (1946) – 'Lolling or larrikin that unsoiled, boiling beauty . . . in the hot, bubbling night'

10. *Travelling*
   Jack Kerouac: *On the Road* (1957), part 3, chap. 5 – 'The car belonged to a tall . . . It was only the beginning, too'
   (After spending their last evening in San Francisco at all-night jazz sessions, Sal Paradise – the narrator of the novel – and his wildly eccentric 'beat' friend, Dean Moriaty, begin their journey back east to New York. They are travelling with strangers: in the States at the period in which the novel is set travel bureaus offered places in cars going to stated destinations, the travellers paying a percentage of the cost in return for their seats.)
   Vladimir Nabokov: 'First Love' (1948) – 'When, on such journeys as these, the train changed its pace . . . until it departed of its own accord'
   (The narrator is recalling journeys he made as a child before the First World War on the Nord Express which connected St. Petersburg with Paris.)

11. *Proposals of marriage*
   Jane Austen: *Pride and Prejudice* (1813), chap. 34 – 'In a hurried manner he – Mr Darcy – immediately began . . . it is of small importance.'
   Charles Dickens: *Bleak House* (1852–53), chap. 9 – 'Mr Guppy sat down at the table . . . entirely out of the question.'

12. *Child chimney-sweeps*
   Charles Kingsley: *Water Babies* (1863), chap. 1 – 'Once upon a time . . . the jolliest boy in the whole town'
   Charles Lamb: 'The Praise of Chimney-Sweepers' from *The Essays of Elia* (1823) – 'I like to meet a sweep . . . more in these sympathies than philosophy can inculcate'

13. *Eating habits*
   Samuel Beckett: 'Dante and the Lobster' from *More Kicks Than Pricks* (1934) – 'Lunch, to come off at all . . . scorching his palate, bringing tears'
   Anthony Trollope: *The Warden* (1855), chap. 8 – And now let us observe the well-furnished breakfast-parlour . . . and so passed the archdeacon's morning on that day'

14. *Accounts of the plague*
   Daniel Defoe: *A Journal of the Plague Year* (1722), opening section – 'But the city itself began now to be visited too . . . the doors of such houses as were shut up'
   Samuel Pepys's *Diary* (1665): 'August 31st. Up; and, after putting several things in order to my removal, to Woolwich . . .' and entry for September 10th: 'Walked home; being forced thereto by one of my watermen . . . the fullest of true sense of joy'

15. *Oxford*

Matthew Arnold: *Essays in Criticism* (1865) – 'No, we are seekers still . . . and will wage after we are gone?'

Thomas Hardy: *Jude the Obscure* (1896), part second, chap. 6 – 'The other course, that of buying himself in . . . not Christminster in a local sense at all'

(Jude Fawley, a poor young man brought up in the countryside not too far from Christminster – the name Hardy uses for Oxford in the novel – has long dreamed of attending the university as a student; but though he has prepared himself as best he can and worked hard, largely on his own, at his studies, there seems to be no hope of his gaining a scholarship.)

16. *Versions of romantic love*

Emily Brontë: *Wuthering Heights* (1847), chap. 9 – 'I was superstitious about dreams then . . . I was out of patience with her folly'

(Catherine Earnshaw confides her feelings about marriage to Edgar Linton; she is addressing Nelly Dean, the housekeeper of Wuthering Heights. Catherine has been raised with Heathcliff, now a wild, passionate young man, whom her father brought to Wuthering Heights as a waif and reared as one of his own children and who has met with harsh persecution from Catherine's brother since Mr Earnshaw's death.

Edward Gibbon (1737–94): *Autobiography* – 'I hesitate, from the apprehension of ridicule, when I approach the delicate subject . . . healed by time, absence, and the habits of a new life'

17. *Discovering the corpse*

Mickey Spillane: *I, the Jury* (1952), chap. 1 – 'I shook the rain from my hat . . . I'm going to get the one that did this'

Joseph Conrad: *The Secret Agent* (1907), chap. 12 – 'Comrade Ossipon avoided easily the end of the counter . . . away from the glazed door, and retched violently'

(Ossipon, an anarchist, enters the back room of Mr Verloc's shop believing that Verloc met his death some time previously in a bomb outrage in Greenwich Park.)

18. *Religious meditation*

John Donne (1572–1631): *LXXX Sermons*, Sermon II – "God made sun and moon to distinguish seasons . . . and all times are his seasons'

Jeremy Taylor: *Holy Dying* (1650–51) – 'At the end of seven years our teeth fall . . . but you tread upon a dead man's bones'

19. *Quirks of consciousness*

Laurence Sterne: *Tristram Shandy* (1760), Volume 1, chap. 1 – 'I wish either my father or my mother . . . what was your father saying? – Nothing'

James Joyce: *Ulysses* (1922), the final section of the novel – 'let me see if I can doze off . . . yes I said yes I will Yes'

(As Molly Bloom lies in bed, her 'stream of consciousness' takes in preparations for the next day and memories of her childhood in Gibraltar and of her courtship.)

20. *Sexual encounters*

James Boswell: *London Journal* (1762) – 'Thursday 25 November. I had been in a bad situation during the night . . . I could know nothing certain of my commission'

Flann O'Brien: *At Swim-Two-Birds* (1939), 'Biographical reminiscence, part the third' – 'Three nights later at about eight o'clock . . . beneficial to my health'

21. *Two hunts*

William Golding: *The Lord of the Flies* (1954), chap. 12 – 'The cries, suddenly nearer, jerked him up . . . "Fun and games," said the officer'

(A group of English schoolboys, isolated on a deserted island, have reverted to a kind of tribal savagery. Ralph, their former leader, is being hunted down; he has gone into hiding in a thicket of bushes, but the other boys have started a fire in order to force him from his cover.)

Fielding: *The Adventures of Joseph Andrews* (1742), chap. 6 – 'The master of the pack was just arrived . . . by assaulting his dogs in that manner?'

22. *Ways of death*

Evelyn Waugh: *The Loved One* (1948), third section – 'Dennis was a young man of sensibility . . . his name and Sir Francis's'

Thomas Hardy: *The Mayor of Casterbridge* (1886), chap. 18 – 'Meanwhile Mrs Henchard was weakening visibly . . . her wishes and ways will all be as nothing!'

23. *Two heroines*

George Eliot: *Middlemarch* (1871–72), chap. 1 – 'Dorothea knew many passages . . . teach you even Hebrew, if you wished it'

G. B. Shaw: 'Preface' to *Saint Joan* (1924), 'Joan Summed Up' and 'Joan's Immaturity and Ignorance' – 'We may accept and admire Joan . . . reacts against that romance'

24. *Would-be writers*

James Joyce: 'A Little Cloud' from *Dubliners* (1914) – 'He turned to the right towards Capel Street . . . he passed his street and had to turn back'

(Little Chandler's friend, Gallaher, has returned to Dublin on a visit after leaving for London eight years earlier.)

Katherine Mansfield: 'Je Ne Parle Pas Français' from *Bliss* (1920) – 'Ah, I can see myself that first evening . . . it does sound so, but then it is not all'

25. *A victim's letters*

Richardson: *Pamela* (1740), Volume 1, Letter XV – 'Dear Mother, I broke off abruptly my last letter; for I feared he was coming . . . his foul proceedings might not be known'

Fielding: *Shamela* (1741), Letter X – 'Now, Mamma, what think you? . . . a full hour and a half, about my virtue; As soon as I had breakfasted, a coach and six came to the door . . . and then what will become of poor me?'

26. *Servants and masters in colonial India*
Rudyard Kipling: 'At the End of the Passage' from *Life's Handicap* (1891) – 'Four men, each entitled to "life, liberty, and the pursuit of happiness", sat at a table . . . for any man to possess that knowledge'
  E. M. Forster: *A Passage to India* (1924), chap. 2 – 'A servant in scarlet interrupted him . . . Call me a tonga'
  (Aziz is a doctor and a native Indian, subordinate to Major Callendar. At the beginning of the passage, Aziz is entertaining some of his friends.)

27. *Hunting at sea*
Hemingway: *The Old Man and the Sea* (1952) – 'Then the weight increased and he gave more line. He tightened the pressure of his thumb . . . is just as desperate as I am'
  Melville: *Moby Dick* (1851), chap. 134 – 'The ship tore on; leaving such a furrow in the sea . . . but one man at the fore. The boats! – stand by!'

28. *Strange cities*
Mervyn Peake: *Titus Groan* (1946), 'The Hall of the Bright Carvings' – 'Gormenghast, that is, the main massing of the original stone . . . housed in the Hall of the Bright Carvings'
  Olivia Manning: *The Great Fortune* (1960), chap. 2 – 'The light was failing. He was beginning to doubt his direction . . . here he was afraid'
  (Yakimov has just arrived in Bucharest.)

29. *Places to drink in*
H. G. Wells: *The History of Mr Polly* (1910), chap. 9 – 'It was about two o'clock in the afternoon . . . so manifestly sweet and satisfying'
  Dreiser: *Sister Carrie* (1900), chap. 5 – On this particular evening he – Drouet – dined at Rector's . . . supplies ordered and needed'

30. *Things of beauty*
North's *Plutarch* (1579) – 'For Caesar and Pompey knew her (Cleopatra) when she was but a young thing . . . with the god Bacchus, for the general good of all Asia'
  Richard Hughes: *In Hazard* (1938), chap. 2 – 'The day was fine and clear . . . as the naked dolphins had done'

Index of authors of extracts